W9-ANE-811

I Am a WITNESS

KALIE KELCH • GCA STUDENTS AND STAFF

Pacific Press®
Publishing Association
Nampa, Idaho | www.pacificpress.com

Cover design by Gerald L. Monks
Cover design resources from iStockphoto.com | Steve Debenport
Inside design by Aaron Troia

Additional copies of this book may be purchased by calling toll-free 1-800-765-6955 or by visiting AdventistBookCenter.com.

Library of Congress Cataloging-in-Publication Data

Names: Kelch, Kalie, 1977- author.
Title: I am a witness / Kalie Kelch ; GCA Nancy Gerard.
Description: Nampa : Pacific Press Publishing Association, 2019. | Summary: "A 366
    entry devotional for teenagers"— Provided by publisher.
Identifiers: LCCN 2019027620 | ISBN 9780816364510 (paperback)
    | ISBN 9780816364527 (kindle edition)
Subjects: LCSH: Teenagers—Religious life—Meditations.
    | Devotional calendars—Seventh-Day Adventists.
Classification: LCC BV4531.3 .K44 2019 | DDC 242/.63—dc23
LC record available at https://lccn.loc.gov/2019027620

June 2019

Dedication

To Jesus, who calls us His friends
and invites us to partner with Him
in sharing with others the good news
of His life, death, and resurrection.

About the Authors

Georgia-Cumberland Academy's (GCA) mission is to foster an educational environment of excellence where students, faculty, and staff pursue a shared goal: to know Jesus as Savior and Friend, to love God and those He brings into our lives, and to serve the church and society. GCA endeavors to pursue this mission of academic excellence in the context of a positive Christian environment with shared values that include spiritual growth; commitment to academic integrity; respect for God, people, and our world; and a healthy lifestyle. The school is located in rural northwest Georgia about an hour north of Atlanta and an hour south of Chattanooga, Tennessee, and is home to approximately 250 students.

Kalie Kelch is the assistant chaplain and a coinstructor of Magnify Worship at GCA. She is passionate about mentoring youth and helping them fall in love with Jesus and use their God-given talents to serve others. Kalie is also author of *Grab Your Boarding Pass*, the junior-earliteen devotional for 2014.

Dear Reader,

There is an Indian parable about a group of blind men who are brought before a mystery animal and asked to identify it. The men request to touch the creature, and as they do so, a colorful description emerges. The first man takes hold of the trunk of the elephant and says that it must be a thick snake. Another man feels the ear and says it seems like a giant fan. A third man touches the leg and says it feels like a tree trunk. Another man stationed by the side of the elephant identifies the creature as simply a wall. Finally, the man by the tail says it feels like a rope. One creature had many different descriptions because each man had a unique experience with the elephant and "saw" things from his own perspective.

Each of us has our own story to tell about our relationship with Jesus. We each have a distinctive perspective because we've encountered Him in a way that is special to us.

After Jesus' resurrection, He spent forty days on earth, many of which were spent with His disciples. Right before His ascension into heaven, He told His disciples, "You will be my witnesses, telling people about me everywhere—in Jerusalem, throughout Judea, in Samaria, and to the ends of the earth" (Acts 1:8).

Witnesses tell what they have seen and heard, which means that one witness may see the same event differently from another witness because we are all unique individuals. That's the beauty of how God made us. We each bring something different to the table. The four gospels are all unique and yet tied together by the common thread of Jesus Christ. Some stories are the same, and sometimes one author includes different details from another one.

The disciples had a job to do, and so do we—we are to share with others our encounter with Jesus. This book is filled with stories and thoughts about Jesus' life from the students and staff at Georgia-Cumberland Academy. As you take a journey through the gospels and the first few chapters of Acts, our prayer is that you will get to know Jesus more fully.

We encourage you to read our words as well as the daily passage of Scripture that is noted with each devotional. Just as we connect with friends by hanging out with them and texting or talking or Snapchatting, we connect with Jesus by hanging out with Him in His Word, in prayer, and in friendship with other Christians.

Kalie Kelch
Assistant Chaplain
Georgia-Cumberland Academy

So Much More
Revelation 1:8

I f I were to ask you the question, Do you know Jesus? your answer would probably be yes. I'm also assuming that if I were to ask you to describe Jesus, you would use words such as *kind, loving, humble,* and *compassionate.* I agree with all of those adjectives. Jesus was very kind to those He met, and He certainly was the epitome of love—the perfect representation of God the Father and His infinite love for us.

However, Jesus was way more than a nice guy. I mean, what do you do with the story of the Canaanite woman whom Jesus called a "dog" (Matthew 15:21–28)? And how about when Jesus lambasted the Pharisees and called them, among other things, "Snakes! Sons of vipers!" (Matthew 23:1–36)?

Don't get me wrong. Jesus was kind, loving, humble, and compassionate, but He was also bold, radical, outspoken, and controversial. He pushed back against societal norms and made people think. He wasn't content to leave people the way they were. He challenged His listeners, oftentimes shoving them out of their comfort zone and into a whole new realm of thinking.

So back to my original question. Do you know Jesus? You may have grown up singing "Jesus Loves Me" and saying "Dear Jesus . . . " before meals and bedtime, but singing about Jesus or saying standard prayers is not the same as knowing Him. Do you truly know the Man who walked on water, healed the sick, interacted with outcasts, called people out for sinning, proclaimed the gospel with boldness, prayed all night, touched the untouchable, and offended people He came to save? Or maybe a better question is, Do you want to know Jesus? Do you want to learn more about this intense Man who was both fierce and gentle?

I know this isn't a new concept. I'm sure you've heard it all your life. But if you want to know Jesus—the One who is, who always was, and who is still to come (Revelation 1:8)—you need to spend time with Him. So that's exactly what we are going to do this year. We are going to explore the Gospels in an effort to get to know Jesus better. We are going to pay attention to what He did and said and whom He interacted with. In the process, I not only hope that you grow deeper in your friendship with Jesus but that you will also learn more about yourself and who you are as a child of God.

—Chaplain Kalie

Spread the Word

John 1:1–18

God gives every Christian gifts we can use for His glory. We all have talents that we can use for Him. Personally, I am a pianist and have been playing music in the church for as long as I can remember. I love playing the piano for Jesus, and it has been my method of witnessing throughout my life.

I think about many things before leading in worship. Our praise band has to work on dynamics, timing, and verbal and musical transitions in order to be prepared for the worship service. In the end, when I get up on stage, I am not the one doing the work. Instead, God is working through me. He is the One who makes the difference.

The light that shines on us and inspires us is the same light—His light—that radiates out of us, His vessels, when we use our talents for Him. This is what drives us to share our God-given gifts in the church.

I believe this is a real-world example of what John is talking about in the beginning of John 1. Using our gifts for God is one way that the light of Christ can shine through us. "In him was life, and that life was the light of all mankind. The light shines in the darkness, and the darkness has not overcome it" (John 1:4, 5, NIV).

John introduces Jesus as the Creator, Sustainer, and Author of everything. John compares Him to light, which is an essential component of life. We cannot live without light. John recognized that he was nothing compared to Jesus, and he took seriously his role of spreading the knowledge of God, the One who is above everything, to the world.

Just like John, any of us can spread God's Word by using the gifts God has given us. God wants us, like John, to take the Word, which comes to us through Jesus, and give it to other people. Yes, you may not be recognized or you might go through trials, but those who recognize Jesus will be changed.

—Nathan Begley, junior

A Living Testimony
Matthew 1:1–17; Luke 3:23–38

At some point every year, I begin to read through the book of Matthew, telling myself I will study and explore God's Word in a new way. However, the first seventeen verses of Matthew are not what I consider particularly interesting reading material. After reading through the first few names on the list of who was whose father, I skim or entirely skip the genealogy that seems to plague the beginning of the New Testament. Yet the inspired Word of God says this in 2 Timothy 3:16: "All Scripture is breathed out by God and profitable for teaching, for reproof, for correction, and for training in righteousness" (ESV). This causes me to stop and ask myself, How are the genealogies in Matthew and Luke "breathed out by God"? What significance is found in these long genealogical lists?

Historically, the Jews were very good at tracing their lineage. By knowing who one's ancestors were, one could claim property and an elevated status. Family trees were extremely important back then because they established the identity of a Jew. Today, not many people can trace their ancestry back more than four or five generations, if that. In Jesus' time, everyone could trace their ancestry back hundreds, if not thousands, of years. Because one's ancestry established their validity, it makes sense that Matthew and Luke would include genealogies in their writings.

If we take a look at some of the names in the genealogy of Christ, we find that Abraham is mentioned. God promised Abraham that through his offspring all nations would be blessed (Genesis 22:18). The crazy thing about that promise is that it is still being fulfilled today. Jesus Christ is blessing millions of lives this very day, and that is a direct fulfillment of God's promise to Abraham. Rahab, a prostitute, is listed in the ancestry of Jesus Christ, showing that God can use those who submit to Him, regardless of background. Ruth, a Moabite, is also listed, demonstrating that God uses those who step out in faith, regardless of nationality or heritage. The genealogies in Matthew and Luke reveal God's faithfulness to His people and show that God keeps His promises. They are a testimony of the saving grace of God, seen in His Son, Christ Jesus.

—Andrew Boyd, senior

The Silent Promise
Luke 1:5–25

The thought of instantly gaining millions of dollars through a game of chance seems exciting to most people. Many buy lottery tickets, hoping they will be the lucky one who gains instant wealth. However, the chances of winning the lottery jackpot are extremely low, with only a 1-in-a-175-million chance. You are more likely to be crushed by a meteor, struck by lightning, or hit by pieces of a falling plane. Sometimes things seem impossible, like a one-in-a-million chance, and yet with God all things are possible.

Zechariah was righteous in the eyes of God, but he and his wife, Elizabeth, were very old and had never been blessed with a child. In fact, they had given up on the idea of raising a little bundle of joy. The odds seemed to be against them, just as they are for whoever thinks they can win the lottery. Having a child seemed so improbable at their advanced ages that even as Gabriel stood before Zechariah explaining the coming blessing, the priest doubted God's word.

Many times in our lives, we face mountains or obstacles that seem enormous. Beating the odds feels impossible. However, in the face of insurmountable odds, we cannot let the devil cloud our judgment and convince us that God's power is insufficient. Once we doubt God's power, we are putting Him on our human, sinful level. Yet God is so much more than we can ever imagine. He is powerful and gracious. He turns impossible situations into realities.

Of course, there are times when we question God and wonder how impossible things can become possible. As soon as those thoughts cloud our minds, we need to push aside the lie and rely on the truth of God's Word that all things are possible with Him (Matthew 19:26). Give it all to God; He promises that He wants only what is best for us. In this life we will face struggles, but we must hold strong to the promise that God makes all things new (Revelation 21:5) and takes our challenges and turns them into joy (Isaiah 61:3).

—Javiera Alquinta, senior

Taking a Step Back
Matthew 14:22–36

We live in a fast-paced world that pushes us to juggle more and more things, leaving us stressed and overwhelmed by the weight of the responsibilities we shoulder. In addition to the responsibilities of school, and maybe work, we have extracurricular activities to keep up with, such as sports teams, music groups, church, Pathfinders, and exercise (not to mention keeping up with the hundreds of friends we have on social media). The list goes on and on.

Don't get me wrong; many of the things that occupy our time are valuable. But if we don't take time to connect with the One who made us and sustains us, we have the potential of burning out or heading down a path that leads to nowhere.

So what do we do about it? Taking a cue from Jesus, we need to step back and, in the quietness, ask Him to speak into our lives. Jesus often retreated from the crowds and the busyness of ministry to spend time with His Father (Matthew 14:23; Mark 1:35; 6:46; Luke 5:16; 6:12). He knew that in the stillness He would be rejuvenated and revived, ready to take on whatever God had in store for Him, whether it was meeting the needs of the people who clamored for healing, dealing with those who hated Him, or teaching the multitudes who flocked to hear His every word.

That's why we will often hit the pause button on our devotional readings and spend time talking to Jesus in a creative way that involves your imagination. We're calling this moment of reflection "Meeting With Jesus." It may take some practice to slow down and talk and listen because we are so used to the constant buzzes, chirps, and dings from our phones and the world around us, but I encourage you to set aside a bit of quiet time to talk with the One who truly cares about you. Just as Jesus was transformed by spending time in God's presence, may we walk away changed because of the time we spend with Him.

—Chaplain Kalie

Right There With Us

Luke 1:26–38

I enjoy sports, so when girls' soccer tryouts came around in the fall, I decided to give it a shot. Even though I didn't know how to play soccer, I figured I would just do it for fun. Well, I tried out—and was shocked when I discovered that I made the team as goalie. I was excited but also really scared—I didn't know all the rules for soccer, so I felt a bit overwhelmed! I finally prayed about it and asked God to send someone who could help me figure things out. I thanked Him for giving me the opportunity to play another team sport, and I left things in His hands. A few days later, as I was talking with my friends, some of them said they would teach me all I needed to know about soccer. I immediately felt more confident knowing that I had the support of my friends. I thanked God for answering my prayers and sending me people who would teach me what I needed to know.

It must have been a great honor for Mary to have an angel come and tell her that she would be the mother of the Son of God, but it must have also been terrifying. Mary must have felt a great amount of pressure as the magnitude of the news settled in. She was very young and was engaged to be married to Joseph. What was she going to tell him and their families? She knew there could be dire consequences once the story got out, but she surrendered to God's plan and trusted that He would work everything out. She said, "I am the Lord's servant. May everything you have said about me come true" (Luke 1:38). God knew Mary would need support, and that's why He told her about her relative Elizabeth's pregnancy.

The nervousness I felt at learning a new sport pales in comparison to Mary's experience, but we each face things every day that scare or intimidate us. The question is, What do we do when we aren't sure what tomorrow brings, and to whom do we turn?

God gives us many opportunities in life, many of which seem daunting. But when He gives us these gifts, He places people—and the Holy Spirit—in our lives to help guide us through the unknown.

—Faith Bispham, sophomore

Ultimatums and Surrender

Luke 1:39–56

Last summer I worked as a colporteur selling Christian literature in California. One day I had only sold three books in six hours, and I was starting to get frustrated. It was well above one hundred degrees, and I was hot and tired. I knew I had to keep going, so I sat down on the side of the road, unloaded my irritation on God, and asked Him to reveal His purpose for me. I was so worn out that I bargained with God, telling Him that if He didn't help me to sell at least one book on the next street, I was going to quit and fly home the next day.

I finished my prayer and headed to the next street. God made His plan for me to stay in California clear. I sold a cooking set at my first door and a set of children's books two houses down. Then someone signed up for Bible studies! In that moment, I saw my prayers answered, and it cemented in my mind that He will never leave us or forsake us (Deuteronomy 31:6). After these three successes, I stopped before going to the next house and thanked God for His blessings. I surrendered myself to Him and asked Him to use me to bring light to the rest of the people I would meet that summer.

God is faithful and worthy to be praised, which we see in the story of Mary and Elizabeth. After being barren her entire adult life, Elizabeth became pregnant as an old woman. Her prayers were answered! When Mary showed up at Elizabeth's house, Elizabeth was filled with the Holy Spirit, and, without Mary saying a word about her own unusual pregnancy, Elizabeth prophesied about the baby that Mary was carrying. Then Mary began to sing a song of praise for God's majesty and faithfulness.

Elizabeth gave birth to a baby boy who grew up to be known as John the Baptist, a man of God's Word who brought many people to Jesus' feet. Elizabeth had gone through a tough season when she thought she couldn't have a baby, but she kept holding on to God. In the end, He worked a miracle through her, because she remained connected to Him. Elizabeth was no different from any one of us. God can use people like you and me. He doesn't take into account our social status, race, or background. He accepts us as we are, and if we surrender ourselves to Him, He will use us in ways we can't imagine.

—Genesis Arteta, senior

Everyone Has a Story
Acts 1:8

I have always loved reading true stories. Don't get me wrong; I enjoy a good fictional book from time to time, but I'm drawn to stories that have actually happened, where you know the blood, sweat, and tears are real.

I've heard it said that everyone has a story to tell, and it's true. If you take the time to ask someone about the high and low points of his or her life, you'll learn a lot about that person. Of course, some people clam up and don't want to talk about themselves because they feel like they don't have anything interesting to say, but we all have something to share about the events that have shaped our lives.

Right before Jesus returned to heaven, He told His disciples to share with the whole world what they had observed and all the things He had taught them (Acts 1:8). We have favorite stories from our lives that we tell again and again; I wonder what stories Peter, James, and John repeatedly told. What was their favorite bit of truth to share with new believers?

As followers of Jesus, we are called to share our testimony with other people. This testimony includes stories of God's providence, protection, and provision. It also includes truths that God reveals to us in His Word. If we don't, who will tell others about Jesus' presence and influence in our lives, and how will they get to know Him?

Once a week, you will read stories that celebrate God's faithfulness and love. Each story will end with a four-word sentence: I am a witness. These simple words carry such power because without each of us attesting to God's goodness today, He remains a legend or a fable. The disciples started rolling the ball, and we get to keep pushing it forward until Jesus returns. Just as God lived and moved while Jesus walked the earth, He still works in the lives of His people today through the power of the Holy Spirit. In the weeks to come, you will read a variety of stories that end with a common theme: I am a witness.

—Chaplain Kalie

Strange Stuff
Luke 1:57–80

There are many abnormal things about the story of John the Baptist. First, his parents, Elizabeth and Zechariah, were really old and had been unable to have kids their whole lives. Then God allowed Elizabeth to get pregnant. Then, when Zechariah doubted what the angel told him, he was struck mute and couldn't speak.

After the baby was born, per the custom of the time, there was a party on the eighth day to celebrate his circumcision and naming. Elizabeth insisted that the baby be named John as the angel had instructed. It was the custom to give the baby a family name, and because no one in their family was named John, the neighbors and relatives were shocked at this piece of information. They turned to Zechariah to ask his opinion, and he asked for a writing tablet. He confirmed what Elizabeth said, writing, "His name is John" (Luke 1:63). Immediately, he was able to speak again!

Zechariah praised God and prophesied about his son and the Messiah. He told how God was coming to save the Jews from their enemies and said that He would remember His holy covenant with Abraham. This prophecy provides a little glimpse of God's character, which is wonderful! Speaking about Jesus, Zechariah said,

> "You will tell his people how to find salvation
>   through forgiveness of their sins.
> Because of God's tender mercy,
>   the morning light from heaven is about to break upon us,
> to give light to those who sit in darkness and in the shadow of death,
>   and to guide us to the path of peace" (verses 77–79).

This prophecy gives us the assurance that even when we mess up, God still comes back for us, dusts us off, and helps us. I personally want to serve a God who loves us even though we are sinful creatures compared to Him. He wants to help us no matter how big our mess is, and He cleans us up so we don't make the same mistakes again.

—Kalen Anderson, sophomore

The Best Fairy Tale

Matthew 1:18–25

H onestly, this story sounds like it could be a fairy tale, but it's the beginning of the best story ever told. I know you've heard it a hundred times, but follow along . . .

Once upon a time, there was a girl named Mary. She was engaged to a man named Joseph. One day an angel came to her and said, "You are going to have a son, and His name will be Jesus." She was obviously shocked because she wasn't married and had never slept with a man. When people found out, which would naturally happen within a few months, she could be stoned to death for adultery.

Mary nervously told Joseph all that had happened. He wasn't exactly thrilled about her little revelation, but he cared about her, so he decided to end their relationship quietly. God had other plans. He sent an angel to Joseph in a dream and said, "Do not be afraid to take Mary as your wife. For the child within her was conceived by the Holy Spirit. And she will have a son, and you are to name him Jesus, for he will save his people from their sins" (Matthew 1:20, 21). Joseph married Mary, and in time, she gave birth to Jesus.

Because we are so familiar with this story, I think we often gloss over Mary and Joseph's faith, but their faith means everything to this story. They wouldn't be part of the Bible if they hadn't embraced the role that God gave them.

Mary and Joseph stuck by each other and held on to God through a very confusing time during which people looked down on them. Their faith was rewarded when Jesus was born. He came into a world of sickness, death, and sin, and He changed it into a world of hope and endless possibilities.

So when you are faced with challenges, and it feels as if everyone is looking down on you, hold on to your faith and remember that Jesus loves you so much that He came to this world to save you.

—Cole Boggess, freshman

Looking Back; Looking Forward
Psalm 2

If I were to ask you what books you should read in the Bible to learn more about Jesus, I'm guessing you would say Matthew, Mark, Luke, and John. Those would be the most obvious choices because Jesus' life story fills their pages. However, throughout the Old and New Testaments we learn about Jesus and His heart for the human race. In particular, the books of Psalms and Isaiah are full of prophecies that refer to the Savior of the world.

Some people discredit the Old Testament, but it validates what we read in the New Testament! The words of David and Isaiah come to life in the stories that Matthew, Mark, Luke, and John penned hundreds of years later.

In Psalm 2, we read about David as God's anointed king, but there are parallels that point to Jesus. Verse 2 talks about how kings and rulers are laying plans against God and His Anointed One. The religious leaders of Jesus' day certainly went after Him and, in the end, had their way when they hung Him on the cross.

There are always people out to get us. I'm sure you can name a few people in your life who you feel are constantly picking on you, pushing your buttons, trying to get you in trouble, or teasing you, even because of your relationship with God. Persecution is inevitable, but read this promise:

The king proclaims the LORD's decree:
    "The LORD said to me, 'You are my son.
Today I have become your Father.
    Only ask, and I will give you the nations as your inheritance,
the whole earth as your possession' " (Psalm 2:7, 8).

David was chosen by God for a purpose. Jesus was chosen by God for a purpose. You and I are chosen by God for a purpose. We can hold on to the same truth that Jesus held on to—we are children of God, and He promises that one day we will possess the earth as His heirs. We have the assurance of His presence here on earth to help us through the tough times, and we have the guarantee of eternity because of Jesus' death and resurrection. What could be better than that?

—Chaplain Kalie

Meeting With Jesus
Zephaniah 3:17

Y ou are sprawled out on your bed, staring up at the ceiling, when you hear a knock at your door. "Come in," you say, not moving from your position. You're so tired! It's the start of a new week, but you're honestly not ready to face another Monday. *Why are there so many responsibilities in life?* you wonder.

You're lost in your thoughts when you remember that someone has just entered your room. You turn your head toward the door, and you see Jesus standing there with a smile on His face despite the fact that your room is not clean.

"Do you have a minute?" He asks in a gentle voice.

"Sure," you say as you push yourself up to a sitting position. You're slightly embarrassed at the mess, but Jesus doesn't seem to care. He moves the pile of clothes off your chair and takes a seat.

"I just wanted to see how you were doing," He says.

You're not sure whether you should dive into everything that is overwhelming you. You avert your eyes from His tender, steady gaze, which seems to read your very soul.

"Life can be rough. Trust Me—I understand!" He says. "When I was walking this crazy planet, there were days that felt like too much to handle. One day a mob tried to stone Me; another day the crowd wanted to crown Me king; and there was the night in Gethsemane before My death. Those were just a few of the moments in my life that felt overwhelming. But I kept My eyes on My Father, and He was always there to see Me through. We're there to see you through too. So tell me, how are you doing? What's going on that seems like more than you can handle?"

Take some time to talk to Jesus or write down your response to His question.

Read the verse for the day and think about the promise it offers or what it tells you about God.

If you were to talk about this verse with Jesus, what would you say? What would you ask Him?

More Than a Day
Luke 2:1–20

People of all ages celebrate the birth of Jesus, but I especially remember the excitement from when I was a child—participating in the school or church Christmas pageant, reading the story, and hearing everyone buzz with joy about the true meaning of Christmas. After the holidays are over, people tend to forget about the beautiful story until the next December.

The story of Jesus' birth shouldn't be reserved just for the holidays. After the excitement of the season has faded and we return to our routine lives, we shouldn't forget about the gift God gave to us—His one and only Son, Jesus. God allowed Jesus to come into this world as a baby to save us from sin. We should celebrate this precious gift year-round.

The shepherds were the first people on earth to hear the good news that the Savior of the world had been born. I can only imagine that, long after that evening in the field, they talked about the angels disappearing into the night sky after singing to them, the joyous trek to Bethlehem, and meeting the Messiah. I'm sure they didn't just celebrate this miraculous event for one day. They probably talked about their experience every day for weeks and months and years to come because they recognized that something significant had taken place that starry night.

Our human minds cannot fathom the tremendous sacrifice that Jesus made on our behalf when He came to this earth. We are alive because of His life and death, yet we often express our gratitude only during the Christmas season, and even then, we make the holiday about ourselves, getting lost in the commercialism and materialism of the season. It's absurd that there is only one holiday to thank God for His ultimate sacrifice.

I choose to celebrate and be thankful for God's sacrifice every single day of my life. I hope you will join me in encouraging everyone around you to remember Jesus' birth all year-round. May we, like the shepherds, praise God for His perfect gift.

—Gabriela Alvarez, senior

Something We Can't Live Without
Luke 2:21–38

We use it every day, and we'd be lost without it. What is it? No, it's not your phone—it's the lightbulb. Every day we rely on Thomas Edison's invention. Imagine what life would be like without the lightbulb. Candles aren't exactly useful to light a soccer field or basketball court at night. We would not be able to work or play indoors or drive at night without this useful invention.

Jesus is referred to as the Light of the World, but when Mary and Joseph took Jesus to the temple to dedicate Him and offer a sacrifice as the Law of Moses required, Jesus looked like just another baby. He didn't seem special in the eyes of the priests, but there was a man who saw Him differently.

Simeon was righteous, and the Holy Spirit was with him. God had revealed to him that he would not die before he had seen the Messiah. The Holy Spirit moved him to go to the temple, and that day he saw Jesus, the Lord's Chosen One. Simeon approached Mary and Joseph and took Jesus in his arms, saying,

"Sovereign Lord, as you have promised,
    you may now dismiss your servant in peace.
For my eyes have seen your salvation,
    which you have prepared in the sight of all nations:
a light for revelation to the Gentiles,
    and the glory of your people Israel" (Luke 2:29-32, NIV).

Simeon's dream had come true—he saw the Son of God, the Light of the World, before he died.

This story confirms to me that God has plans for us, just as He had a plan for Simeon. He has a purpose for each one of our lives if we will simply ask daily for the Holy Spirit to fill us and move us according to His plans. God's ultimate goal is that we will accept His gift of salvation and share the good news with others.

Just as we can't live without light, we can't live without the Light of the World. What would you do if Jesus came today? Are you ready to meet Him?

—Chris Barrera, sophomore

Letting Go
Proverbs 3:5, 6

It had been a rough day, and just as I closed my eyes to sleep, my phone dinged with an incoming text. I could tell from the tone that it was my mother. I was tempted to look at it in the morning, but then I decided to read it in case it was something important. It was.

My mother and I have always been super close, and she is one of my biggest role models. She has been battling skin cancer since before I can remember, but it had always been benign. This time was different. She had been diagnosed with melanoma, a very aggressive type of skin cancer that can be fatal. As I read the text, I was filled with dread about the unknown. Would she be okay? What if it had spread? I don't think I slept much that night.

In the days that followed, I kept asking God why He would let this happen. I was scared stiff that I would lose her. I tried to trust Him with her life, but I couldn't let go. My mom kept reassuring me that God would take care of her and reminding me to trust Him. I tried to; I really did. Yet I continued to take back my trust. I clung to my fears about what would happen if she died.

The doctors scheduled a date for her surgery to remove the skin cancer. By the time the day came, I was a nervous wreck. I convinced myself that I would never see her again. I did my best to be strong for her, but on the inside, I was falling apart. Despite my fears and lack of trust in God, she made it through the surgery, but she wasn't out of the woods yet. We still had to wait for the test results to see whether the cancer had spread. During this waiting time I realized I couldn't do anything to help her and was refusing to trust the One person who could. As I let go of my worries and turned my fears over to God, I finally found peace. Praise God; the tests came back clear, and the doctors declared her cancer free.

We often find ourselves holding on to something or someone we think is too precious to put in God's hands. We tend to forget that He is the safest place they could be. God wants us to trust Him completely so that He can give us peace, and that means letting go.

I am a witness!

—Savannah Cantrell, senior

Obedience Is Key

Matthew 2:1–18

H ave you ever stopped to think about the story of the wise men from the East? They traveled a great distance to see the Messiah. What would drive them to leave their homes and risk such a long journey to see a baby? I think the answer lies in the fact that they knew, in their souls, that this Baby was the answer to all of life's deepest questions. They obediently followed their consciences and set out for a foreign land.

As Matthew records, their journey wasn't easy. When they arrived in Jerusalem, they met with the devious King Herod. Herod was paranoid and angry when he heard their story and who they were looking for. In his thirst for power, Herod had already killed three sons and a brother whom he was afraid might overthrow him—he was not about to let a baby king usurp the throne. After meeting with the priests, King Herod called a private meeting with the wise men and instructed them to go on to Bethlehem and look for the Baby. When they found Him, they were to come back to Jerusalem and tell Herod where the Baby was so he, too, could go and worship Him.

The wise men set out for Bethlehem, and the star guided them to the home where Mary and Joseph were staying. The wise men worshiped Jesus and gave Him presents of gold, frankincense, and myrrh. After visiting with Mary, Joseph, and little Jesus, the wise men were told by God via a dream to return home by a different route because Herod wanted to harm Jesus. The wise men did as the angel instructed them.

If you think about it, the wise men were obedient to their consciences. They followed the star from their homeland; they went to Bethlehem based on Herod's orders; and then they listened to the angel and changed their travel plans to avoid King Herod.

This story could have ended a lot differently if the wise men hadn't been obedient and risked everything to see Jesus. Obedience is key in our personal relationship with Christ, and we must be willing to risk it all for Him.

—Terrell Basden, junior

Fighting Against Fear
Matthew 2:19–23; Luke 2:39, 40

Fear is an emotion we all experience, but we don't have to let it control our lives. I'm sure Mary and Joseph experienced fear when they fled to Egypt, and yet they chose to trust God and follow His plan, which He sent Joseph in a dream.

After spending years in Egypt, Joseph received another dream. This time the angel of the Lord told him that the ones who were trying to kill Jesus were dead and it was time to return to Israel. Joseph did not question God. He did not doubt Him. He simply did what God instructed. Joseph learned that the new ruler of Judea was Herod's son, which, naturally, made him afraid, but he didn't run, turn back, or doubt the dream. Instead, Joseph waited for further instruction. God gave him another dream and told him to head to Nazareth, which fulfilled the prophecy that Jesus would be called a Nazarene.

Just like Joseph, we often face the unknown, and fear threatens to overwhelm us. I knew of a boy named Thomas. His mother and father were struggling, so the state took Thomas and his siblings and placed them in a foster home. For a whole year, Thomas's father worked really hard. He went to classes to learn how to be a better father. He also worked hard to earn enough money to buy a house. Thomas's father got to know God and tried to have faith that everything would work out. Sadly, he made another mistake, and the state said his children could not return home to him. Thomas and his siblings were moved to another foster home. Fortunately, Thomas's dad never gave up. He had faith in God and trusted that He would help him do the work he needed to do to become the man he needed to be. He continued working, and, eventually, the family was reunited. Thomas's dad didn't let fear win. He didn't know what the future held, but he kept working and trusting.

Joseph didn't let fear control him. Instead, he chose to trust that God had a plan. What are you afraid of? What threatens to control you? What will it take for you to trust Him?

—Marc Briggs, freshman

Learning by Watching
Luke 2:41–52

My dad is the head doctor at a walk-in clinic in our town, and since I want to become a nurse, he lets me come help in the office so that I can see what it's like before college.

One particular day, I was running all over the office helping my dad's nurse. I was calling the patients to the examining room and taking their blood pressure. On occasion, I even got to hang out with Diego, my dad's nurse, in the examining room. As I followed Diego around, I asked questions when I didn't know what was going on or about what was causing a patient to have the symptoms they were describing. Diego explained everything to me, and I soaked up all the information.

One time a patient came in, and I noticed he had oily hair. In my mind I was thinking, Why would someone not want to shower and stay clean? After getting the patient situated, I privately mentioned my thoughts to Diego. He informed me that the person had schizophrenia. He told me about the psychological battle raging inside of a person with schizophrenia. I learned that people with this mental health disorder are scared that others are out to get them. This becomes a big problem when showering because they feel very exposed, and they imagine that someone is going to harm them.

We learn by observing and asking questions from people who are more knowledgeable than we are. Jesus grew up just like you and me, and He learned from God the Father, Mary and Joseph, and many other people. When He was twelve years old, Jesus attended the Passover celebration in Jerusalem. During this visit, He ended up at the temple where His parents found Him sitting at the feet of the teachers. Not only did Jesus listen to what the teachers said, but He asked questions and shared what He knew to be true from Scripture. At age twelve, Jesus was preparing for the job God had planned for Him.

Like Jesus, God has a special job for us. In order to learn what to do and how to do it, we need to listen to God and ask questions when we are confused. He will help us and guide us through everything. We just have to be willing to learn and grow.

—Merlyn Balboa, junior

Meeting With Jesus

"Whatever is good and perfect is a gift coming down to us from God our Father, who created all the lights in the heavens. He never changes or casts a shifting shadow" (James 1:17).

What stuck out to you in this verse?

_____

_____

_____

_____

_____

_____

What question would you like to ask God about this verse?

_____

_____

_____

_____

_____

_____

How can you apply this verse to your own life?

_____

_____

_____

_____

_____

The Only Way
Matthew 3:4–6; Luke 3:1–14

John the Baptist lived and died all in the name of Jesus. You can actually say that his whole purpose in life was Jesus. Matthew 3:4–6 gives us a very general idea about who John was. It tells us that he lived in the wilderness and completely relied on nature for his needs. He ate locusts and honey, and he wore camel skins. John distanced himself from the sins of society by staying in the wilderness, but he didn't shy away from talking to the people who came to him. The Bible tells us that people from Jerusalem and the surrounding region came to the Jordan River to hear John preach and to be baptized.

One of the messages that John the Baptist taught is found in Luke 3:8, 9: "Produce fruit in keeping with repentance. . . . The ax is already at the root of the trees, and every tree that does not produce good fruit will be cut down and thrown into the fire" (NIV). Talk about an intimidating message! No one wants to be thrown into the fire! As the people listened to John speak, they asked, "What should we do then?" (verse 10, NIV).

John presented a solution. Repent. Make things right. Then allow the Holy Spirit to fill you. In John 15:5, 6, Jesus explained the key to this process of transformation: "I am the vine; you are the branches. If you remain in me and I in you, you will bear much fruit; apart from me you can do nothing. If you do not remain in me, you are like a branch that is thrown away and withers; such branches are picked up, thrown into the fire and burned" (NIV).

The Pharisees believed that the way to salvation was through works: good deeds and strictly following the law. They thought they could do things on their own. They weren't connected to the Vine and were in danger of being cut down and thrown into the fire if they didn't repent and attach themselves to God.

The first step to salvation is repentance and recognizing that we mess up all the time and need God's help. Jesus died to save us, and He freely offers us forgiveness. We just have to say we're sorry and accept the gift. When we do that, we attach ourselves to the Vine. We won't be cut down because we'll naturally produce fruit as a result of being connected to God.

—Jacob Brown, junior

A Defining Moment
Matthew 3:13–17; Mark 1:9–11; Luke 3:15–23

As I read about Jesus' baptism, I tried to imagine what it would have been like if I had been there in the crowd. It would have been an unreal experience. I mean, you come to listen to John the Baptist preach, but in the end, you witness the baptism of the Messiah and hear the voice of God. Whoa! Imagine it from the beginning . . .

You arrive at the Jordan River with some friends and find a place among the crowd. John is preaching fire to the Pharisees, the leaders of the church, calling them a brood of vipers. You and your companions are whispering about his harsh message and what it could mean when John says these words: "I baptize you with water, but he who is mightier than I is coming, the strap of whose sandals I am not worthy to untie" (Luke 3:16, ESV). Everyone gets quiet as John continues to preach about this Prophet who is to come. You are intrigued, but you have so many questions about who and when and what. You keep listening.

Suddenly, John stops talking. His eyes are fixed on something in the distance. You turn to follow his gaze, and you see a Man walking through the crowd. All eyes are on Him. The crowd parts, and the Man walks down to where John is standing and asks to be baptized. John resolutely refuses. He insists that he needs to be baptized by this Man (Matthew 3:14). However, the Man replies that "It should be done, for we must carry out all that God requires" (verse 15).

After the baptism, things get even more interesting. As the Man is coming out of the water, a thundering Voice from heaven says, "This is my dearly loved Son, who brings me great joy" (verse 17). You get goosebumps as you realize the sanctity of this moment.

The Bible doesn't record what happened in the moments immediately following Jesus' baptism, but I like to think that John didn't preach for the rest of the day. Instead, he let the magnitude of the moment sink in for all the people who had witnessed Jesus' baptism. He left them to mull over the words he had been preaching for so long about the coming King.

Jesus' baptism was a public display of His commitment to God and the mission set before Him. He gave us an example to follow. What's stopping you from committing to God and being baptized for all to see?

—Josh Burgess, sophomore

Shattered Dreams

Psalm 6:2

Growing up, there were times I questioned God's existence. I am very analytical, so I questioned any teachings about Him. My stubbornness was sometimes a poor quality, but God used it for good when I faced the fight for my life.

I had always been an active kid, but when I was in the fifth grade, I began to struggle with running and exercising. What started out as fatigue became utter weakness and exhaustion. I couldn't even do the dishes without sitting down to rest. In only a few months, my life had completely changed. I couldn't even walk up a flight of stairs without getting dizzy. Day in and day out, my heart and body were slowly deteriorating. I soon fell into a state of depression. I felt hopeless. My dreams of growing up and becoming a doctor, nurse, photographer, director, teacher, or whatever were gone. My life had no meaning.

Finally, I was hospitalized. I was passing out left and right and experiencing the most intense pain ever. I could tell by my family's eyes that they thought I was going to die. Ironically, it was that realization that brought me to life. It wasn't quite like the movies, but I had a moment of clarity—I realized that it didn't matter that I was sick or that I could die, but it did matter that God was not an active part of my life.

I didn't die that summer. It took almost another year before the doctors finally diagnosed me with Hashimoto's disease. They put me on medication, but they said it would only help a little bit. They told me I would always be exhausted. Their prognosis cut me like a knife. I thought I'd never get better, never be able to run again. Then I decided that a disease was not going to end my life. I went gluten free, took the proper meds, and, most importantly, prayed desperately to a merciful God every day. As Christians, we have to go through difficult things to build a strong faith.

Today I climb flights of stairs on a daily basis with no breaks. I smile, knowing that my health is better than I ever imagined. God has blessed me more than this brief testimony does justice. I don't know what you are going through, but God can turn anything the devil intends for harm into something utterly beautiful. Trust me; I can attest to His awesomeness.

I am a witness!

—Sydney Hoffman, sophomore

Standing Strong

Matthew 4:1–11; Luke 4:1–13

Sometimes I think I have it rough, but nothing compares to what Jesus went through on this earth. We often focus on His brutal death, but He faced countless other hardships and challenges, including being tempted by Satan in the wilderness.

The story of the temptation of Jesus is an example of discipline and conquering the desires of the flesh. Human nature is corrupted by sin, but through Christ we are able to overcome any obstacle that is set out for us. If Christ is for us, no one can stand against us (Romans 8:31). This being said, we must discipline ourselves not to fall to the temptations that the devil throws our way.

While Jesus was in the desert, He was tempted by the devil in every way, just like we are. Because He was starving after fasting for many weeks, He was tempted by the basic human need for food. He was tempted to test God and His Word. And He was tempted by the benefits of power and authority. In all of these areas, Jesus was tempted to rely on Himself and take control of the situation instead of trusting His Father.

Yet Jesus prevailed through a strong faith in God and His Word. Through Scripture, Jesus was able to counter the attacks the devil threw at Him. He had to rely on God for strength. His example proves the point that with God all things are possible (Matthew 19:26).

This can make a difference for each one of us. We can learn how to resist the devil and succeed in life by praying daily for the power of the Holy Spirit and by staying connected to God through the study of His Word. Jesus knew that friendship with the world was enmity with God, and He could not afford that separation. He gave up the desires of the flesh so that He could overcome temptation.

Christ lived His life as an example for us to emulate. The devil wanted nothing more than to defeat Jesus, and he wants the same with you and me. His whole goal is to distract us and get us off track until we find ourselves worshiping him. We must take time to look deep within ourselves to see what we need to say no to and what is keeping us in bondage. We must look to Jesus, call upon His name, and cultivate discipline in ourselves if we want to withstand the temptations that Satan sends our way.

—Pedro Campbell, senior

Mistaken Identity
John 1:19–34

H ave you ever had someone confuse you for someone else? This spring we had a pastor come speak for our spiritual emphasis weekend, and he looked just like the owner of Papa John's Pizza. A bunch of students kept joking around with him, asking him if he was Papa John. One student even edited a picture of the speaker and put a pizza in his hands and then did a side-by-side comparison of the two men. It was really funny.

In this passage of Scripture, we find the priests and Levites confronting John the Baptist about his identity. They ask him whether he is Christ, Elijah, or a prophet. John's response to every question is no. They finally ask, " 'What do you say about yourself?' He [says], 'I am the voice of one crying out in the wilderness, "Make straight the way of the Lord," as the prophet Isaiah said' " (John 1:22, 23, ESV).

John knew who he was. He was confident in his purpose and in what God had asked him to do. He didn't let the priests sidetrack him from his mission of preaching about repentance and baptizing people in the name of God. Because he remained focused, he had the privilege of baptizing Jesus and introducing Him as the "Lamb of God, who takes away the sin of the world!" (verse 29, ESV).

Do you know who you are and what your purpose is? That's the big question we have to answer as we go through high school and head off to college. Are we going to define ourselves based on whom we hang out with, what we like to do in our free time, or what we're good at in school? Or are we going to define ourselves by who God says we are and the path He wants us to follow?

—Dylan Cannon, sophomore

Overturning Injustice
Psalm 11

Have you ever thought, *Of course Jesus was perfect; He had infinite wisdom, He always knew what to say, and He knew what people were thinking. God gave Him the power and authority to perform countless miracles?*

It's true that He had all these things, but they didn't just happen. Jesus spent time with God. He cultivated His connection with Heaven, and that relationship developed the wisdom and power that He displayed during His life.

Let's not forget the hardship that came with the blessing. Jesus was a target. Satan had his sights set on Jesus, and every move He made was met with opposition and hatred. The devil and his minions stirred up the hearts of the people, especially those of the religious leaders, against Jesus. He faced injustice, hatred, and ridicule. He endured slander, and His words were misunderstood. His was not exactly an easy life.

When we see or experience injustice, we want to make things right. We want justice to prevail. But often we try to take these things into our own hands. We fire back at the perceived offender or talk behind his or her back, stirring up support for our side of the story. We try to control the situation and make things right.

Instead, we need to take a cue from Jesus' playbook. He lived by the principle that David wrote about in Psalm 11. Jesus acknowledged the sovereignty of God:

The LORD is in his holy Temple;
    the LORD still rules from heaven.
He watches everyone closely,
    examining every person on earth.
The LORD examines both the righteous and the wicked (verses 4, 5).

Remembering this helps us to keep things in perspective. God sees every injustice, and in time the wicked will receive their punishment. In the meantime, we have to trust, like Jesus did, in God's divine plan and His ability to take care of those who are only living for themselves. What do you need to let go of and give to God today? I guarantee that He is still on His throne in heaven and sees all that goes on down here. He has the final say in everything. Will we trust Him to do what is right?

—Chaplain Kalie

Meeting With Jesus

"For I am not ashamed of this Good News about Christ. It is the power of God at work, saving everyone who believes—the Jew first and also the Gentile" (Romans 1:16).

What did you learn about God from this verse?

_____

_____

_____

_____

_____

_____

How should we relate to others based on this passage?

_____

_____

_____

_____

_____

What spiritual principle can you take from this reading?

_____

_____

_____

_____

_____

Teach Me

John 1:35–42

Why is it that we so often forget who God is? We know He is omniscient—He knows all of our sins; He knows what we are doing at all times; He even knows the number of hairs on our heads. We know He is omnipotent, having all power in heaven and on earth to do anything He wants. He is also omnipresent, meaning He can be everywhere at the same time. We talk about His authority, but do we forget that He is our Teacher?

I think we often forget that we need to learn from God by reading the Bible, studying His character, and then duplicating those characteristics in ourselves. God also teaches us by allowing challenging situations that we can learn and grow from to come our way.

When I arrived on campus my freshman year, I discovered that my work assignment was the nursing home. I didn't choose that job, and I was not happy about my work placement. The first month was horrible because I had such a negative attitude. But once I decided to make the most of my situation, I began to see that I was making a difference in the lives of the patients at the nursing home. I saw how happy it made them when I spent time with them. I also met some very nice people who reflected God's character. One of the residents I regularly visited was the kindest and most gentle person I had ever met. I loved spending time with him and listening to him tell stories.

The hardships I experienced at my first job were all God's way of preparing me for bigger challenges. He was molding me to be a better follower and servant. Once I accepted God as my Teacher, I had a much better experience and gained valuable lessons from the people around me.

When John pointed Jesus out of the crowd, two of John's disciples followed Jesus. They called out to Him, saying "Rabbi . . . where are you staying?" (John 1:38). *Rabbi* means teacher. They recognized His ability to teach them and lead them into all truth. We need to be like the disciples in this passage and be willing to follow Jesus and learn from Him.

—Kevin Burgess, junior

Optimism Wins

John 1:43–51

I like driving "junk" vehicles. I mean, they aren't junk to me, but other people may think so. Even though it isn't a bright, shiny new vehicle, I see the life left in the car, and I'm willing to take the chance on it, even driving long distances. Of course, I must admit that there is usually that thought in the back of my mind that wonders if we might not make it this time. However, I don't linger on those thoughts. I push them out of my mind and simply get the car ready for the trip.

While I am extremely optimistic about my car and long-distance trips, everyone else I know is extremely pessimistic—my dad being the main doubter. He is always questioning my sanity regarding long trips and the cars I choose to make those trips, even though I have a good track record with minimal breakdowns.

Just as my dad doubts me, Nathanael doubted that Jesus was the Messiah that Moses and the prophets had written about (John 1:45). Philip is convinced that Jesus is who they've been looking for, but Nathanael asks Philip, "Can anything good come out of Nazareth?" (verse 46, ESV). Philip persuades Nathanael to come and decide for himself, so they head off to find Jesus. When Nathanael meets Jesus face-to-face, Jesus states, "Behold, an Israelite indeed, in whom there is no deceit!" (verse 47, ESV)

Nathanael proceeds to ask how Jesus knows him, and Jesus blows his mind by telling him that He saw him sitting under a fig tree before Philip called him (verse 48). At this, Nathanael declares, "Rabbi, you are the Son of God! You are the King of Israel!" (verse 49, ESV).

Jesus doesn't get after Nathanael for doubting. Instead, He gives him a promise—He says, "You will see greater things than these" (verse 50, ESV).

It's easy to be pessimistic and doubt God's goodness when we live in such a broken world, but we need to hold on to God's promise that when we believe, we will see miracles take place that we never thought possible because God is in the business of taking junk and turning it into something amazing.

—Andrew Burnham, junior

The Missing Wheel
Psalm 34:7

Bumping along on the washboard roads of Nicaragua, our old farm truck slowly meandered along the banks of the Rio Coco. Three other students and I were student missionaries taking about forty village women fishing to supplement their sparse diets. We'd been on the road about two hours and were almost at our destination. The trip would have taken less than an hour back in the States, but the rough roads made traveling time consuming, dusty, and jolting.

Slowing near the river, we bumped to a sudden stop and careened to one side. We carefully climbed down from the truck and discovered our right front tire had broken off at the axle. We were in a very remote area, so there were no phones or help of any kind nearby. After assessing the damage, we decided to camp where we were for the night and go for help the next morning. We unloaded our supplies and began to set up camp while the village women scattered to fish in the river with their large nets.

As soon as the sun was up the next morning, two of us began walking for help. Eventually, we found someone with a couple of small jungle ponies. We paid to borrow them and set off, hoping we'd be able to find help soon. After hours of riding, we were able to locate someone with equipment to fix our wheel. They came back to camp with us and soldered the wheel back on.

We loaded our supplies and all the village women into the bed of the truck and set off for the mission station. Because the wheel was patched but not really fixed, we could only go in one direction and had to make a circle to turn, but we were happy to be on our way. We were bumping along when we suddenly noticed something very odd. Our right front tire was bouncing down the road in front of us, but we were still driving down the road as though we had all four tires. Then we felt the truck come to a gentle rest on the road. There was a deep ditch on one side of the road, and all of us could have been killed, but not one person was hurt. Not even a scratch! That day I saw God work in an unmistakable way, and it has carried me through other times when I wondered where God was. He is amazing, caring, and powerful!

I am a witness!

—Jeanne Hartwell, registrar

Ordinary to Extraordinary
John 2:1–12

No one could have anticipated that the Son of God's first miracle would take place at a party—a wedding feast, to be exact. At the request of His mother, Jesus jump-started His ministry, ushering in redemption and salvation. Many firsts cannot be expected, predicted, or planned, and in this, there is beauty.

I began walking at fourteen months of age. My mom recalls me wobbling from the bathroom to bedroom, teetering but taking off all the same. A few weeks later, I'm sure both heaven and house rejoiced upon realizing that I had learned to pray. Clasping my hands and tightly closing my eyes, I began to conclude our morning worships in the best way I knew how.

Later, my mom discovered I had learned to read when she heard me mumbling behind my brother's bedroom door. She opened the door to find me sitting on his desk, surrounded by books. Trying to decipher what exactly I was doing, she asked, "Juliet, what are you reading?" I replied, "Oh, books, baby!"

My parents celebrated their only daughter's "firsts" as they occurred—they never knew when I'd accomplish something new for the first time. That's the thing with firsts; sometimes they are unexpected, while other times we are forced to face a new situation we may wish we didn't have to face. I have often wondered whether Jesus knew His time was coming. Did He know His mother was going to catapult Him into the limelight, instructing the servants to follow whatever directions Jesus gave them? Jesus said to His mother, "My time has not yet come" (John 2:4).

Yet Jesus did as Mary asked, and in one fell swoop, the Messiah became a miracle worker. Jesus' time of teaching and transforming began. I believe Jesus did not intend for His first miracle to take place at a wedding reception. Yet He used this ordinary setting to showcase His Father's love and power. To me, this seems so right. With His mother by His side and friends nearby, Jesus left His first mark on His ministry by saving the best for last. Jesus turned the ordinary (water) into the extraordinary (wine), a process He still works today when He transforms us into all that we are meant to be.

—Juliet Bromme, senior

The Right Motivation
John 2:13–25

I think it's safe to say that your church doesn't have oxen, sheep, pigeons, and greedy money changers sitting in the foyer. This was the scene at the temple when Jesus was alive. God's house had become nothing more than a marketplace for livestock.

Jesus saw the temple as a sacred place—it was His Father's house. He was not satisfied with the lack of respect that people were showing in it. He saw that worldly things, such as greed and skepticism, motivated them, and He was not pleased with that. Jesus drove the animals and people out of the temple, turning over their tables and scattering their coins in the process. He did this to get their attention and wake them up to their true motives. The people were using the temple as a place to make money and show off, and they were not showing any respect to God.

Jesus knows how important motives are and how we need to put God first in everything we do and say. It is easy to slip into living for ourselves and not for God. We may start by doing something for God, but slowly our motivation changes, and we shift the focus onto ourselves. It is easy to get distracted by things of this world, so we need to be careful and make sure we are staying connected to God.

Jesus knows our hearts; He reads our minds. He is the only One who can lead us to salvation, but we have to be willing for Him to overturn things in our lives if they are getting in the way. The money changers had a choice to make that day when Jesus came crashing into their world, upending their way of doing things. Likewise, we have a choice to make every single day. Are we going to allow Jesus to lead in our lives even if that means disrupting our way of doing things? Or are we going to ignore Him and do things our way? Today, allow the Holy Spirit to change your heart. He will be right there with you, and He will help you to have the right motives and focus if only you ask.

—Taylor Brossfield, sophomore

A Personal Relationship
John 3:1–21

What's the most commonly quoted Bible verse? This same verse is often plastered on posters and displayed at sporting events. If you guessed John 3:16, you're right.

I've read this verse my whole life. In fact, along with the Lord's Prayer, it was one of the first verses I memorized. The beauty of this verse is that it sums up the whole gospel. Within one passage of Scripture, you find the essence of what we believe in. In summary, God loves us a ton. He loves us so much that He sent us Jesus, who lived and died for us. If we just believe in Him, we receive the free gift of eternal life.

As I read this verse in the context of the story in which it is found, I discovered something I had never thought of before. The central verse of salvation was not preached to a multitude of people. It was not included in the Sermon on the Mount. It wasn't shared with the five thousand. Instead, this beautiful message was shared in a personal conversation with Nicodemus. Did you catch that? We talk about Jesus being a personal God, but this proves it. In the secrecy of a private meeting at night, Jesus revealed the truth about His mission to a Pharisee who was seeking meaning in life.

Jesus wants to meet with us too! He wants to have those late-night talks in which He reveals more of who He is to us. The key to all of this is that we come to Him. Nicodemus sought out Jesus. Granted, he came to Him at night because he was fearful of what others would think and how it might hurt his reputation, but nonetheless, he came.

If something is holding you back from truly seeking God, let it go. What matters is that you come to Him. Whether it is in secret or in a crowd, simply come. Jesus is ready and willing to meet you where you are, how you are. He wants to get to know you. In turn, He wants you to know Him.

So, what's standing in your way from developing a personal relationship with Jesus? What steps do you need to take to come, like Nicodemus, to the One who knows you better than you know yourself?

—Chaplain Kalie

Meeting With Jesus
Hebrews 11:1

You are heading to your favorite restaurant. The minute you walk in the door, your stomach starts to grumble as the good smells hit your nostrils. This is definitely your favorite place to eat.

You're meeting some friends, but they aren't here yet. A host seats you at a table, and you peruse the menu as you wait. The server introduces herself and brings you your favorite drink. You check your watch. Where could they be? They're ten minutes late. You text them, but they don't answer. You are starting to get frustrated, partly because your stomach is growling and you want to order soon. Not wanting to be rude, you sit there and mess with your phone. You play a few games, check your social media accounts, send another text to your delinquent friends who don't seem to own a watch—and you wait.

As you're sitting there, absorbed with your phone, you sense that someone is standing beside the table. You look up, and you're surprised to see Jesus. Your first thought is, "Wow, I didn't know He liked this kind of food!" Then you remember your manners and invite Him to take a seat. I mean, your friends clearly aren't there yet anyway.

"It looks like you're waiting on your friends," Jesus says. "I know the feeling. I love hanging out with My friends, but many times it seems like they are busy and have other things going on. I understand the waiting game."

The words sink in as you realize that you often make Jesus wait.

"While you wait for your friends, do you want to chat? How are you doing? What's been going on in your life this last week?"

Take some time to talk to Jesus or write down your response to His question.

- -

Read the verse for the day and think about the promise it offers or what it tells you about God.

- -

If you were to talk about this verse with Jesus, what would you say? What would you ask Him?

- -

Face Value
John 3:22–36

When I was a lot younger, maybe eight or nine, I went through a phase in which I really liked to imitate people, mostly my mom and my older sister. I said my favorite color was the same as my sister's, or I tried to be interested in the things she was, which at the time was horses. When my mom was out of the house, I played dress up in her clothes or try to cook like her. I wasn't very successful in my attempts to be like my mom, but she was never mad at me when I tried. The funny thing is that over time I began to reflect the things that made my mom who she was. I naturally developed similar likes and dislikes. I said things she said, and I believed in the things she believed in. As I grew older, I became a reflection of my mom's character—anyone who knows my mom knows I am her daughter; it's obvious.

Today's passage talks about how John the Baptist was a mere reflection of the One who sent him. Likewise, Jesus was a reflection of His Father. And we are called to be a reflection of Jesus. How do I become like Christ? It happens the same way I began to reflect who my mom was. By spending time with God and making His ways our ways, we begin to reflect His character of love and sacrifice.

Because John the Baptist had a relationship with God, he was able to say, "I am filled with joy at his success. He must become greater and greater, and I must become less and less" (John 3:29, 30).

As humans, we tend to look to the world for our value because our culture has programmed us to do so—the boss is paid more than the employee, the teacher deserves more respect than the student, and the inventor receives more pay than the people who put together his ideas. However, as John showed us in his life of ministry, the kingdom of God doesn't work that way. When we place our value in what the Bible says about us, we see a different picture. Even though we are sinners and mess up all the time, we have been given the same task as Jesus—to point people to the Father. We can find our value in our mission. As we spend time with God, we discover our true value and imitate Him more.

—Kristin Burgess, junior

Jumping to Conclusions
John 4:1–26

When I was younger, my friends and I used to think that we were hot stuff. We thought we were so cool and that everyone wanted to be like us. If I'm completely honest, I used to judge people very quickly, no matter who they were. My friends did the same thing, which meant we were all a bad influence on each other.

Toward the end of my junior year of high school, while on our class history trip, a rumor about my friends and me started spreading. We were accused of something we hadn't done, but the gossip spread fast. When we got back to school, other students immediately began asking if it was true or not. I felt attacked. There were so many different stories flying around that we were pulled into the vice principal's office to sort through the whole thing. I was so mad! I could not believe that people I'd gone to school with for years believed these stories and helped spread the rumors. After a while, things died down.

Since then I've thought about how I often do the same. I hear a story, and I get caught up in the drama and judge others based on what I have heard without verifying the facts. I often contribute to the gossip and lies. I have to admit to myself that when the tables were turned on me, I felt horrible.

From that point on, I have tried to give people a chance and not jump to conclusions about them or believe everything I hear from others. It's not my natural inclination, but I'm trying to look at others like Jesus did: with love instead of judgment.

In today's passage, Jesus was resting at Jacob's well when a Samaritan woman came to get water. He asked her for a drink. She reminded Him that Jews did not like Samaritans. She'd been judged before for her race, and she thought it was odd that He was speaking to her. But Jesus didn't judge her for her race or the fact that she had been married five times and was living with a sixth man. He called her out on this, but He did so in love, and He offered her hope and a future in getting to know God.

I encourage you to start your day by treating others with kindness. Follow Jesus' example, and be quick to love instead of to judge.

—Alexandra Candamil, senior

Sirens and Prayers
Deuteronomy 31:6

What am I afraid of? Tornados! I remember hearing the blaring siren as a small child and being terrified because I knew it signaled that something bad was going to happen. When we heard that piercing warning, my parents and I headed downstairs, where I curled up on the couch by my mom while my dad joked (more like tormented me) about how a tornado was going to suck me up and swirl me around.

One spring day the weather was pretty bad. Afraid it was going to get worse, my dad picked me up from school early and took me home. I hadn't really seen my dad that worried before, which escalated my anxiety. My dad's nervousness grew worse as he and my mom monitored the weather and tried to decide whether she should ride out the storm at school or try to drive home and be with us. My mom, being more chill about it, decided to come home, which didn't sit well with my dad.

At this point, I was a bundle of nerves. My dad took me downstairs and told me we needed to pray for my mom's safety because the weather was steadily getting worse. A few minutes later, the wind picked up, and the warning siren went off. I was horrified, knowing that a tornado had been spotted somewhere close. We hid in a closet and continued to pray for my mom and our safety. As soon as we were done praying, it seemed as if the storm went from complete chaos to peace. We waited a few minutes before leaving the closet. As we emerged, we discovered that the storm had indeed died down. That's when my mom pulled into our garage. We thanked God for keeping all of us safe.

There's a verse in Deuteronomy that reminds us of Who's in control when life seems overwhelming: "Be strong and courageous. Do not be afraid or terrified because of them, for the LORD your God goes with you; he will never leave you nor forsake you" (Deuteronomy 31:6, NIV). When hard times come, remember that God is always there to help you through.

I am a witness!

—Cherise Piotrowski, freshman

Jumping in the Deep End
John 4:27–42

Dig into the recesses of your memory and think about a time when you were afraid to try something just because you'd never done it before and it was scary. I remember the first time I did a high ropes course. I was twelve, and I was nervous! I wasn't terrified of heights, but I can't say I loved the idea of climbing up a tree and walking across a thin cable strung between two towering pine trees twenty feet above the ground! My determination overcame my fear, and I slowly climbed the tree and inched my way across the cable.

Since then I've done many ropes courses and zip lines, but I can't say I've ever grown completely comfortable being that high off the ground. There's always a tinge of fear that I have to shove down, and I must remind myself that I can trust the safety equipment and the people who operate the facility.

I think this translates into how most of us feel about sharing the gospel with someone else. There is a tinge of uncertainty about what to say or how to say it or how the person will react to us talking about God and our faith. And yet there's merit in jumping in with both feet and just doing it, letting our determination to share Jesus with others overcome our hesitations.

The story of the Samaritan woman proves that you don't have to know everything. She had one conversation with Jesus, and yet she went and told others what He had done. John 4:39–41 says, "Many Samaritans from the village believed in Jesus because the woman had said, 'He told me everything I ever did!' When they came out to see him, they begged him to stay in their village. So he stayed for two days, long enough for many more to hear his message and believe."

Too often we want to feel comfortable before we try something new or scary, but if we always waited for comfort, we'd never drive a car, ride a roller coaster, go white-water rafting, go to college, or try out for the soccer team. The same goes for sharing Jesus with others. We're never going to know enough—even if we become pastors—because we're always learning something new! So what's it going to take to jump in and share what you do know? What's it going to take to overcome your fears and tell others about what Jesus is doing in your life?

—Chaplain Kalie

Vending Machine or Friend
John 4:46–54

How would you describe your relationship with God? Do you treat Him like a vending machine, only coming to Him when you want something and expecting that if you put in enough currency, you'll get what you want? Or do you treat Him like a Friend, talking to Him throughout the day and spending time with Him every chance you get?

It seems that the official in today's passage who goes to Jesus and begs for healing for his son is treating Jesus like a vending machine. " 'Unless you people see signs and wonders,' Jesus [tells] him, 'you will never believe' " (John 4:48, NIV).

The official responds by pleading with Jesus to heal his son, and Jesus tells him to go and that "[his] son will live" (verse 50, NIV). The official has faith that what Jesus said will happen, so he heads back home. Sure enough, the next day when he arrives, his servants run to meet him and tell him that his son is better. The official asks what time the boy recovered, and the servants tell him at one o'clock, which was the very hour that Jesus told him that his son would live. The Bible then says that the official and his whole family believed in Jesus.

Jesus is our best Friend, and He comes to us when we need Him the most, even when we sometimes slip into treating Him like a vending machine and just asking Him for stuff. The official put his faith on the line when he chose to believe Jesus' words and head back home. That one step of faith resulted in his son's healing and a whole family believing in Jesus.

With faith, anything is possible. With God, we can accomplish anything in the world.

—Christian Butler, freshman

Your Enemies
Psalm 18

Who are your enemies? It's an honest question, and I'm guessing you can name a few people who seem bent on making your life miserable. Of course, a follow-up question is, Have you done anything to make them hate you? If so, you need to fix how you are treating others. But sometimes it doesn't matter what you do; there just are certain people who dislike you for no apparent reason.

There was a girl a class below me all through elementary school and into my sophomore year of high school whom I could not figure out. One day she was nice to me, and the next day she was talking behind my back and trying to steal my friends. It was messy and weird. I always smiled and was nice to her, but she was mean and vindictive. I often came home crying to my mom because I just didn't know how to handle being in a small school with this girl, and my mom told me I needed to shower her with kindness no matter how she treated me. I can't say I always succeeded, but I tried to follow my mom's advice because deep down I knew that's how God wanted me to act.

My measly relationship challenges with this classmate pale in comparison to what Jesus dealt with on this earth. He had real enemies—people who were trying to kill Him—as did David. I wonder whether Jesus found comfort in David's psalms. Psalm 18 is full of promises of God's goodness, strength, and ultimate victory in the midst of an evil world where people seek to harm us. Check out these verses and remember to let God fight your battles. Our job is to be like Jesus, to trust in God, and to love those around us, whether they are our friends or enemies.

> The LORD is my rock, my fortress, and my savior;
> > my God is my rock, in whom I find protection.
> He is my shield, the power that saves me,
> > and my place of safety.
> I called on the LORD, who is worthy of praise,
> > and he saved me from my enemies. . . .
> God's way is perfect.
> > All the LORD's promises prove true.
> > He is a shield for all who look to him for protection. . . .
> The LORD lives! Praise to my Rock!
> > May the God of my salvation be exalted!
> He is the God who pays back those who harm me;
> > he subdues the nations under me
> > and rescues me from my enemies (verses 2, 3, 30, 46–48).

—Chaplain Kalie

Meeting With Jesus

"So letting your sinful nature control your mind leads to death. But letting the Spirit control your mind leads to life and peace" (Romans 8:6).

What can you share with others from this verse?

What truth is God sharing in this passage?

What stuck out to you in this reading?

Making It Right
Matthew 4:12–17; Luke 4:14–30

The goal of every religious person is to go to heaven. It's paradise, right? Who wouldn't want to go to such a wonderful place? Of course, the obvious question that arises among non-Christians, and even some Christians, is How do you get there?

Some people are under the impression that once you accept God's love, you are saved forever and will go to heaven no matter how you act after you accept Jesus. Others believe that you must be a good person and that you earn your way into the kingdom of heaven through good works and by keeping the commandments.

John 3:16 tells us that God sent His only Son to the world in order to save us and that if we accept His loving gift of salvation, we can be saved. This is indeed true; however, there is something we must do in order to receive this free gift—people often forget that we must repent and allow the Holy Spirit to change our ways. John the Baptist, whose job was to prepare the way for Jesus' ministry, proclaimed this idea. It was at the core of his message. He said, "Repent, for the kingdom of heaven is at hand" (Matthew 3:2, ESV).

Then, when Jesus started His ministry, He preached the same message: "Repent, for the kingdom of heaven is at hand" (Matthew 4:17, ESV). The first message Jesus shared at the start of His ministry was to repent and accept God's forgiveness.

Throughout the Bible, we see stories about repentance, which always leads to restoration and forgiveness. Think about the stories of David, Elijah, Moses, and Solomon. Even though these people sinned and made mistakes, they repented and made things right with God. He went on to use them for remarkable things. If we acknowledge our sins, repent, and accept the love of Jesus, one day we will be with our Savior in heaven. That's the beautiful promise of the gospel.

—Daniel Burke, junior

Gaining More

Matthew 4:18–22; Luke 5:1–11

Matthew and Luke both record stories of how Jesus called His first disciples—Peter, Andrew, James, and John. The stories are documented differently, which provides us with distinctive insights.

In Matthew 4, we find Jesus walking along the shore of the Sea of Galilee. As He passes by Peter and Andrew, He calls to them and says, "Come, follow me, and I will show you how to fish for people" (verse 19). Peter and Andrew drop all that they are doing and follow Jesus. That says a lot about Jesus' character and the authority He exudes. Peter and Andrew must sense that Jesus is no ordinary man. There is something different about Him that attracts the brothers to Him. This leads them to stop fishing and leave everything to follow Jesus. I imagine that they were excited that a Man with such great authority would ask simple fishermen to follow Him. Then Jesus calls James and John, who are fixing their nets with their father. The Bible tells us that they immediately dropped their nets, right in front of their father, and followed Jesus (verses 21, 22).

Luke tells the story slightly differently. Jesus is once again walking by the Sea of Galilee, and a large crowd is following Him. Jesus sees two empty boats, so He asks the owner, Peter, whether he can push Him out a bit from the shore so Jesus could preach from the boat to the crowd of people. Peter agrees. After Jesus finishes preaching, He says to Peter, "Now go out where it is deeper, and let down your nets to catch some fish" (Luke 5:4). It is midday, and Peter knows there will be no fish because they come out at night. Peter tells Jesus this but then sets aside his doubt and does as Jesus tells him. Jesus blesses Peter for his faith, and he catches so many fish that the nets are breaking and the boats are almost sinking because they are so full of fish. Then Jesus calls the four men to follow Him, and they leave everything and follow Jesus.

What do we need to give up to follow Jesus? What is standing in the way of dropping everything and doing what Jesus asks us to do? I believe that if we set aside our wants and desires and take what Jesus offers, we will be blessed to the extreme for it.

—Will Cantrell, sophomore

Little Signs Mean Big Things
Psalm 18:1–6

It had been a stressful day as I found myself preparing for Thanksgiving, running to the airport to pick up family members, helping my husband with his business, and juggling things at home. To add to the fatigue, I was three months pregnant with our first child. I had been in the car or on my feet since before the sun had come up. It was now evening, and finally I could rest. I headed to the bathroom, and that's when I noticed that I was bleeding.

It wasn't a lot of blood, but when you're pregnant, any amount of blood is cause for alarm. I panicked and called my husband. We were young and inexperienced, so we had no idea what this could mean. We decided to call the midwife. She sounded somewhat worried, but she asked some questions and reassured me that things would probably be fine. She asked me whether I was feeling contractions, and I didn't really know. My stomach was tight, so she recommended that I take a nice warm bath and see whether I could get my body to relax. Contractions are necessary when the baby is ready to be born, but if they happen too early, it can be a sign of the body trying to abort the baby.

I was terrified. I wanted this baby. I didn't want it to die. I prayed hard. And I cried harder than I've ever cried before. I also realized that some things were best given to God, even things we want so desperately. After what seemed like hours of crying and praying, I took a deep breath and told God I was giving Him my baby. If He knew something about its future that I didn't know, I wanted Him to handle it in the best way. I told Him I wouldn't be angry if that meant I couldn't have this baby.

I could hardly get the words out, even in prayer, and as soon as I said them, I sobbed uncontrollably. I chose to surrender my will to His plan. With my head down, I looked at my stomach, and I gasped. It was moving! I couldn't believe it. I looked again because it was ever so slight, but sure enough, right near my navel, there was a very slight movement of the skin. My baby was moving! It was the most reassuring and wonderful sign God could have sent. I just knew God had heard my prayer and that no matter what He was in control. I laughed and cried and called my husband, and we prayed in thanks together. Six months later, we had a beautiful, perfectly healthy baby girl.

I am a witness!

—Shannon Scott, science/technology/art/journalism teacher

The Road to Salvation

Mark 1:21–28

S ometimes it is easier to hide behind the walls of comfort and security rather than to leave our comfort zone. Confidence and authority are very admirable traits, although, at times it is easier to let another person take the lead for fear of the unknown.

Because of His close relationship with God the Father, Jesus did not hesitate to show His authority with confidence, which He always attributed to God. This stood out to the people because the other religious leaders of the day relied on tradition or statements such as "this Rabbi said" or "as teacher so-and-so put it" instead of focusing on Scripture and clearly interpreting it as Jesus did.

When Jesus spoke to the people in the synagogue, they were astonished by His confidence and wisdom. The authority of heaven was with Him, and it was evident in the way He preached. Not only did Jesus speak with clarity, but when a demon-possessed man entered the synagogue, Jesus cast out the evil spirit from the man.

Jesus' action was not by chance, of course, but was part of God's plan. Jesus came from heaven to relieve humankind of the burdens of sin and to save humanity from the raging war between good and evil. He was beginning the wonderful and merciful work of salvation, and He used this miracle as an example of that work.

Because of Jesus' close connection with God, He stepped out boldly and proclaimed the gospel. He didn't try to play it safe or look for the easy way out. He did with confidence what God called Him to do. Just as God led Jesus, He is constantly working to piece together His plan for our lives. Something may seem insignificant now, but later, when we can see more of the bigger picture, we realize that it was part of God's greater plan. Will we play it safe? Or will we give God our all, step out of our comfort zone, and do whatever He asks us to do?

—Olivia Carlson, junior

A True Superhero
Mark 1:29–34

Our society is obsessed with superheroes. There are movies, books, TV shows, toys, clothing, and all kinds of other merchandise dedicated to these fictional characters who can save the world. Kids and adults debate about the best superhero and the coolest superpower.

Of course, none of these hold a candle to the one and only true Superhero—Jesus. Mark 1:29–34 shares the story of how Jesus healed Peter's mother-in-law and many others right after He displayed His authority over an evil spirit while teaching in the synagogue.

Jesus and the disciples left the synagogue after the service and headed to Peter's house for Sabbath lunch. When they got there, Peter's mother-in-law was sick in bed. Someone alerted Jesus to the fact that she had a fever. He walked into the bedroom and simply took her by the hand and helped her sit up, and the fever left her. She immediately felt well, so she got up to serve lunch to Jesus and His friends.

The Bible doesn't tell us what they did for the rest of the afternoon—maybe they took a Sabbath afternoon nap! But it does tell us that after sundown, the whole town showed up at Peter's house. They brought people who were sick and demon possessed to Jesus to be healed. Others just came to watch Jesus work. We don't know how many people were healed, but I can't imagine that Jesus turned anyone away.

The very last verse of this passage reminds us of Jesus' ultimate authority. It says, "He cast out many demons. But because the demons knew who he was, he did not allow them to speak" (Mark 1:34). Did you catch that? Jesus wouldn't allow the demons to speak because He wasn't ready to reveal that He was the Messiah, the Son of God. Jesus controls everything. Even the demons are still under His authority!

Whom are we worshiping? Whom are we giving our time and attention to? Are we mesmerized by the fictional superheroes of society? Or are we enamored by the God of the universe who knows all, sees all, and has all power?

—Chaplain Kalie

The Mission Field
Mark 1:35–38; Luke 4:42, 43

I was so excited I could hardly contain myself. It was the spring break of my junior year, and my sister and I were about to go on our first mission trip, which also happened to be our first trip outside the country. After an eighteen-hour plane ride and a six-hour car ride, we finally made it to the Maasai Mara in Kenya, Africa.

We settled into our accommodations, and the next day we headed to the work site. I had so much fun that first day working on the dormitories we were building that I didn't want to leave. I was excited to continue the building project the second day, but I ended up jamming my finger, so they moved me to helping with Vacation Bible School.

At first, I was a little sad about having to work with the kids every day because I really wanted to work on the building site or with the medical crew, but as the week wore on, my outlook changed. I began to get to know the kids. I began to build relationships with them—not only the young kids but also the students who were my age and the adults at the school. I began to see the impact I was having on them, and it was amazing to me. Growing up in the church, I was always surrounded by people who knew Jesus. Working with those kids, I found out that not everyone knows about God and not everyone knows the basic things I had been taught from the time I was little.

I left Africa with a new outlook on God and His call to share the gospel with everyone. When Jesus was on this earth, He showed us what it's like to be a missionary. In Mark 1:38, Jesus told His disciples, "Let us go somewhere else—to the nearby villages—so I can preach there also. That is why I have come" (NIV).

Christ was our ultimate example of what being a missionary should look like. Shouldn't we follow Jesus' example, share the message of Christ with everyone and not just keep it to ourselves? The good news of the gospel is made to be shared.

—Alexis Castro, senior

Meeting With Jesus

"Dear brothers and sisters, when troubles of any kind come your way, consider it an opportunity for great joy. For you know that when your faith is tested, your endurance has a chance to grow. So let it grow, for when your endurance is fully developed, you will be perfect and complete, needing nothing" (James 1:2–4).

What question would you like to ask God about these verses?

How can you apply these verses to your own life?

What can you share with others from these verses?

Just Ask

Matthew 8:1–4; Mark 1:40–45

I am a very shy person, so my mom decided that it would be good for me to go away for high school. We live in South Korea, and in addition to working on my social skills, she thought it would be good for me to learn English, so she began looking for a school for me to attend in America. She began praying about it, and people recommended a school in California and one in Georgia. She kept praying, not sure which school to choose. One morning, God answered her prayer. She had just finished talking to God about the schools and had opened her Bible. As she was reading, she came to a verse that talked about going south. Georgia is obviously in the South, while California is in the West. My mom decided right away to send me to Georgia-Cumberland Academy (GCA). It was a hard adjustment for me, and I struggled, but over time, I have settled into life at school and am enjoying my time here.

If my mom hadn't asked God to guide her, I wouldn't be at GCA. God wants to help us. He is ready to help us. We just have to ask.

In today's passage, a leper came to Jesus and asked for healing: "If you will, you can make me clean" (Mark 1:40, ESV). The Bible says that Jesus had pity on the man. Jesus wants to help us overcome sin and the things we struggle with. But we have to believe, like the leper, that Jesus can help us. The man with leprosy believed that Jesus had the power to heal him. As a result, he approached Jesus confidently, and Jesus healed him.

In addition to helping us with whatever we are facing, this story is also about being cleansed. We may not have physical leprosy, but we have other things in our lives that we need to be cleansed of. The leper recognized his need and came to Jesus. We need to see the problems in our lives and come to Jesus for cleansing, and then we need to stay close to Him. Whenever I focus on reading and studying the Bible and staying away from the stuff that people usually do for entertainment (which sometimes is inappropriate), I learn truths that help me become a better person. We each need to ask ourselves, What do I need to be cleansed from? Talk to God about it today.

—Alex Choi, junior

Spiritual Paralysis

Matthew 9:1–8; Mark 2:1–12; Luke 5:17–26

There are about 5.4 million people in the world who are paralyzed.* When I think of a paralyzed person, I mostly think of someone who cannot move a part of his or her body. But if you think about it, you could also be spiritually paralyzed. As Christians, our job is to tell the world about Christ, but many of us just sit around and do nothing. We wait for someone else to do it, but we don't seem to want to do it ourselves.

The four friends who brought the paralytic to Jesus to be healed didn't sit around discussing how to help their friend. They took action. They rigged up a stretcher they could carry, and they physically carried their friend to Jesus. Then, when they couldn't get into the house, they climbed up on the roof, took the tiles off, and lowered the bed through the ceiling in front of Jesus.

The Bible says the following: "When Jesus saw their faith, he said to the paralytic, 'Son, your sins are forgiven' " (Mark 2:5, ESV). It was because of the faith of the four friends and the paralyzed man that Jesus healed him not only physically but also spiritually.

Jesus wants us to actively share our faith and spread His Word. We talk about Jesus in church and school, but we need to share that with the world. I know that most of us won't travel around the world, but we can go to our family and friends and tell them what we are learning about God from our religion classes or in Sabbath School or church. Doing little things like that can cause a ripple effect and turn into something huge.

We make too many excuses about why we can't share God with others, but they are just excuses. God calls us to stop being paralyzed spiritually. What are you going to do about it?

—Kaiden Coker, sophomore

---

* Brian S. Armour et al., "Prevalence and Cause of Paralysis—United States, 2013," *American Journal of Public Health* 106, no. 10 (October 2016), https://ajph.aphapublications.org /doi/10.2105/AJPH.2016.303270.

So Many Decisions

Isaiah 58:11

S ome people know from childhood what they want to be when they grow up. Not me. At one point, I thought I wanted to be a hairstylist because I liked fixing my friends' hair. Then I thought I could be a physical education teacher because I was good at sports. In college, I started out as a music major because I was a decent pianist. That lasted one term, and then I switched to pre-physical therapy. I finished my prerequisites and was accepted into PT school. I thought I'd finally figured it out, but I struggled with science classes and often felt like a fish swimming against the current, struggling to keep up with my classmates.

In the middle of my junior year of college, I panicked as I thought about the future. Getting the strong sense that physical therapy was not for me, I spent hours thinking about my options. Making the decision to drop out of the PT program wasn't easy, but it gave me a huge sense of relief. But now what? Assessing my interests and abilities, I became open to the idea of teaching. But what could I teach? Stressed by the weight of this life-altering decision, I pleaded with God to show me what to do.

As the winter term began, I slipped into the church for a chapel service. I was scared and frustrated. The organist played quietly as noisy college students entered. Opening the hymnal, I read the words of the familiar hymn "In the Heart of Jesus" as he played. "In the mind of Jesus there is thought for you, Warm as summer sunshine, sweet as morning dew; Why should you be fearful, why take anxious thought, Since the mind of Jesus cares for those He bought?"*

Comforting words, for sure. Then, when I came to the third verse of the hymn, tears came to my eyes. "In the field of Jesus there is work for you; Such as even angels might rejoice to do; Why stand idly sighing for some lifework grand, While the field of Jesus seeks your reaping hand?"† God spoke to me through the words of a simple hymn, reassuring me that my life and my career were in His hands.

Many years have gone by since that wintry day in chapel. As I look back, I can see how God faithfully kept His promise and provided a wonderful career in education for me. You can trust God to help you make career decisions or any other decision. He has a place for you to work where you can make a difference for Him.

I am a witness!

—Nancy Gerard, alumni and development director

---

* Alice Pugh, "In the Heart of Jesus," *SDA Hymnal,* no. 577, public domain.
† Pugh, "In the Heart of Jesus."

Follow Me!

Matthew 9:9–13; Mark 2:13–17; Luke 5:29–32

When I first read these passages, I thought, *Yeah, I know what this is talking about. Jesus asks Matthew to be His disciple. I've read this before.* But then I stopped and wondered, *Why would Jesus ask* him? I mean, seriously, why Matthew? He was a tax collector, and nobody liked tax collectors. They cheated people, they were greedy, and they were just jerks in general. I didn't understand why Jesus would pick one of the dirtiest and the worst people of that time. What's the deeper meaning?

That's when it hit me. Jesus was making an example of Matthew. He was showing the Pharisees, and me, thousands of years later, that He has the power to transform anyone who believes in Him. Jesus didn't care how badly Matthew had messed up, and He doesn't care how badly we've messed up. All He cares about is whether we answer the call when He says, "Follow Me."

Last year I had just finished taking an algebra retake test. I had done poorly on the previous test, and my teacher allows one retake test per semester, so I decided to use it for that one. I walked out of the building, and two of my friends were standing there. They asked me whether the retake test was easy because they were going to take it later. They asked me what kind of problems were on the test, and I decided to tell them. As I was explaining the questions, another teacher walked out of the building and caught me red-handed. She then told my math teacher. I was embarrassed and ashamed of myself. I prayed and cried as I walked home. I then told my dad, who encouraged me to go apologize to both teachers. I talked to the girl to whom I told the answers, and we went together. We told our math teacher that we were sorry. I then went and found the teacher who had caught me. I apologized to her, and she forgave me too.

Matthew messed up when he stole from people. I messed up when I told my friend the answers to the test. The bottom line is that we all need Jesus. In this same passage, Jesus told the Pharisees: "Those who are well have no need of a physician, but those who are sick. I came not to call the righteous, but sinners" (Mark 2:17, ESV). We are all sinners, which means we all need Jesus. God will never, never stop loving us. We just need to repent of our sins and choose to follow Him.

—Haydn Collins, sophomore

Keep Moving Forward

Matthew 9:14–17; Mark 2:18–22; Luke 5:33–39

An old drunk sat in his usual spot on the sidewalk. He was down to the bottom of his last bottle, and he had little chance of getting more. He watched the people pass by, sipping slowly on his cheap wine. Soon he spotted a young man carrying a bag of groceries, and he thought, *I bet he'll have some good stuff. Maybe he'll give me some.* So he said to the young man, "Hey fella, you got any good stuff? I'm almost out."

The young man had seen this guy before, and he knew that the "good stuff" he was talking about was wine, but all he had in his bag was grape juice for his kids. *Maybe if I give him a bottle of grape juice, he'll stop drinking wine,* the young man thought. The young man turned to the old man and said, "Sure, I'll share some of my good stuff with you."

As you can imagine, the old man wasn't pleased with the grape juice. In his estimation, it wasn't the "good stuff" he was looking for. Someone who has drunk wine for a long time may not like grape juice instantly. For them the wine is sweet and the juice is bitter.

When Jesus was on this earth, the Pharisees didn't understand His new way of thinking. They struggled to accept His teachings and the way He interpreted Scripture. They were stuck in their old way of thinking. They needed to come to Jesus and let Him fill them with the truth. They were religious, but they were trapped in wrong thinking.

This is the same as people who are stuck in the world and are constantly tempted to fall back into their old way of doing things, whether it is stealing, lying, anger, prideful behavior, or any other vice. People often get frustrated with themselves and give up, thinking they are too far gone for God to save them. But we need to be patient. There is a reason living in faith is sometimes called "the Christian walk." It takes many steps to get where we are going; it takes time, and that's OK.

—Savannah Cantrell, senior

Abandoned
Psalm 22

I attended a junior academy in Florida, and I was on the yearbook staff my freshman and sophomore years. It was March, and we were working to get the yearbook finished and sent off to the printer. My best friend and I, along with a few other classmates and my brother, who was two grades below me, were diligently working on the yearbook one evening until 10:00 P.M. Quitting time arrived, and we began cleaning up the mess we had made. My mom showed up, and my brother headed to the car. I had a bag of trash, so I told them I would meet them by the dumpster. I walked around the side of the school building, expecting them to follow me. Instead, as I approached the dumpster, my mom pulled out on the main road and took off toward home.

I quickly threw the trash away and, don't ask me why, went running after them. (This was before cell phones, so I couldn't just call her and remind her that she had left me behind.) I had been forgotten. Abandoned. Left behind. Apparently, they made it to the second stoplight before my brother blurted out, "Hey, didn't you forget Kalie?" My mom immediately turned around and came back to the school where she found me sitting on the curb.

OK, I know I'm being dramatic when I say that I was abandoned. I obviously knew my mom would figure it out eventually and return for me. But we face times in our lives when challenges come and bad stuff happens, and we often feel abandoned by God. We cry out and ask Him where He is. Jesus did the same thing on the cross. He said, "My God, my God, why have you abandoned me?" (Matthew 27:46), which are the same words David uses in Psalm 22:1. David goes on to say, "Every day I call to you, my God, but you do not answer. Every night I lift my voice, but I find no relief" (verse 2).

Have you ever felt like God wasn't answering you? Have you felt like He has abandoned you? When we feel this way, we have to remind ourselves of the truth, which David does in Psalm 22:3–5:

> Yet you are holy,
>> enthroned on the praises of Israel.
> Our ancestors trusted in you,
>> and you rescued them.
> They cried out to you and were saved.
>> They trusted in you and were never disgraced.

We have to hold on to what is true when we are in the midst of a trial. And the truth is that God is good and He loves us very much.

—Chaplain Kalie

Meeting With Jesus

"Give your burdens to the LORD, and he will take care of you. He will not permit the godly to slip and fall" (Psalm 55:22).

What did you learn about God from this verse?

_____

_____

_____

_____

_____

_____

What spiritual principle can you take from this reading?

_____

_____

_____

_____

_____

_____

What can you share from this verse with others?

_____

_____

_____

_____

_____

_____

The Reflection of Christ
John 5:1–15

I was in Pathfinders for about five years, and throughout those years, we learned how to make fire in different ways. Our Pathfinder leader showed us one way to start a fire with a magnifying glass. He aligned the magnifying glass with a beam of light from the sun, and as the light hit the leaves, it started a small fire that we could then build up.

Just the same, if you sit and shine something against a mirror, you know that the light will bounce off the mirror onto other surfaces in the room. The truth is that many things on earth reflect light, such as water, polished metal, or anything smooth and shiny.

The Bible tells us that Jesus is the true Light of the world, and He shines on everyone so that they may know Him and reflect His light to other people, just as a mirror or magnifying glass does. When Jesus healed the man by the pool of Bethesda, the man had a story to tell of God's goodness. He had been sick and crippled for thirty-eight years, but now he could walk again. Although the Bible doesn't tell us what he did with his life after being healed, I can only imagine that he told everyone he knew that Jesus had made him whole again. Jesus brought light into his life, and the man let it bounce off him onto other people by sharing his story.

God created us to be in relationship with Him, and He's given us a job to do. He's asked us to tell others about Him and what He has done for us. If you shine a light onto a dull surface that has no shine or smoothness, you will not get a reflection. Just the same, if you turn away from God, there is no way for His light to reflect off you onto others. People won't know who God is if His light doesn't reflect from us onto others.

What are some ways that God shines through you? How can you reflect Him today?

—Kiera Coker, senior

Work for God

John 5:16–30

T he Father and Jesus are one and the same—They are both God. And yet Jesus didn't do anything that God the Father didn't tell Him to do. He obeyed His Father. Jesus makes this clear in John 5:19: "Very truly I tell you, the Son can do nothing by himself; he can do only what he sees his Father doing, because whatever the Father does the Son also does" (NIV).

Jesus came to earth to save us from our sins and deliver us from evil, but He didn't carry out this mission by Himself. Jesus and the Father worked together as a team. Jesus worked where, when, and how the Father commanded. He never worked for the approval of people; He always worked for God (verses 41–43, NIV). If He had worked to please the Pharisees or the people, Jesus would have failed to save us because He would have succumbed to teaching the people exactly what the religious leaders were teaching or He would've been crowned king by the people.

In addition to talking to the Pharisees about His connection with God, Jesus also reminds them what is at stake—eternal life. "Very truly I tell you, whoever hears my word and believes him who sent me has eternal life and will not be judged but has crossed over from death to life. . . . For as the Father has life in himself, so he has granted the Son also to have life in himself. And he has given him authority to judge because he is the Son of Man. . . . By myself I can do nothing; I judge only as I hear, and my judgment is just, for I seek not to please myself but him who sent me" (verses 24–30, NIV).

Jesus recognized that He was nothing without the Father. This seems kind of ironic because He is God, but He was also totally dependent on God the Father. While Jesus was on this earth, They were in partnership to save us. And They continue that mission in heaven. How will we respond?

—Briana Castro, senior

A Life of Service

James 1:27

I have seen God work in my life in many different ways, but He specifically led me to my future career path. I'm one of those people who likes to have a plan in place. When I was younger, I often felt lost, wondering what God had planned for my life. I wanted purpose. I wanted to know I was helping others. When you're a kid, people often ask you what you want to be when you grow up, but it gets even worse when you are in high school. Everyone wants to know what your future plans include.

In the midst of all these questions, one could usually find me asking myself, What am I supposed to do with my life? How can I make a difference? The older I became, the more nervous I was about what my future held for me.

One Sabbath morning, our pastor talked about the future and how it could be scary if no one was there to guide you down the right path. He then told us that all we had to do was pray and ask our heavenly Father for guidance. I felt terrible as I thought about all the time I'd spent worrying about my future career. I had forgotten that all I had to do was go to God in prayer. That afternoon I begged God to show me what I should do with my life to glorify Him. Sometimes you receive your answer right away, but other times you have no choice but to be patient and wait. God tested my patience.

Finally, after three weeks, I began to see my prayer being answered in little ways. People began to come to me with their troubles. Through prayer and the thoughts God put in my mind, I was able to help them. All of these instances solidified the idea that I should become a counselor. I was at peace when I settled on this career path. I knew that I could help people come to Him in the midst of whatever struggle they were facing.

I hope that, as a counselor, I can bring people to Jesus. Prayer is powerful, and God will guide you to where you need to be if you will ask.

I am a witness!

—Heather Morris, junior

Authentic

John 5:31–47

It seems that every time I sit down to watch TV, a charity commercial comes on. You've seen them advertising their need for money to stop the extinction of the panda bears or feed children in developing countries or take care of dogs in animal shelters. Don't get me wrong; these are real needs that we should support, but it is hard to know whether they are trustworthy. If I give money, will it really go to the cause?

My dean recently shared a video with us during dorm chapel about the journey of one man to provide clean water for people around the world. As I watched the video, I was impressed with his commitment to helping people and the detail he provided about his charity. He talked about water sensors to show how much water was being used and map tags to show where in the world the donated money went to bring clean water for those in need. He provided tangible, visible evidence to convince his audience that his company is authentic.

As I reflected on this, along with the Bible passage for today, I gained a better understanding of what Jesus was saying in John 5:39, 40: "You study the Scriptures diligently because you think that in them you have eternal life. These are the very Scriptures that testify about me, yet you refuse to come to me to have life" (NIV).

We can be very skeptical of things, whether they are charity organizations or something else. But the kicker is, when we have enough information to know whether something is authentic and reliable, what do we do? More often than not, we come up with excuses not to get involved.

Are you skeptical of God and the Bible? Or do you believe?

I can assure you that as I've studied, I've found that God is real, Jesus is alive, and the Holy Spirit lives within us. He has given us the Bible to help guide us on the right path, and trust me, it is the most dependable thing on the planet. Sometimes we don't want to follow what the Bible says because it requires us to give up things we've grown attached to, which often leads to us make excuses about why we should be allowed to do this or that, even though we know God says no for our greater good. God wants us to follow what the Bible says because He wants the best for us. Even though it may seem impossible, God is right there to help us, and the reward is far greater than anything on earth.

—Aleah Clarke, junior

Made for Man

Matthew 12:1–8; Mark 2:23–28; Luke 6:1–5

When I was a kid, I always thought that the Sabbath was full of rules. My siblings and I longed for sunset so we could watch a movie or play a game that wasn't approved for the Sabbath. Sure, I did recognize the benefits that Sabbath held, like being able to go to church and visit with friends, having no schoolwork, playing outside, and eating good food, but I always seemed to focus on the disadvantages. My parents, along with all the other adults I knew, made me think that Sabbath was all about what I couldn't do.

In today's passage of Scripture, we find the Pharisees blaming Jesus and the disciples for harvesting grain on the Sabbath. The Pharisees were so focused on the law that they couldn't open their eyes to see what the Sabbath was actually made for. They were blind to the blessing of the Sabbath.

As I've grown older, I have realized that Sabbath isn't a burden—it actually lightens the load. Someone told me a few years ago that our bodies naturally get tired on Friday because we need the rest of Sabbath. Now, whether that is true or not, it helped me feel the true importance of the Sabbath. My body definitely gets tired during the week, and I now long for the Sabbath. Many times, we look at the Bible and the fourth commandment and think, *How can the Sabbath be considered a blessing when there are so many laws to be followed?*

But in Mark 2:27, Jesus said, "The Sabbath was made for man, not man for the Sabbath" (NIV). To me, this verse is telling us that we weren't made just to worship and follow the rules of Sabbath for God's sake. God knew from the beginning of time that we needed a day to rest. Our weeks can be rough, and we can't carry the weight indefinitely, so we have the gift of the Sabbath to ease our burden. It is our special day when we can worship, praise, and have an intimate relationship with Him because we love Him. God knew that we needed the Sabbath—a day with Him, a day of rest. And so He gave us the Sabbath—and He saw that it was good (Genesis 2:2, 3).

—Stephanie Davis, sophomore

A Prayer at Thirty Thousand Feet
Matthew 12:9–14; Mark 3:1–6; Luke 6:6–11

Two years ago, I boarded a plane to travel home to China from school. I had made the trip before, and this flight felt like all the others. The flight was scheduled to take approximately sixteen hours. I always try to take a long nap on the plane to help avoid terrible jet lag when I land. I would only wake up when the flight attendants started passing out food.

However, this flight was different. I fell asleep, but I did not wake up to the kind voice of the flight attendants asking me what I wanted to eat. Instead, I woke up to violent shaking. We had hit very bad air turbulence. The flight attendants were trying to comfort people, but they could hardly stand, so they sat down and spoke to us through the PA system.

People were scared. Some people crying or whispering. Others tried to comfort those around them. I heard many people praying in different languages. Suddenly, the old lady sitting beside me picked up my hand and asked me if I wanted to pray with her. At that time, I was not a Christian, so I personally wasn't sure how prayer worked, but I said yes anyway. The old lady held my hand and slowly started talking to Someone. I don't remember what she said, but I do remember feeling comforted. From then on, I began to believe in the God I was learning about at school.

In Matthew 12:9–14, the Pharisees try to trap Jesus by asking Him whether it is OK to heal on the Sabbath. Jesus answers by saying, "If you had a sheep that fell into a well on the Sabbath, wouldn't you work to pull it out? Of course you would. And how much more valuable is a person than a sheep! Yes, the law permits a person to do good on the Sabbath" (verses 11, 12).

The Pharisees were more worried about tradition than helping people. The old lady who prayed with me could've worried about how I would respond or whether it would be awkward, but she didn't. Because she took the opportunity to share her faith, even in a small way, she showed me Jesus, and it made a difference in my life.

—Cinsilia Yang, senior

Meeting With Jesus

Isaiah 54:10

Y ou sink into the couch and flip on the TV. You scroll through Netflix, looking for a show to binge watch, but after fifteen minutes of searching, nothing looks entertaining. You turn off the TV and grab your phone. You play a few games, and then you open Snapchat and Instagram.

After scrolling through the latest posts, you come to the realization that everyone else's lives seem so interesting. Your friends are traveling, hanging out at each other's houses, going out to eat, or doing something fun while you are stuck at home by yourself, desperately trying to fill the time with something to do. You turn off your phone and lie on the couch in silence.

Psst!

You turn over and see Jesus sitting in the recliner across the room.

"What are you doing?" He asks.

"Not much." *Isn't that obvious?* you think sarcastically.

"Hey, I wasn't trying to push your buttons. I just figured I'd stop by and hang out for a while if you weren't busy," Jesus says.

Oh, right! I forgot He can read me like a book and knows my thoughts! Sometimes I wonder if that's a good thing or a bad thing.

Jesus' gentle voice brings you back to the moment. "So, what's on your mind today? I'm here to listen to whatever you want to talk about. Even though I know you better than you know yourself, I'm not here to analyze you—I'm here to spend time with you."

Take some time to talk to Jesus or write down your response to His question.

Read the verse for the day and think about the promise it offers or what it tells you about God.

If you were to talk about this verse with Jesus, what would you say? What would you ask Him?

Don't Say a Word

Matthew 12:15–21; Mark 3:7–12

Jesus came down to earth and did many extraordinary things. In today's verses, a great multitude was following Jesus, and "He healed all the sick among them" (Matthew 12:15). As I was reading, one thing that stuck out to me in these passages is that Jesus told the people not to spread the news about Him. At first this sounded odd, especially since our job is to tell the world about Jesus and His love, so I decided to dig deeper.

The passages say that people were coming from all over the place to be healed by Jesus; however, we know that healing people was not Jesus' sole purpose on earth. Jesus ultimately came to provide us with spiritual healing, not just physical healing. I think He wanted to minimize the attention He received as a physical healer so as not to diminish His true purpose of taking away the sins of the world.

Another thing that stood out to me was the amount of power Jesus holds, not only over the earth but also over evil spirits. We cannot generally see evil spirits physically because they are invisible, but we can see their effect as they manifest themselves in the people they control. The evil spirits mentioned in Mark 3 knew who Jesus was. As soon as the evil spirits saw Jesus, they took control of the people they were in and fell down before Jesus, crying out, "You are the Son of God" (verse 11, NKJV).

Although the evil spirits knew that Jesus was the Son of God, He would not allow them to tell the truth to the people. This may sound weird until we realize that the job of revealing the nature of Christ was specifically given to the Holy Spirit, not to the evil spirits. Evil spirits are under the control of Satan, who is the father of lies. And even though Satan knows and can quote Scripture, his main goal in life is to deceive us, so Jesus commanded the evil spirits to be silent.

Jesus knew exactly what He was doing. He had good reasons for His command, even if it didn't make sense to the people. Jesus still knows exactly what He is doing, and He has good reasons when He tells us to, or not to, do something. The question is, Will we listen?

—Mei Chin, senior

The Chosen

Mark 3:13–19; Luke 6:12–19

Jesus had a lot of people following Him, but He called twelve to be His disciples and to carry on His work of preaching and healing the sick and casting out demons (Mark 3:14, 15). Jesus was only one person, and although He was healing whole crowds of people, He empowered His disciples to perform good works in God's name, thus being able to heal that many more people.

The disciples were ordinary people like us, but because they allowed God to fill them, they could do the impossible. God gives to all people this power to do good things in His name, but many times we don't see it or use it.

I've had moments when I knew I could help someone, like the day my mom and I were going to get a pizza. We saw a homeless man, and my heart started to ache. I felt a tugging, and I asked God if He wanted me to help the man. I felt certain the answer was yes, so I gave the man some money. I know some people say, "How do you know whether he used it for something good or bad?" But I don't think it matters. It's not our job to worry about how a person in need uses the help we give them. It's our job to show God's love to others when they are in need.

The bottom line is that God wants us to help others. That might mean giving away money, or it might mean simply being there for someone during a really tough time.

Not only do we give God's love away, but we also receive it. I've had many moments in life when I needed someone to be there for me and give me strength, and God brought me a second family and people to care for me. I have a friend who gives me a job whenever I need money to bring home. I have another friend that I consider family, because they brought me into their home and cared for me.

Just as Jesus gave the disciples a mission, God asks us to serve the people around us. And just as Jesus gave the disciples the power and resources they needed, God gives us His love and strength so that we, too, can share Him with others. How are you using the gifts God has given you to make a difference?

—Tristan Collins, sophomore

Choosing to See
Isaiah 41:13

When I was in the third grade, a new girl joined our classroom. As she stood beside our teacher on that first day, I was struck by how different she was from the rest of us. The new girl was fourteen, so she was much older than my friends and me, and she was as tall as our teacher. Her dress, hair, and skin were dirty. She wore extremely thick glasses that almost hid her eyes, which constantly raced back and forth. Our new classmate suffered a type of blindness that limited her sight range to that of the head of a nail.

I remember her holding the magnifying glass she used to aid her thick glasses when she read. Reading was painstaking work because she could only see three to four letters at a time. The schoolwork we did took her three to four times longer to complete. Because of this, it wasn't long before our teacher, in desperation, asked some of us to help her with her schoolwork when we finished our own. We dreaded the time when it was our turn to help, because it meant we had to sit next to her and wait as she tried to see the words on the page and answer the questions. She would tell us her answer, and we'd write it down. It was agonizing—until our teacher made a new rule. Whoever helped her with her schoolwork also got to help her at recess.

You see, freeze tag had become much more exciting since our new classmate joined us. Playing tag with her was like playing with a Kamikaze pilot. She was fearless, running at top speed on the uneven, gravel-strewn asphalt, unable to see anything in her path or where she was going. We envied her excitement, and we wanted in on the action, so we took turns running with her. We held hands and tried to coordinate our movements so as not to trip each other. But it was to no avail. Almost every time she played tag, she tripped and fell, resulting in skinned knees and elbows. It wasn't long until everyone in the third grade began to admire her not only for her courage at recess but also for her patience and stamina in the classroom. Every day she showed up to school, ready to face the same difficulties all over again.

As I think about her today, I am reminded that when we are faced with difficult circumstances in life, whether they are short-term or long-term, we have two choices. We can choose to show up or we can give up. Fortunately, Jesus has promised to help us if we choose to show up.

I am a witness!

—Melanie DiBiase, science teacher

Not What We Expected
Matthew 5:1–12; Luke 6:20–26

Imagine this. It's a beautiful day in Israel. You and some friends are walking in the hill country outside of the city of Capernaum. With the sun shining and the birds singing, you stop for a moment to take it all in. Then you notice something. There's a figure sitting at the top of the mountain—no, there are several figures. Actually, there are quite a lot of people at the top of the mountain. *What is going on?* you wonder.

As you draw closer, your eyes are drawn to the focal point of all the commotion. It's that Man, the one people have been talking about for months. Could it be? This is the guy everyone is so excited about, the one they call Messiah. It's rumored He will finally bring an end to the Roman oppression and conquer the whole world in the name of Israel! He is a mighty warrior. With power, royalty, and destruction, He is going to raise up an army and fight for the rights of the people. Israel will finally win the respect they deserve, and it's about time.

A hush falls over the crowd as He opens His mouth to speak. What will He talk about? War plans, fighting strategies, or a call for soldiers? When He speaks, you hear, "Blessed are the poor in spirit, for theirs is the kingdom of heaven" (Matthew 5:3, ESV). What? Confused, you listen closer. "Blessed are those who mourn, . . . blessed are the meek, . . . those who hunger, . . . the merciful, . . . the pure in heart, . . . the peacemakers, . . . those who are persecuted." (verses 4–10). *Well, this isn't what anyone had in mind,* you think.

Jesus was anything but what people expected Him to be. When the world called for a war hero, He came as the Good Shepherd. He taught them to count others as more significant than themselves and to love their enemies. He was completely the opposite of what they intended, and yet those who got to know Jesus adored Him.

As followers of Christ, we have been called to stand out as Jesus did. We have been called to be different, to be bold, and to speak freely about the gospel. The world tries to convince us to fill the mold they've built for us, but God has shown us where the true reward lies: not in revenge or greed, not in money or status, but in humility and love. Those who come to understand these things are truly blessed. Are you blessed?

—Desiree Clemons, senior

No Salt, No Taste
Matthew 5:13–16

During the teen years, it seems inevitable to struggle with finding oneself. Our culture doesn't make it any easier with all the images and messages that bombard us.

I grew up listening to God's Word and His voice, but I lost myself this last year. I had no idea what to do with my life or who I was. I was consumed with other things, and the darkness pulled me away from who I actually was. I was tired of all the negative forces in my life, but I had distanced myself from God and kind of shut Him out.

One day as I was sitting in chapel, my ears perked up as one of my friends spoke. He quoted from Matthew 5:13, 14: "You are the salt of the earth, but if salt has lost its taste, how shall its saltiness be restored? It is no longer good for anything except to be thrown out and trampled under people's feet. You are the light of the world. A city set on a hill cannot be hidden" (ESV).

As he read the passage, it was as if something inside me woke up. After chapel, I looked up the rest of the passage, and something began to change in me. The darkness was once again replaced with the light. The next weekend after that chapel experience, I went on a Pathfinders retreat, and the theme passage for the weekend was Matthew 5:13–16! I felt as if God was reminding me that I am the light of the world as long as I stay connected to Him, even when I struggle.

God made us with a purpose, even when we don't understand all of the pieces because we're still growing up. With God's help, and with His Word, that purpose will unfold before us. We need to be a light in the darkness and salt to the world. Without these two things, the world would be miserably dark and tasteless, neither of which would be good. Without God, this world would be miserable, too, and many people live as if He doesn't exist. It's our job, no matter how broken we are, to seek God and to share whatever He has done in our lives with others. How are you being salt or light to those around you?

—Francesca Cuenca, sophomore

A New Perspective
Psalm 23

As a kid, I used to love looking at optical illusions, and there was one that always got me. It's a picture of a woman's face. Some people see a young woman while other people see an old woman. It's all a matter of what you focus on. It drove me crazy because I could only see the old woman! I could never see the young woman's face until one day when I stared at it for a really long time, taking cues from my brother, who was the exact opposite of me and could only see the young woman's face. I was so glad when I finally saw what was in front of me the whole time—a different perspective on the picture.

Sometimes I think we look at Scripture passages we've heard all our lives and think we know everything because we are used to a certain perspective, but God is always revealing new things to us when we study His Word. For example, look at Psalm 23. It is a classic passage of the Bible that is often memorized. But have you ever read it with Jesus in mind, looking at the different characteristics David outlines? Here's what I found after studying each verse.

Verse 1—As our Shepherd, Jesus has our best interest in mind, and He leads us through life, protecting us, caring for us, and loving us.

Verse 2—Jesus provides for us. Not only does He take care of our daily needs, but He also gives us rest during the week and especially on Sabbath.

Verse 3—Jesus sustains us. He gives us strength when we lack it, and He guides us in the direction we should go.

Verse 4—Jesus protects us and comforts us. We will go through rough patches, but Jesus will always be with us.

Verse 5—Jesus lavishes us with good things. He wants to bless us, even in the presence of those who want to harm us. He gives us more than we can imagine.

Verse 6—Jesus pursues us. He loves us so much that He seeks us out and invites us to spend time with Him.

Which of these characteristics of Jesus have you experienced? Which ones are hard for you to relate to? What other things caught your eye as you read it?
—Chaplain Kalie

Meeting With Jesus

"The LORD is my strength and my song;
   he has given me victory.
This is my God, and I will praise him—
   my father's God, and I will exalt him!" (Exodus 15:2).

How can you apply this verse to your own life?

_____

_____

_____

_____

What spiritual principle can you take from this reading?

_____

_____

_____

_____

What did you learn about God from this verse?

_____

_____

_____

_____

Following the Law
Matthew 5:17–20

W e live in a world with laws. See how many laws you can name in the next thirty seconds. I'll wait. Pretend there is suspenseful game show music playing in the background.

Here are a few of the laws I know. It's against the law to steal. When you go to a store and pick something up, you need to pay for it and not just walk out. When you get into the car, you need to wear your seat belt. It may seem like this is common sense, but it's also the law. No matter how old you get, you always have to wear a seat belt. Also, it's against the law to run a red light. When you're driving (with your seat belt on, of course), and the light turns yellow, you slow down. You don't go faster because if the light turns red while you're speeding through the intersection, you could get a ticket for breaking the law.

As citizens of the United States of America, we are required to obey the laws of our country. If we choose to break the laws, we are subject to the consequences of our actions. We all know that by keeping these laws, we are doing what is right. Of course, America and other countries around the world aren't the only ones with laws. Before any earthly government was formed, God set forth His perfect law in Exodus 20.

God gave us these laws, also known as the Ten Commandments, to help us live the best lives possible. In Matthew 5:17–20, Jesus says that He came to fulfill the law, not to take it away. Jesus lived a life that showed us how to obey God's law, not do away with it.

Look at what Psalm 119 says about the law. Here are just a few verses. "The law of your mouth is better to me than thousands of gold and silver pieces" (verse 72, ESV). A little further down it says, "Oh how I love your law! It is my meditation all the day" (verse 97, ESV). And verses 105 and 106 say,

> Your word is a lamp to my feet
>> and a light to my path.
> I have sworn an oath and confirmed it,
>> to keep your righteous rules (ESV).

The writer of this psalm asks God to open his eyes so that he can behold the most wondrous things in the law.

We need to be like the author of Psalm 119. We should study God's law, and when we know it, we should live it. This is the example that Jesus gave us when He came to save us. God wants us to live out His law. Will we listen?

—Jadyn Davis, freshman

The Next Level
Matthew 5:21–26

Jesus has a way of taking things to the next level. In Matthew 5:21, 22, we find an example of this: "You have heard that our ancestors were told, 'You must not murder. If you commit murder, you are subject to judgment.' But I say, if you are even angry with someone, you are subject to judgment! If you call someone an idiot, you are in danger of being brought before the court. And if you curse someone, you are in danger of the fires of hell."

Jesus was quoting from the sixth commandment, which everyone knew. He reminded them that they would be subject to judgment for breaking the law. I'm sure the people listening must have thought, *Yeah, we know. We get it. We've been taught this all our lives. We're not murderers. We're not guilty. We're good, moral, ethical people.*

But Jesus took it a step further. He told the crowd that if they got angry, they were subject to judgment. In this translation, it says "if you call someone an idiot," you are subject to judgment! That's a whole different ball game!

I don't know about you, but it's hard not to get angry. Whether you're out on the soccer field and someone intentionally fouls you, your teacher falsely accuses you of cheating, or your parents won't let you go out with friends, it's hard not to let your emotions get the best of you.

As Christians, we can fall into the trap of thinking we are superior to others because we haven't murdered anyone and we obey the other commandments. But Jesus takes it to the next level and calls us to love our enemies and be patient with people who frustrate us. He challenges us to live like He lived, which requires us to have a relationship with God because it's only by staying connected to Him that we can replace anger with love.

—Filippe Da Silva, senior

Spirit Moving
Psalm 34:8

Last summer as I was preparing for the start of another school year, many others and I were praying that God would lead us to the students, or lead the students to us, who needed to be at GCA. I was in the process of communicating with every potential student I could. As I was going through the possible names to call or call again, I laid them before the Lord, meditating on whom God wanted me to contact as I spent time with Him in my morning devotions.

One particular morning, God put a name on my heart. The family seemed like they would fit into life at GCA very well, but they had stopped the process of applying and decided to go in a different direction. As I headed to work that day, this family kept coming to my mind. I decided I would call them when I had time during the day. That day was busy, and I never seemed to have extra time to call.

Time flew by, and before I knew it, it was almost time to go home. The entire day this family had been on my heart, and I told myself I would call them later, but I hadn't gotten around to it. Then the phone rang. The caller ID revealed that it was a call from this family. I couldn't believe it. I quickly answered the phone with a joyful hello and proceeded to hear about how God had spoken to them that day.

I couldn't believe what I heard. They had heard and felt the same words I had heard and felt that morning. They felt God telling them to reengage with us at GCA. After I listened to their story, I had the chance to tell them my side of the story and what I had heard God say that morning. Together we rejoiced in the knowledge that God simultaneously speaks the same message in multiple places.

On that day, GCA received some new, great students, but even more importantly, God showed His power, goodness, and mercy. The Spirit of God that moved that day is still moving today and can move in your life too.

I am a witness!

—Jeff Freeman, recruiter

Love Beyond Limits

Matthew 5:38–42; Luke 6:27–31

Retaliation is celebrated in our culture. Think about popular movies or TV shows. Many of the plots focus on getting even or settling a score. This plays into the human emotion that wants revenge when we have been wronged. But is that really the right thing to do? Will getting revenge benefit anyone involved, or are we just satisfying our desire to protect our pride?

In Luke 6:27, 28, Jesus says, "Love your enemies, do good to those who hate you, bless those who curse you, pray for those who abuse you" (ESV). Jesus calls us to do what may sometimes feel impossible. He calls us to overcome the instinct for revenge and to forgive people who have wronged us. Jesus takes it further when He says, "To one who strikes you on the cheek, offer the other also, and from one who takes away your cloak do not withhold your tunic either. Give to everyone who begs from you, and from one who takes away your goods do not demand them back. And as you wish that others would do to you, do so to them" (verses 29–31, ESV).

Jesus goes beyond forgiveness of people who hurt us and tells us to go the extra mile. I've wondered why He would take it this far, and this is what I've decided. This type of behavior shows people that we are not afraid of them and that our love goes beyond our words and is alive through our actions. Our goodwill toward others, especially those who hurt us, will not only build respect for us within their hearts but also may cause them to ask questions about why we act the way we do. They will be curious about what could motivate someone to do something so unusual and go so far as to allow misfortune to fall upon them for the purpose of glorifying God. By showing our willingness to go to such lengths, we are a beacon of God's character to those around us.

—Harrison Wyatt Cross, senior

A Love That Is More Than Love

Matthew 5:43–48; Luke 6:32–36

Love and hate. It's an age-old topic, but Jesus ramps up the requirements when He says, "Love your enemies and pray for those who persecute you" (Matthew 5:44, ESV).

When your best friend needs a pencil, there is absolutely no hesitation; you chuck a wooden number two her way. Now let's say that the one person you hate for completely legitimate, not at all petty, reasons has the same request. You're not so ready to give them your trusty lead stick now, are you? It's easy to do things for people you care about. They have never wronged you, and trust runs deep.

But Jesus painted a different picture with His life. He never cared about what others thought about Him, and He certainly never did anything to hurt anyone, nor did He hate people, even though He had every right. Those for whom He was to die ridiculed Him. Those whom He came to save tortured Him. At His death, as He was pushed past the limit that any human should bear, He asked God to forgive them. Forgive them, His enemies.

Jesus reminds us of how much He loves us, and He challenges us to show that same love to other people. He says that the Father "makes his sun rise on the evil and on the good, and sends rain on the just and on the unjust. For if you love those who love you, what reward do you have? Do not even the tax collectors do the same? And if you greet only your brothers, what more are you doing than others? Do not even the Gentiles do the same?" (verses 45–47, ESV).

I need this passage to sink into my own life. I love my friends and family so much. However, I also hate with a passion. I won't be overtly mean or anything, but will I let someone cut in front of me in line? No. I need to take the time to stop hating in general, but more specifically, I need to treat those I don't love quite as much as my friends and family with respect. Beyond respect, I need to move to kindness, and maybe with the Holy Spirit's help, one day I will love them as Jesus does.

—Abigail Davis, junior

A Gift of Sacrifice
Matthew 6:1–4

My family has worked in children's ministry for as long as I can remember. Whether it's in the community, at a church, or for the conference, my parents have dedicated themselves to serving kids and teaching them about Jesus. Even though we sometimes get tired of dealing with kids who often ignore us, our goal is to help kids learn about Jesus and see them smile as they sing and play and learn. Many people come up to my parents and ask, "How much money do you receive to put in this program?" And they respond, "None. All of this comes out of our pockets."

When I was five years old, I remember a time when we didn't have food, and my father's boss hadn't paid him yet. Our fridge was empty, and everybody was hungry. We went to the bank to see whether we had any money in our account, but it was empty, so we headed back home. I was frightened that we wouldn't be able to eat. My young mind immediately wandered to the thought that I might eventually die of hunger. As my father parked the car, we noticed that the porch of our small trailer home was packed with bags. I ran over to see what was in them, and it was food! Bags and bags of different food items! It was everything we needed. My parents asked our neighbors and church members whether they knew anything about the mystery groceries, but no one knew who delivered the food. God knew what our family needed, and He took care of us.

God doesn't want us to brag about our good deeds toward others because then they would get the wrong picture about giving. Jesus said, "When you give to the needy, sound no trumpet before you, as the hypocrites do in the synagogues and in the streets, that they may be praised by others. . . . Your Father who sees in secret will reward you" (Matthew 6:2–4, ESV).

Giving is about sacrificing what you have without expecting anything in return. Giving only what is left over after you've had everything you want isn't truly giving because there is no sacrifice in that. My parents give up what they have—their jobs, time, and health—so that they can help kids learn about Jesus. They do it quietly without seeking praise or compensation. Sure, there have been times when it has felt like we hit rock bottom, but God has always been there, and He will continue to be there to keep our family afloat through His blessings.

—Sergio De La Cruz, junior

Meeting With Jesus

"They refused to obey and did not remember the miracles you had done for them. Instead, they became stubborn and appointed a leader to take them back to their slavery in Egypt. But you are a God of forgiveness, gracious and merciful, slow to become angry, and rich in unfailing love. You did not abandon them" (Nehemiah 9:17).

What truth is God sharing in this passage?

_____

_____

_____

_____

_____

What question would you like to ask God about this verse?

_____

_____

_____

_____

_____

How should we relate to others based on this passage?

_____

_____

_____

_____

_____

Lost in Conversation
Matthew 6:5–15

We haven't talked in a few months. She's busy keeping up with three little boys. I'm busy keeping up with hundreds of teenagers. She lives in Ontario. I live in Georgia. It's complicated to connect, and yet we've been friends for years. This particular evening, we set up a time to FaceTime at 8:00 P.M. after her kids had gone to bed, and we talked and laughed and caught each other up on the latest happenings in our lives. We kept saying we should go, but then we'd start talking about a new subject. Before we knew it, we'd talked for more than three hours.

That's the beauty of a close friendship. No matter how long it's been since you last talked, you pick up where you left off and fall into a comfortable conversation. Some friendships are like that, while with others you may talk every day. I talk to my best friend, who happens to be my husband, every day. Sometimes they're brief conversations that simply deal with the details of our day, while other times we have long conversations about our dreams or struggles, but whatever form our conversations take, they are constant, and they are comfortable.

Jesus talked with God every day, multiple times a day. He was in constant communication with His Father. He encourages us to develop the same type of relationship and ongoing conversation with God. In the Sermon on the Mount, Jesus talked about prayer. He reminded His listeners that it wasn't about putting on a show or reciting a script or saying the right words. Prayer is about spending time with God. Jesus said, "When you pray, go away by yourself, shut the door behind you, and pray to your Father in private. Then your Father, who sees everything, will reward you" (Matthew 6:6). Jesus then went on to teach the crowd what we call the Lord's Prayer (verses 9–13).

When we pray, we connect with God. Whether it's a three-hour conversation like I have with my friend in Canada, a five-minute update on my life, or a long talk about my dreams like I have with my husband, when I talk to God, in whatever form and for however long it takes, I am building a relationship with Him. I'm connecting with Him on a deeper level, which means that whether it's a good day or bad day, He's a part of it with me.

What does your prayer life look like? Do you find it easy or hard to talk to God? What can you do to develop a closer connection?

—Chaplain Kalie

Investing in Heaven
Matthew 6:19–21

F lip on the television or read the latest news article, and it becomes very evident that our world is approaching the end of time faster every day. The media bombards us with tragic stories that make us long for Jesus to come back and take us to heaven. Yet at the same time, we try to cling to this fading world and the treasures we've collected. We see the hurt and the pain, but we have also grown accustomed to it because it often doesn't directly affect us. This world, even with all the tragedy, is comfortable—it is where our possessions and families are. This earth is where we've earned success and where we've made our memories. This world makes us feel as though we are capable of reaching high levels of status and wealth. So why would we feel the need to prepare to leave this place that we love so much?

In Matthew 6:19–21, Christ urges us to look to heaven rather than to this world, which can only give us fleeting wealth and pleasure. "Do not lay up for yourselves treasures on earth, where moth and rust destroy and where thieves break in and steal; but lay up for yourselves treasures in heaven, where neither moth nor rust destroys and where thieves do not break in and steal. For where your treasure is, there your heart will be also" (NKJV).

As Jesus instructed, we should store our treasures and invest our hearts in heaven, not in this earth. While this world seems comfortable and satisfying, it is easily stripped away, leaving us lost and without anything. We have a Savior who gave His life so that we may have a perfect place to dwell when He returns. However, if we're going to be ready, we need to give up what we now hold dearly, remembering that the things we own on this earth are unstable and cannot give us the happiness that Christ brings. When we choose to give our lives to Christ, our hearts become invested in His will and our goal of reaching heaven. Instead of remaining comfortable with our uncertain lives in this world, we receive an assurance of a better life that is awaiting us.

What are you investing in? Where is your treasure? Better yet, what would it look like if you invested in heaven instead of this earth?

—Isabella Dempsey, senior

Perfect Peace

Psalm 29

I decided to go canvassing in California the summer between my junior and senior years of high school. Through this literature ministry, God revealed Himself to me many times, but I want to share one story in particular.

We worked late into the evening because that was when most people were home. It was the last hour of our workday (8:00 to 9:00 P.M.), the "power hour," as my leaders called it. They said anything could happen in the final hour. As I got ready to knock on the last few doors of the day, I asked God for a divine appointment, which is what literature evangelists call a situation that God orchestrated in which someone can be reached for Him.

I ran from door to door that last hour, which I normally didn't do, but I sensed that God had a divine appointment ready for me. I wasn't sure when it would happen, so I hurried from one house to the next as soon as I finished speaking with the person who opened the door. Then it happened. I knocked on the door, and an elderly woman opened it and asked what I wanted. I went through my opening script: "Hi, my name is . . ."

She cut me off and said, "Go away! I don't want anything. Now is not a good time."

As she said this, she was trying to turn on her porch light, but it didn't seem to be working. "What's wrong? Maybe I can help," I said.

Her facial expression changed, and she looked confused for a minute. Then she spoke. "My husband has Alzheimer's. I just came back from the hospital."

I gave her words of comfort and told her about God's love and that He always has a purpose for every struggle. I told her I had something that could help her through this difficult time. I pulled out a book titled *Peace Above the Storm*, which talks about the struggles of life and how God reveals Himself to us in the midst of these trials.

"This book will be a light in the darkness," I said. Tears filled her eyes, and at that very moment, her porch light turned on. We both stood in shock. I then gave her a big hug, and she told me that she believed I had been sent to her house for a reason. I couldn't have agreed more.

I am a witness!

—Genesis Arteta, senior

Wandering Eyes
Matthew 6:22–23

What comes in through our eyes shapes us into the type of person we are. Jesus made this clear in Matthew 6:22, 23: "The lamp of the body is the eye. If therefore your eye is good, your whole body will be full of light. But if your eye is bad, your whole body will be full of darkness" (NKJV).

God lets us decide what kind of people we want to be. He doesn't force us to follow Him or His laws. God wants us to choose Him willingly because He wants our love for Him to be genuine. He lets us choose good or bad. It's completely our choice. However, He warns us that what our eyes take in is what we will become, which is what we will then reflect to others.

I've seen this concept at work in my own life. I was raised in a place that wasn't an ideal environment to grow up in. I lived in a city with a high crime rate, and many people did drugs, including my friends. I was surrounded by people who were making poor choices. I was surrounded by darkness. But I fought against what was around me, and I chose a different path.

I decided to take my eyes off those distractions and focus instead on becoming a better person. Although most of my immediate family weren't active Christians, my mom (luckily) concluded that the city wasn't the best place for me because of all the negative influences vying for my attention. She decided to send me away for my eighth-grade year to live with a friend; then I could attend a Christian school. She said we'd test it out to see whether it would help me develop a relationship with God. Going to this new school helped a lot. I was exposed to good things, and I got to know Jesus. I also began going to church and was able to get involved, which helped me to see even more good things.

What are you putting into your mind? What are you allowing your eyes to see? It makes a difference what you look at.

—Juan Duarte, senior

Shallows
Matthew 6:24

There once was a man who won the lottery. He was ecstatic. Everything seemed so good! This man quit his job and spent the money believing it would never run out. He bought alcohol, drugs, and everything else he wanted. Then the money disappeared. He had to sell all his fancy stuff to pay his debts. He couldn't get a job and ended up living in a shack. His health declined, and his appearance grew shabby. Many days this man wandered around alone. All the neighborhood children knew him as the guy who couldn't afford a haircut.

This person had a good life—he had a job, money, and friends. But after a few bad decisions, all that rapidly vanished. In Matthew 6:24 Jesus says, "No one can serve two masters; for either he will hate the one and love the other, or else he will be loyal to one and despise the other. You cannot serve God and mammon" (NKJV). *Mammon* can be defined in two ways: wealth regarded as an evil influence or a false object of worship and devotion. In the above illustration, the man did not serve his money. In fact, he used it rather foolishly. But he did serve another master. He served his own pleasure. Serving anything other than God can be dangerous.

A devotional is meant to be a guide, or a starting point, for worship. Many people forget that, and they use a devotional as their entire worship. After a three-minute, Bible-related reading, it's off to the computer or phone or friends. So many things in this world are taking the place of God in people's hearts. Whether they want to admit it or not, they aren't serving God. People today are serving their own pleasure, just like the guy who couldn't afford a haircut.

Don't let this world confuse your mind or occupy all your time so that you don't have anything left for God. I encourage you not to stop with this devotional—dig deeper. Do not push God to the side like a despised master. Serve God the way He is meant to be served. Leave the shallows and enter the deeper water.

—Natalie Draia, sophomore

The Disappearing Path
Psalm 25

A few summers ago, my family and I visited Glacier National Park in Montana. We spent three days exploring various parts of the park. On the second day of our stay, we planned to hike to Grinnell Glacier, which was a ten-mile, round-trip hike to one of the last known glaciers in the United States. The sky was overcast, and the air was cool the day we set out, but it wasn't raining, so we decided to go for it. I can't even begin to describe the beauty of the mountains and lakes along the trail. Because the lakes were glacier fed, the water was bright turquoise blue. There were purple and orange wildflowers dotting the landscape and waterfalls cascading down the mountains. We even spotted a grizzly bear down in the valley.

The trail was easy to follow, but at one point, while I was in the lead, the trail went straight and then started to disappear. I stopped and commented about how it suddenly was harder to spot which way to go. My adventurous and outdoorsy husband said it was fine. He could still see a path, so we should keep going. I felt like we had gotten off course, but he took the lead, and we began picking our way along. A bit further and it became very clear that we had veered off the path and were now following some wildlife path through the underbrush. I kept praying that we wouldn't stumble across a bear! Eventually we popped out into a clearing, and we caught sight of the actual trail.

In Psalm 25, David talks about following the right path and staying close to God.

> Show me the right path, O Lord;
>> point out the road for me to follow.
> Lead me by your truth and teach me,
>> for you are the God who saves me (verses 4, 5).

Jesus became a human and lived out David's request. Jesus is the path to God. In John 14:6, He says, "I am the way, the truth, and the life. No one can come to the Father except through me."

What path are you following? If you're on the road that leads to God, keep going! If you're on the road that leads to the world, make a U-turn, get off at the next exit, call a tow truck—do something! Whatever it takes, remember that you can always ask God to help you find your way back home. As David wrote: "The Lord is good and does what is right; he shows the proper path to those who go astray" (Psalm 25:8).

—Chaplain Kalie

Meeting With Jesus

"Each time he said, 'My grace is all you need. My power works best in weakness.' So now I am glad to boast about my weaknesses, so that the power of Christ can work through me" (2 Corinthians 12:9).

What did you learn about God from this verse?

How should we relate to others based on this passage?

What spiritual principle can you take from this reading?

Trust Issues

Matthew 6:25–34

According to a quick internet search about the top things people worry about, money comes up in every list. Whether it is worrying about paying off debt, having enough money to retire, or earning enough to provide for kids and a family, money stresses people out.

Jesus made it clear that we don't need to worry about our basic needs being met. He said, "Therefore I tell you, do not worry about your life, what you will eat or drink; or about your body, what you will wear. Is not life more than food, and the body more than clothes? Look at the birds of the air; they do not sow or reap or store away in barns, and yet your heavenly Father feeds them. Are you not much more valuable than they? Can any one of you by worrying add a single hour to your life?" (Matthew 6:25–27, NIV).

Jesus concluded His speech on worrying by reminding them to keep their focus on God: "But seek first his kingdom and his righteousness, and all these things will be given to you as well. Therefore do not worry about tomorrow, for tomorrow will worry about itself. Each day has enough trouble of its own" (verses 33, 34, NIV).

I know some people who have their kids in church school but who were struggling financially, so they stopped paying tithe. They were mad at God because they felt that He should reward them for sacrificing and sending their kids to a Christian school. However, over time they shifted their thinking. When they started to trust God for their financial needs and once again paid tithe, they received a few donations from people who had no idea about their situation but said they wanted to help them out.

God works in many different ways. I'm not saying He'll work the same way for your family as He did for this family, but I do know that you can trust God to financially take care of your family in His own special way. God has a plan. We are more valuable to Him than anything, which is why He sent His only Son down to this awful world to die for the sins of every single person so that they may live. When we seek God's kingdom first, He promises to take care of all the rest (verse 33). God will always care for you, protect you, and love you. Where are you placing your trust?

—Allison Davis, sophomore

Blinded by the Negative
Matthew 7:1–5; Luke 6:37–42

As a society we've become very good at seeing problems in other people, but we struggle to acknowledge our own problems. It's easy to judge others. We like to point out each other's problems and flaws, but nobody likes to admit their own faults. It makes us feel weak and hopeless. But the truth is, we all have struggles. No one is perfect, which gives us no right to judge others for their imperfections. We're all in the same boat. We are all sinners in need of a Savior.

As Jesus was talking about not judging people, He gave this illustration: "Can the blind lead the blind? Will they not both fall into a pit? The student is not above the teacher, but everyone who is fully trained will be like their teacher" (Luke 6:39, 40, NIV).

God sent us Jesus to save us from our imperfections. He sent us a perfect example to follow so that in Jesus we could have someone to look up to and emulate. We can't lead each other; just as Jesus said, the blind can't lead the blind. Instead, we need to learn from Jesus as our Teacher. He promises that if we will learn from Him, we can be like Him. We can't be saved without Jesus. We can't reach perfection without His help. But with Him we can change the world and be a source of encouragement instead of a source of judgment.

It is our duty as children of God to help each other. We shouldn't discourage each other. Instead, we should offer help and support to whomever God brings our way. We are to be beacons of God's love and mercy and examples of His character. In Galatians 6:2, Paul says, "Carry each other's burdens, and in this way you will fulfill the law of Christ" (NIV). Our job is to help each other in moments of need. When we see someone in distress, we should reach out to them and offer our care and support instead of judging them for how they got into the situation or for how they are handling it.

How are you carrying someone else's burdens? Are you helping? Or are you judging? It's definitely a challenge and something to think about as we start a new day.

—Brandon DeSouza, junior

Provision
Joshua 1:9

When my family told me I wasn't coming back to GCA, I felt like crying. I couldn't believe that God was going to do this to me. But time went on, and I began to accept the reality of the public high school in Arkansas where my family planned to move after my dad retired from the military. I told my friends that I would not be returning, and my family began to pack. However, early in the summer my father came downstairs with trembling knees and a white face. "My retirement got denied," he said.

All of us were surprised. Our entire plan changed in an instant. That wasn't the only challenge going on in our lives. At the time, my mother was battling cancer, my sister was going to begin public school after being homeschooled, and finances were tight—not to mention the struggle I had in deciding where I should go to school. With everything else going on, it seemed to make sense that I should stay home and go to a nearby Christian school instead of going back to GCA.

Partway through the summer, I left for Cohutta Springs Youth Camp for a three-week program called DiscipleTrek. I had received a scholarship, so I decided I should still go and devote myself to growing my relationship with Christ, especially in light of all the trials our family seemed to be going through.

One Sabbath morning during camp, I spent almost an hour pouring out my heart to God in prayer. I surrendered my future to Him. As I prayed, I felt sure that He wanted me to stay at home. I was at peace with this decision as I talked to Him, but at the end of my prayer, I told God that if GCA offered me a scholarship, I'd know that He wanted me to go back to GCA. Miraculously, the next day, the school called my mom and offered me a scholarship!

God showed me that GCA was where He wanted me, but He did more than that. In His perfect time, He's worked things out for His glory. My mother successfully had surgery to remove the tumors, my sister adjusted to school, and God provided for our financial needs.

For those of you who are in the midst of a struggle, remember that God is bigger than your fear. If He can take dirt from the ground and breathe life into it, God can and will provide a way for you.

I am a witness!

—Sydney Hoffman, sophomore

The Faithful Key
Matthew 7:7–12

There will be days when you question God because things haven't worked out the way you wanted them to. You may even quote this verse and tell God that He promised to give you what you asked for: "Ask and it will be given to you; seek and you will find; knock and the door will be opened to you. For everyone who asks receives; the one who seeks finds; and to the one who knocks, the door will be opened" (Matthew 7:7, 8, NIV).

I can testify that I have been guilty of these feelings from time to time. However, when I pray with unselfish motives and trust that God has my best interest in mind, I find peace. Many times in my life when I've prayed for God's mercy, He has granted me relief and safety—not just for me but also for friends and family.

One day at the beginning of my junior year of high school, I was feeling discouraged, and my faith in God was wavering. I called my dad, and I remember him telling me, "God is going to close some doors and open others for you. Just because you can't open this door right now doesn't mean that you should just give up. God can burn that door, knock it down, or help you go under it or over it! Never give up." That's when I remembered 2 Corinthians 12:9, 10, which says, "But he said to me, 'My grace is sufficient for you, for my power is made perfect in weakness.' Therefore I will boast all the more gladly about my weaknesses, so that Christ's power may rest on me. That is why, for Christ's sake, I delight in weaknesses, in insults, in hardships, in persecutions, in difficulties. For when I am weak, then I am strong" (NIV).

Even when I felt defeated and questioned why God wasn't working things out, my dad reminded me to be persistent in prayer and to keep knocking until God took care of the door. I felt weak right then, but God was using that to make me stronger and to develop my faith.

I don't know what door stands in front of you, but keep praying and trusting that God has a plan. Your faith is the key to unlock new doors in life. God's mercy endures forever, and His love for us never ends. He gives "good gifts to those who ask him!" (Matthew 7:11, NIV).

—Evan Diaz, senior

Taking the Right Path
Matthew 7:13, 14

Many people like to cut corners. They want to do things the easiest way possible with the least amount of work. We don't want to be inconvenienced. We don't want life to be hard, so we look for shortcuts. Instead of studying hard, students opt to cheat and take advantage of someone else who put the time in to know the right answers. Adults do the same thing. They cheat on their taxes or at their job to get more money without doing the work. There are many more examples I could list, but the point is that we can be really lazy.

Sometimes I don't want to get up in the morning, do my homework, or finish my chores. Oftentimes my laziness manifests itself in a half-baked job. I also struggle with wanting the easy way out of a situation. One time this got me into big trouble. You see, I had a problem with staying up at night on my phone. My parents warned me that if I didn't stop, there would be serious consequences. I didn't take them seriously. I thought they were just messing around with me, so I decided to continue doing my thing. Big mistake. They caught me and grounded me. They took away all that I thought was good in my life—primarily, my phone. Instead of accepting my punishment and serving my time, I plotted to find my phone and take it back. I reasoned that it was my phone so I could do what I wanted. It really wasn't that hard to find it because my parents didn't expect me be dumb enough to disobey them again. I'm sure you can guess, but they caught me with the phone, and this time my punishment was a lot worse—I lost my phone for a year. Yep, not kidding. I tried to cut corners and not endure my punishment, but that only got me into deeper trouble.

Jesus says, "Enter through the narrow gate. For wide is the gate and broad is the road that leads to destruction, and many enter through it. But small is the gate and narrow the road that leads to life, and only a few find it" (Matthew 7:13, 14, NIV). When we cut corners or try to cheat our way through life, we're following the wide path, which ultimately leads to consequences and, as Jesus said, destruction. It may seem hard, but the narrow path, which represents God's way, is definitely the better path to follow.

—Josh Davis, freshman

Recognizing Fruit
Matthew 7:15–23; Luke 6:43–45

Y ou have probably heard it said that you are what you eat. If you eat fast food three times a day, you'll eventually become fat and sick because of all the grease and nastiness you are putting into your body.

From a spiritual standpoint, it works the same way. What we digest—what fills our mind—will eventually come out in our words and actions. Jesus tells us to beware of people who try to pull us away from the truth. He says that we are to test them by the fruit they bear: "Every healthy tree bears good fruit, but the diseased tree bears bad fruit. A healthy tree cannot bear bad fruit, nor can a diseased tree bear good fruit. Every tree that does not bear good fruit is cut down and thrown into the fire. Thus you will recognize them by their fruits" (Matthew 7:17–20, ESV). We can discern whether people are for God or against Him based on what they say and what they do.

Think of God as a master gardener. We are His trees. He tends us, fertilizes us, waters us, and prunes us. Because of His loving care, we produce flowers, which is the first sign of fruit. He continues to nurture us, and through the work of the Holy Spirit, our flower is pollinated, and the fruit begins to form. Over time, the fruit develops and grows until it is finally ready to be harvested.

Because we have the freedom to choose, we can refuse God's offer to help us grow. But if we accept it, He does what is right and good in our lives. He helps us to grow, and as we learn more about Him, we begin to develop good fruit. We are patient, kind, loving, gentle, helpful, and gracious with the people around us. We speak encouraging words that lift others up instead of tearing them down. All of this is the result of God living in us.

Do you want to know what kind of fruit you are producing? Listen to the words that proceed from your mouth and the actions that go with it. You'll soon see where you stand.

—Karen Dominguez, senior

Meeting With Jesus

"So now there is no condemnation for those who belong to Christ Jesus. And because you belong to him, the power of the life-giving Spirit has freed you from the power of sin that leads to death" (Romans 8:1, 2).

What stuck out to you in this reading?

_____

_____

_____

_____

_____

What question would you like to ask God about this verse?

_____

_____

_____

_____

_____

How can you apply these verses to your own life?

_____

_____

_____

_____

_____

A Firm Foundation
Matthew 7:24–27; Luke 6:46–49

When I was nine years old, my family decided to build a new house. I remember watching the cement truck pull up to our building site to pour the foundation that our house would sit on. It was a perfect outline of the house.

A lot of work goes into building the foundation of a house. First, the workers have to dig deep into the ground. This ensures that the foundation will be sturdy and strong enough to hold the house up. After the cement is poured, it has to have enough time to set before the building process can continue. Without a strong foundation, the house would settle and shift and crack. It would not be able to withstand a storm or any other natural disaster.

Jesus used the example of building a house on a firm foundation to illustrate our connection with Him. "Everyone then who hears these words of mine and does them will be like a wise man who built his house on the rock" (Matthew 7:24, ESV). In His story, Jesus says that the wise man's house, which he built on a strong foundation, stood firm in the storm, but the foolish man's house, built on sand, collapsed.

So how do we build a strong foundation with Christ? It's important that we are deeply rooted in Jesus and in His truths through reading the Bible and memorizing His Word. It's also important that we allow Jesus to "set" in our hearts. Just like the cement for the foundation must set and dry, when we mediate on His Word and allow Him to speak to us through prayer, our relationship becomes strong and solid in Jesus. Finally, the most important part of the foundation of our relationship with Jesus is whose name is written on it.

After the foundation for our house was poured, my family got to write our names in it. It was our house! Our names were written in the foundation. When we allow Jesus into our lives, He writes His name on our hearts. The cool thing is, just like the names of my family are now set in stone and will always be there, Jesus' name will always be on the foundation of our hearts when we invite Him in and choose to build our lives on His Word.

—Taylor Einhellig, junior

What Really Matters

Matthew 8:5–13; Luke 7:1–10

S ome Christians think they have it all together and that they are superior to those who don't know Jesus or even to those of another Christian denomination or faith. However, this is shortsighted because Jesus said that He has "sheep that are not of this fold. I must bring them also, and they will listen to my voice" (John 10:16, ESV).

Christians don't have a market on hearing God's voice. He can speak to and through anyone. We find an example of this in the story of the centurion. This man was a Roman citizen, a hated enemy of Israel because of the oppression the government imposed on the people. Yet we find the centurion coming to Jesus for help to heal his servant.

It may have surprised the disciples, but Jesus agreed to go heal the servant. This is where it got interesting. The centurion said, "Lord, I am not worthy to have you come under my roof, but only say the word, and my servant will be healed. For I too am a man under authority, with soldiers under me" (Matthew 8:8, 9, ESV).

This commander had obviously heard about Jesus and believed in His power and authority to work miracles. He was a sheep from another fold that was listening to God's voice. Jesus rewarded his faith by simply speaking the words right then and there, and the Bible says that the servant was healed at that moment.

Check out what Jesus says to the centurion: "Truly, I tell you, with no one in Israel have I found such faith. I tell you, many will come from east and west and recline at table with Abraham, Isaac, and Jacob in the kingdom of heaven, while the sons of the kingdom will be thrown into the outer darkness" (verses 10–12, ESV).

Israelites weren't guaranteed a place in heaven based on their Jewishness. Just because we belong to a certain denomination doesn't mean we're going to heaven. It isn't about our position or our religious affiliation—it is about our relationship. That's what matters. The centurion believed. He had faith. He listened to God's voice. We have the same opportunity.

—Chaplain Kalie

Campfire Moments

Proverbs 19:21

My parents worked at Camp Heritage when they were younger, and my two older sisters have worked there since they were old enough. This last summer I was old enough to join my sisters and work at camp. When I got there, I figured I would float around and work in a variety of different capacities, but the director informed me that I was going to be a sub-counselor, which is the last job I was expecting!

I moved into a cabin with Isaiah, the head counselor, and I prepared for a crazy summer. The first week was Cub week with the seven- to nine-year-old kids. My day off was Monday, so I had barely met the kids when I left to take some time off. I came back Monday night, Isaiah filled me in, and then he left for his day off. He assured me that we had a good group of guys. I felt a little in over my head, but I told myself it would be fine.

The next morning at breakfast two of my campers said they didn't feel well. I suggested that they eat something, but that resulted in one kid running to the bathroom to throw up. I took him to the nurse's office and headed back to the rest of the group. Partway through the morning, the second camper got sick during his activity, and he went to the nurse's office too. So within a matter of hours, I had gone from seven kids to five. It wasn't looking too good.

As we were heading to the evening fun time, one of my remaining campers tripped and fell and ended up in the nurse's office. That left four campers. I was feeling lousy about how my day had gone, but God showed up at campfire that evening. I was sitting with one camper singing "The Crayon Box Song," when he leaned over and asked me what the lyrics meant. The line was, "Yellow is for the Christian who's afraid to tell."* I had sung this song many times in my life, but I hadn't stopped to think about what the words meant. I prayed that God would give me the right words. I explained that we have the Bible with all its stories and principles, but sometimes we worry about what the rest of the world will think about us if we talk about Jesus, so we don't say anything. We have God with us, and we don't need to be afraid of sharing Him with the world.

I started out the summer unsure of my role as a sub-counselor, but in the end, God opened doors for conversations and amazing memories with the kids He placed in my cabin.

I am a witness!

—Devin Schlisner, sophomore

---

* William V. Mason, "The Crayon Box Song," 1998.

The Ultimate Healer
Luke 7:11–17

It's hard to imagine losing everything because most of us have it pretty good. Most of us live in a home, and our families have a car to drive and food to eat. Most of us have living parents and siblings who care for and love us.

By contrast, put yourself in the shoes of the widow of Nain. We don't know her name. Instead, we know her by her status as a widow, meaning that she'd already lost her husband. For a woman in that culture, that meant she had no worth. All of her husband's property and earthly possessions went to their son. Then her son died, and she was crushed by the loss not only because she loved him but also because she became a nobody in the eyes of society overnight.

Enter Jesus. He and His disciples happened to be near the gates of the town at the very moment that the funeral procession carrying the body of the dead boy was leaving the village. Jesus quickly assessed the scene and saw the heartbroken widow. The Bible says that "his heart overflowed with compassion. 'Don't cry!' he said. Then he walked over to the coffin and touched it, and the bearers stopped. 'Young man,' he said, 'I tell you, get up.' Then the dead boy sat up and began to talk! And Jesus gave him back to his mother" (Luke 7:13–15).

The crowd was in shock! They were in awe and afraid all at the same time. They couldn't believe that Jesus had touched the dead body, which made Him ritually unclean, and that He also had the power to raise someone back to life. News about this miracle spread quickly.

This story is just one of the amazing things Jesus did while He was on the earth. The fact that He has the power to resurrect anyone at His desire is beyond our comprehension and a small sample of His glory. Just because Jesus isn't physically on the earth anymore doesn't mean miracles don't happen. There are modern mission stories of people being brought back to life because of faith in God's power. He is alive and active on this earth just as He was in Bible times. We just have to look for Him and ask God to live and move in our lives.

—Freddy Duran, sophomore

Knowing the Difference
Matthew 11:2–19; Luke 7:18–30

Growing up, I wanted to know the difference between thunderstorms and tornados. It never made any sense why people would hide if a tornado was coming but not if it was a thunderstorm. To me, both were frightening! Every time a thunderstorm came, I asked my older sister if a tornado was coming, and she always told me to learn the difference.

It wasn't until I was seven years old that I learned the difference. The power had been flickering that whole day, and the sky was green. My sister was scared, which frightened me because she never really got scared the way I did. Our parents weren't home, so she was in charge. She took me to the bathroom and told me to lie down in the bathtub. She then covered me with sofa cushions. She told me that there was a tornado warning, which meant that one had been spotted. She said that if anything fell on me the cushions would protect me. She grabbed our dog, some flashlights, a few water bottles, and some food and brought it into the bathroom.

After what seemed like forever, the storm passed, and although there was some intense wind, the tornado didn't touch down near our home. My sister took the cushions off me. That's when I asked her if we had just been through a tornado. She finally explained the difference between a thunderstorm and a tornado and told me the signs to look for. She told me that thunderstorms come before tornados many times.

When John the Baptist was in prison, he sent his disciples to find Jesus and ask whether He was really the Messiah. Jesus told them to go back and tell John about all the amazing miracles He had been doing. As they turned to leave, Jesus said, "What kind of man did you go into the wilderness to see? . . . Were you looking for a prophet? Yes, and he is more than a prophet. John is the man to whom the Scriptures refer when they say, 'Look, I am sending my messenger ahead of you, and he will prepare your way before you'" (Matthew 11:7–10).

John the Baptist was like a thunderstorm, and Jesus was like a tornado. But the people had to be looking for the signs in order to understand His coming. Are you looking for the signs?

—Isabella Eklund, junior

Under Attack
Psalm 27

H ave you ever been attacked? I don't mean physically attacked, although maybe that's happened to you, but verbally attacked. Whether it's friends, your parents, or others, it's probably safe to say that someone has yelled at you for something you did, whether you messed up or not. In those moments, it doesn't matter whether you are right or wrong; the other person is playing the role of the accuser and is hurling accusations at you faster than you can think. They are right, and you are wrong, and they are going to scream at you until they feel like you've been beaten up enough.

If this scenario has ever happened to you, then you know how miserable it makes you feel, and it gives you a small taste of what Jesus went through on earth. The Pharisees and religious leaders were constantly attacking Him. In yesterday's passage, Jesus confirmed this when He said, "And from the time John the Baptist began preaching until now, the Kingdom of Heaven has been forcefully advancing, and violent people are attacking it" (Matthew 11:12).

I wonder whether Jesus took comfort in the psalms because David wrote a lot about his enemies and how he often felt under attack. Yet David always expressed his faith in God, even in the midst of a trial. Psalm 27 says,

> The LORD is my light and my salvation—
>> so why should I be afraid?
> The LORD is my fortress, protecting me from danger,
>> so why should I tremble?
> When evil people come to devour me,
>> when my enemies and foes attack me,
>> they will stumble and fall.
> Though a mighty army surrounds me,
>> my heart will not be afraid.
> Even if I am attacked,
>> I will remain confident (verses 1–3).

David and Jesus were able to remain confident and survive whatever attack was befalling them because they were connected to God. Verse 14 of this psalm sums up their relationship with God the Father: "Wait patiently for the LORD. Be brave and courageous. Yes, wait patiently for the LORD."

Do you feel as if you are under attack? If so, how can you turn it over to God and wait patiently for His provision?

—Chaplain Kalie

Meeting With Jesus
2 Timothy 1:12

This is definitely your happy place! The mountains. The lake. The cool breeze. The vivid blue sky with a few stray clouds. You take a deep breath and drink in the beauty surrounding you as you climb into the kayak resting on the shore and push off. Your paddle slips in and out of the water as you quietly glide across the crystal, clear water. Before you know it, you're in the middle of the lake.

You take a break from paddling and close your eyes. You sink into the seat and feel the gentle rocking of the kayak as the water laps against the sides of the boat. A few minutes go by, and you open your eyes to find another kayak skimming across the water toward you.

"Being in nature always refreshes my soul," the person says as He draws near.

"Definitely! I feel closer to God out here," you respond, not able to see fully Who is speaking but somehow feeling totally at ease.

"Now you're really close—to God—that is."

It only takes a second for you to understand. "Sorry, Jesus, I couldn't see Your face with the sun shining in my eyes! It's so good to see You!"

He smiles and anchors His boat next to yours so that you can sit and talk without drifting apart. "I have many memories of time spent on the lake in fishing boats," Jesus comments.

"I bet you do," you say. "I think one of my favorite stories is the time You walked on water and scared the disciples, and then You called Peter to get out of the boat and come to You."

"That was an experience Peter never forgot! It took a lot of faith for him to step over the edge with the storm still swirling around him, but he trusted in My word, which made the miracle possible."

The two of you sit in a comfortable silence as you think about what Jesus just said, and then He hits you with a question that leaves you speechless. "What do you need to trust Me with, to take a step of faith, and to believe that even though the storm is raging, I have your back?"

Take some time to talk to Jesus or write down your response to His question.

Read the verse for the day and think about the promise it offers or what it tells you about God.

If you were to talk about this verse with Jesus, what would you say? What would you ask Him?

Divided Beliefs
Matthew 12:22–37; Mark 3:20–30; Luke 11:14–23

Many people like to debate things, especially in the church. I'm sure you've seen it or heard it. There's the debate about what style of music is acceptable, what type of worship service is most inspiring, or who should be allowed certain roles in the church. Of course we debate about lifestyle choices—what we should eat, watch, wear, and more.

The Pharisees weren't any different. They debated everything, and they constantly tried to get Jesus involved in their verbal wars. When they weren't trying to debate Him, they were attacking Him and trying to slander His character and reputation. Of course, they were no match for Jesus. He always had a logical and wise response that put them in their place.

One day Jesus healed a demon-possessed man who was also blind and deaf—quite a combination! The crowds were amazed and asked, "Could this be the Son of David?" (Matthew 12:23, NKJV). The Pharisees in the crowd immediately shot back that Jesus was on Satan's side and was casting out demons in the devil's name.

Pretty poor logic, right? Jesus thought so. He was quick to point out to everyone listening that that argument didn't make any sense. Why would Satan remove a demon from a person when his whole point was to possess people? Jesus finished His questioning with this statement: "He who is not with Me is against Me, and he who does not gather with Me scatters abroad" (verse 30, NKJV).

Jesus reminded the crowd that there are only two sides in this world. People are either for God or against Him. Jesus wasn't condemning all those who were listening, but rather He was warning them to figure out whose side they were on.

Although I'm guessing they had tuned Him out, Jesus wasn't through with the Pharisees. He called them a brood of vipers, and then He said, "But I say to you that for every idle word men may speak, they will give account of it in the day of judgment. For by your words you will be justified, and by your words you will be condemned" (verses 36, 37, NKJV).

Each of us, like the Pharisees, has to answer this question: Whose side am I on? A good test to determine the answer is found in what Jesus said: "For out of the abundance of the heart the mouth speaks" (verse 34, NKJV). What is your heart saying?

—Rafael Encarnacion, junior

A Steadfast Love

Matthew 12:38–45; Luke 11:24–32

All throughout the Bible, we are given answers to rattling questions such as why we were created, whether God truly loves and cares for us, or whether He really gave us a purpose. As I read Matthew 12 and Luke 11, I didn't understand the context of the story of the Pharisees and Jesus, but as I talked it over with someone, I discovered a different outlook to the story, and it became very clear to me what kind of person Jesus is.

You see, the Pharisees were seeking a sign from the Messiah, whom we know is Jesus Christ. Jesus had given the Pharisees plenty of signs that He was the Messiah, but they still refused to believe. The fact that He had healed people and cast out demons wasn't enough. The fact that He knew Scripture forwards and backwards and that His birth and life lined up with prophecy wasn't enough. They chose not to believe, and Jesus knew this. So He answered them and said, "For just as Jonah was three days and three nights in the belly of the great fish, so will the Son of Man be three days and three nights in the heart of the earth" (Matthew 12:40, ESV).

Jesus also spoke about unclean spirits and how the expelled spirits will come back and be worse the second time around if the person doesn't replace the evilness with goodness (Luke 11:24–26). I don't think this is just referring to demon possession. When the Word of God convicts us, we must not take it lightly. If we do not respond to our conviction, temptation will come stronger than ever before.

The Pharisees pushed back against what the Holy Spirit was telling them. They refused to believe that Jesus was the Messiah.

It's safe to say that my friends and I have been sheltered a bit from the world by attending a boarding academy. When we leave for college, we will face more challenges than we had in high school not only academically but also socially and spiritually. However, we are equipped with tools to help us when we face a difficult situation. Jesus is there to help us if we choose to believe in Him and His power. His Word is truth. The sign He gave to the Pharisees in Matthew 12:40 came true. We can have assurance in Him because He has kept His word.

—Zoe Dorsett, senior

Stepping Out
John 10:10

I am from Bermuda, and I attended the same school for eleven years. I knew that I was different from the other kids I went to school with, but it wasn't an issue in elementary and middle school. However, when I entered high school, things started to change. I started to feel isolated because many of the things my classmates did or were involved in didn't fit with the lifestyle I wanted to live. It was hard to stay strong and stand for what I believed in.

It was then that I knew I needed a change. As much as I loved my school, my friends, and my teachers, my mom and I decided to look into other schools. We started looking at schools in Bermuda. However, our island is very, very small. There are two public high schools and five private schools. My options were limited. That is when we concluded that I had to step out of my comfort zone and travel abroad.

We continued praying about it and began looking at boarding schools in the US. I began the application process at one school that a friend of my attended, but my heart was not completely set on that school. We continued to look for other schools, and that is when I came across GCA. After looking around the website and checking everything out, we submitted an application. My mom and I continued to pray that if this was the right school for me, He would work out the finances and all the other details.

As the months went by, we continued to work through all the paperwork. Things seemed to be moving forward, and I heard many positive comments about boarding school in general and GCA in particular. Of course, I also heard negative things from some people saying I shouldn't go so far away from home and that boarding school was horrible.

I remember one night just crying to God, wondering what direction I should go and to whom I should listen. God saw my tears, and the next day, He sent confirmation of His plan—my mom received an email from the school saying I had been accepted. I was overjoyed! God had answered my prayers. From that point on, I didn't worry or doubt when things didn't go as smoothly as planned because I knew that this was God's will. I simply waited and trusted because I knew God had a plan.

I am a witness!

—Aleah Clarke, junior

Adopted

Matthew 12:46–50; Mark 3:31–35; Luke 8:19–21

Jesus said some things while He was on earth that people didn't understand. Some might even have thought He was downright rude or crazy. Thousands of years later, we are still scratching our heads sometimes to make sense of what Jesus meant when He said certain things. Today's passage contains one of those instances.

"While Jesus was still talking to the crowd, his mother and brothers stood outside, wanting to speak to him. Someone told him, 'Your mother and brothers are standing outside, wanting to speak to you.' He replied to him, 'Who is my mother, and who are my brothers?' Pointing to his disciples, he said, 'Here are my mother and brothers. For whoever does the will of my Father in heaven is my brother and sister and mother'" (Matthew 12:46–50, NIV).

Jesus was, in essence, stating that the natural relationship we have with our parents and siblings is not as important as the spiritual relationship we have with our brothers and sisters in Christ. We should never allow our earthly family members to keep us from doing the will of God.

This is one of the many moments in Jesus' ministry that sizzles with intensity, drama, and significance. Jesus' words would likely hurt His physical family who were already struggling to understand His ministry. However, these words would've been liberating and joyous to those who had always felt left out of the political order, pushed aside by the religious elite, and excluded by the social structure of their day. Jesus was promising that His family would be determined by obedience—not genealogy, politics, power, or money. That offer still stands today, and the promise is just as true for us as it was for those who first heard Jesus' words. Jesus invites us to become disciples. This means we become cherished members of His family.

—Mike Fisher, senior

Radiate
Luke 11:33–36

It seems so obvious. No one fixes a meal and then throws it in the garbage. No one nurtures a garden simply to toss out all the flowers and produce. No one plans a party hoping no one shows up. No one plans a vacation and then doesn't get on the plane.

Jesus said, "No one lights a lamp and then hides it or puts it under a basket. Instead, a lamp is placed on a stand, where its light can be seen by all who enter the house" (Luke 11:33).

This world needs light, and we all have the ability to let God shine through us if we'll only let Him come in. Your friends need your light. Your parents need your light. The girl who sits alone at lunch needs your light. We need to let God shine so brightly through us that others can see their way out of the dark.

Jesus continued, "Your eye is like a lamp that provides light for your body. When your eye is healthy, your whole body is filled with light. But when it is unhealthy, your body is filled with darkness. Make sure that the light you think you have is not actually darkness. If you are filled with light, with no dark corners, then your whole life will be radiant, as though a floodlight were filling you with light" (verses 34–36).

It's safe to say that we live in a dark world. Sometimes it feels easier to stay in the dark, to blend in with your surroundings. But before you know it, your eyes adjust to the darkness and stepping back into the light seems scary and painful. Jesus promises us that if we are filled with Him and His light, we will live radiant lives.

I want to challenge you to be a source of strength and courage. Share His wisdom. Radiate love. Let your personality blossom. You don't have to be a people pleaser, just a people lover. It's a chain reaction. All it takes today is one act of kindness. True joy is contagious. When we let God fill us, His love spills out to everyone we meet.

—Tylor Einhellig, sophomore

Telling It Like It Is
Luke 11:37–54

Don't you love it when the good guy in a movie sticks it to the bad guy with a one-line zinger that shows him who is boss? We cheer at those moments, applauding the wit of the good guy who finally has the upper hand. I feel like this passage, in which Jesus gives it to the Pharisees and tells them what's what, is similar to the climax of a movie when the hero verbally spars with the villain.

Here are just a few examples out of the many woes, or warnings, that Jesus presents to the Pharisees: "You Pharisees are so careful to clean the outside of the cup and the dish, but inside you are filthy—full of greed and wickedness!" (Luke 11:39). The Pharisees may have become physically pure by upholding all the ceremonial laws, but they were spiritually rotten.

"What sorrow awaits you Pharisees! For you are careful to tithe even the tiniest income from your herb gardens, but you ignore justice and the love of God. You should tithe, yes, but do not neglect the more important things" (verse 42).

Jesus didn't stop there. "What sorrow awaits you Pharisees! For you love to sit in the seats of honor in the synagogues and receive respectful greetings as you walk in the marketplaces. Yes, what sorrow awaits you! For you are like hidden graves in a field. People walk over them without knowing the corruption they are stepping on" (verses 43, 44).

"What sorrow also awaits you experts in religious law! For you crush people with unbearable religious demands, and you never lift a finger to ease the burden" (verse 46).

"What sorrow awaits you experts in religious law! For you remove the key to knowledge from the people. You don't enter the Kingdom yourselves, and you prevent others from entering" (verse 52).

Jesus was blunt with the Pharisees, and He wants to be clear with us too. If He were eating a meal with us as He did with the religious leaders when He said all this, what would He say to you or me? What sorrows, if any, would He say await us because of our actions? What would He say about the state of our hearts?

—Koby Fiebelkorn, junior

Meeting With Jesus

"What shall we say about such wonderful things as these? If God is for us, who can ever be against us? Since he did not spare even his own Son but gave him up for us all, won't he also give us everything else?" (Romans 8:31, 32).

What stuck out to you in this reading?

_____

_____

_____

_____

_____

What can you share with others from these verses?

_____

_____

_____

_____

_____

How should we relate to others based on this passage?

_____

_____

_____

_____

_____

Desiring God
Luke 12:1–12

What are some of the things you desire? Some people desire food or clothes. Other people may desire their electronics. If you asked this question, most people would list their worldly possessions.

I once read a story about a woman who had a deep desire for worldly things, which got her into a lot of trouble. The story goes like this. The woman had been married off to a poor family, and she was very upset about her status in society. She wanted more than anything to have jewels and beautiful clothing. One day her husband brought home an invitation to a party that the minister of education was hosting, but the woman was very upset because she didn't have the right clothes for it. So her husband went and bought her a dress, but she was still upset and didn't want to go. She claimed she needed jewels to go along with the outfit, so she went to her wealthy neighbor and asked to borrow some jewels. Her neighbor was a kind woman, so she let the poor woman borrow a necklace that looked quite expensive.

The poor woman was the center of attention at the party, and she loved every minute of it. Unfortunately, on her way home, she discovered that the necklace was missing! Afraid to tell her neighbor, she spent thirty-six thousand francs and bought a necklace that looked the same. Of course, this put the couple into major debt, and it took them ten years to pay it off. One day, many years after the party, the poor woman finally told her neighbor the truth about the necklace. The neighbor was flabbergasted and told the poor woman that the original necklace was a replica and had only cost five hundred francs.

If our sole focus is on our earthly possessions, then it's safe to say we aren't looking to God. If we aren't looking to God, then we aren't sharing Him with others because He isn't a part of our lives. And if we aren't sharing Him with others, then what's the point? It's a domino effect. Jesus said, "And I tell you, everyone who acknowledges me before men, the Son of Man also will acknowledge before the angels of God, but the one who denies me before men will be denied before the angels of God" (Luke 12:8, 9, ESV).

What do you desire, and what effect will it have on you, now and long term?

—Kenzie Everts, freshman

Battling Our Stuff
Luke 12:13–21

If the green-eyed monster is jealousy, then its cousin greed must also be a monster.

Greed is part of the human struggle whether you are rich or poor. It slowly eats away at you if you let it. Think about this. A man's wealth begins to increase. He likes the fact that he can buy whatever he wants and that money isn't an issue. He desires more and more wealth to satisfy the craving inside of him. On the other hand, a poor man doesn't have much, but greed and jealousy push him to want what he doesn't have to the point where he may do something wrong in order to get what he wants.

Now, we need to remember that money isn't the problem. The sin is in the love of money, which is another way of talking about greed. Paul wrote to Timothy about this problem: "For the love of money is the root of all kinds of evil" (1 Timothy 6:10).

In Luke 12, Jesus told a parable to illustrate the problem with greed. Before He started the story, He said, "Guard against every kind of greed. Life is not measured by how much you own" (verse 15). Then He talked about a farmer who was very rich. The man's crops did so well that when he brought in the harvest, he didn't have enough space in his barns to store it. So he decided that he would build more barns. He reasoned that if he did that, then he could kick back and relax and not have to work because he would have more than enough stored in his barns to make him money in the years to come. Jesus finished the story with these words: "A person is a fool to store up earthly wealth but not have a rich relationship with God" (verse 21).

Jesus' point is that the material things we have on this earth won't get us to heaven. Our relationship with Him is all that matters in life. He asks us to not invest in the world but to invest in heaven. In heaven, everything lasts forever, death plays no part, and greed has no hold. What are you investing in today?

—Anthony Ferreyra, sophomore

A Little Bit of Love

John 15:15

When I graduated from college, I heard a story that changed my perspective on the penny. Inscribed on the penny are the words "In God We Trust." Instead of looking at it as a worthless coin or a good luck charm, I began to view it as a reminder to trust in God. Whenever I found a penny or another coin, I imagined that God was sending me a hug from heaven and reminding me to trust in Him.

I have many penny stories in which God has sent me a coin at just the right moment when I'm down or lonely or facing a difficult situation. One of my favorite stories is from when my son, Ryan, was six months old. He was in the hospital for the second of three surgeries. It had been an exhausting few days, and I was naturally worried about my baby. I headed to the cafeteria to grab some food, knowing I needed to eat. I ordered a sandwich and looked for an empty table to sit at. I wasn't in the mood to make small talk with others.

I found a completely empty table and set my tray down. I glanced up at the TV across the cafeteria. When I looked back at my tray, there was a penny sitting right beside it, which I am certain wasn't there when I set my tray down. Tears sprang to my eyes as I thought about how God loved me so much that He sent me a special reminder, just for me. I knew that He was in control, and my job was to simply trust.

It's no secret that life is full of good and bad days, so it all comes down to how we handle the days we are given. Do we focus on the negative? Or do we trust in a God who loves us beyond anything we can comprehend? The Bible promises that as we seek God, we will find Him. Our relationship with Jesus is not about a formula, it's about a friendship—an amazing friendship that is full of adventure, growth, shared dreams, and late-night talks.

When we take the time to get to know God, we will find that He shows up in unexpected ways that are unique to us. One way He shows up in my life and reminds me of His love is through pennies and other coins that literally appear when I need them the most.

I am a witness!

—Chaplain Kalie

The Cure for Anxiety
Luke 12:22–34

A s high school students, we face stresses every day. There is a lot of pressure for a teenager to make good choices, get good grades, and figure out what college to go to and what career to pursue, not to mention navigating the world of friends and boyfriends or girlfriends.

That's the type of drama and pressure we deal with. If I asked my parents or another adult what they worry about, it would be their job, having enough money, relationships, health, and maybe even retirement. It's easy to focus on our earthly needs and feel like we need to control the situation in order for things to work out instead of trusting in God.

Jesus said,

"Therefore I tell you, do not worry about your life, what you will eat; or about your body, what you will wear. For life is more than food, and the body more than clothes. . . . Consider how the wild flowers grow. They do not labor or spin. Yet I tell you, not even Solomon in all his splendor was dressed like one of these. If that is how God clothes the grass of the field, which is here today, and tomorrow is thrown into the fire, how much more will he clothe you—you of little faith! . . . For the pagan world runs after all such things, and your Father knows that you need them. But seek his kingdom, and these things will be given to you as well" (Luke 12:22–31, NIV).

Jesus reminds us that if we keep our focus on Him and His kingdom, He will provide everything else we need. I have often wondered what the world would look like if everyone lived by the golden rule. Imagine how quickly things would change. The wealthy would care for the poor, giving their riches to help those in need. The gang members would stop fighting and get rid of their guns in the name of love. The adulterers would stop cheating, return to their families, and focus on their wives.

Jesus was just one man, but He proved that one person can make a change. Imagine what would happen if each of us lived like Jesus and focused on His kingdom instead of _____ (fill in the blank with a worry, habit, or distraction). Imagine how we would change the world!

—Sam Fanelli, junior

Be Ready for Anything
Luke 12:35–48

I used to be afraid of Jesus' second coming. I thought the whole earth would destroy itself before He came to get me, which seemed pretty scary for a little kid. Then when I was in the third or fourth grade, I read a fictional story that was written from the point of view of a girl living during the end times. This story changed my perspective of Jesus' return.

The story was full of miracles and close calls. One time her car ran out of gas, but it kept going even though her tank was empty. At the end of the story, she was strapped to the electric chair, and the person pushing the button told her she had one final chance to give up on God. She told him she would never betray Jesus. Just before he pushed the button to kill her, there was an earthquake that destroyed the building. She got out of the chair and ran outside. When she looked up into the sky, Jesus was coming in the clouds!

This story inspired me when I read it. I want to have courage to stand up for God. I want to be ready for Jesus' second coming because it is going to be magnificent. It's not something to be afraid of, but it's not something to take lightly either. We need to pay attention and always be ready. Jesus instructed His disciples about this when He said, "You also must be ready, because the Son of Man will come at an hour when you do not expect him" (Luke 12:40, NIV).

I believe that Jesus is coming very soon and that we need to tell others about His return. Of course, this means that we need to have a relationship with Jesus so that we have something to share. We don't have to be a pastor or a Bible scholar to share Jesus with others. We just have to know Him.

Trust me, enduring persecution for my faith isn't exactly something I get excited about. I have to remind myself that if that happens to me, I'm just experiencing what Jesus went through. God will be with me just as He was with Jesus. Jesus died for us. He gave everything so that we can live. What are you doing to be ready for Jesus' soon return?

—Olivia Fisher, sophomore

All in His Hands

Psalm 31

I first met Randy at Mt. Aetna Camp in Hagerstown, Maryland, where he was the rock-climbing instructor and I was the camp secretary. We started hanging out the first few weeks of camp, and we began dating shortly thereafter. I had never been rock climbing, but I had done some high–ropes course activities, so I was definitely open to trying a new sport when Randy offered to teach me how to climb.

On one of our days off, we headed up to Annapolis Rock on the Appalachian Trail, not too far from camp, and he found an easy route for me. I watched as he expertly secured the rope above the rock face and set out all the equipment we would need for the day. He seemed very thorough, double- and triple-checking his knots and anchor points. I wasn't worried about my safety because Randy took so much care in setting everything up.

He gave me a harness and adjusted it to fit me. He then secured the rope to my harness and took the other end so that he could belay me as I climbed up the rock face. He checked the carabiner and rope attached to my harness multiple times before teaching me the correct climbing commands and sending me to pick my way up the rock face.

In essence, my life rested in Randy's hands. I trusted that he had properly secured everything and that he would keep the necessary tension on the rope while I climbed to help me feel safe. If I called for slack or tension, I knew he would listen and adjust as needed.

David wrote the following words in Psalm 31: "Into your hands I commit my spirit; deliver me, LORD, my faithful God" (verse 5, NIV). In the midst of the trials David faced, he trusted that God was still holding his hand and walking beside him. Jesus uttered the same words when He hung on the cross (Luke 23:46). In the midst of the most horrific moment of Jesus' life—when He experienced separation from His Father and felt the weight of the world on His shoulders, not to mention the torture of crucifixion—He chose to trust in God the Father. Jesus chose to rest in the knowledge that God loved Him, and even though He couldn't see the other side, He would walk that road, believing that God would be faithful.

What wall are you facing in your life? What could happen if you believe that God is securely holding the rope and won't let you fall?

—Chaplain Kalie

Meeting With Jesus

"So be strong and courageous! Do not be afraid and do not panic before them. For the LORD your God will personally go ahead of you. He will neither fail you nor abandon you" (Deuteronomy 31:6).

What stuck out to you in this reading?

_____

_____

_____

_____

_____

What question would you like to ask God about this verse?

_____

_____

_____

_____

_____

What truth is God sharing in this passage?

_____

_____

_____

_____

_____

Consequences
Luke 13:1–9

Whether it's at home or at school, we grow up hearing about consequences. When we're little, it starts with basic commands, such as "Don't touch the stove or you'll get burned." As we grow older, it turns into stuff like "Don't do drugs because they fry your brain and mess up your life" or "Don't have sex before marriage because you could end up with a kid or catch an STD." For each of these actions, there are potential negative consequences attached to them.

This is basic cause-and-effect thinking, but it gets us in trouble when we attach this rationale to spiritual matters. In an effort to explain why bad things happened, the Jewish people reasoned that the person suffering must have sinned or done something to make God angry. In Luke 13, we find Jesus addressing this wrong thinking. "Do you think that these Galileans were worse sinners than all the other Galileans because they suffered this way? I tell you, no! But unless you repent, you too will all perish. Or those eighteen who died when the tower in Siloam fell on them—do you think they were more guilty than all the others living in Jerusalem? I tell you, no! But unless you repent, you too will all perish" (verses 2–5, NIV).

In these verses, Jesus was essentially answering the question of why bad things happen to good people. He made it clear to His listeners that these people weren't suffering tragedy because they were worse than anyone else. Jesus sought to draw their attention to a different cause-and-effect principle, and here it is. We are sinners, and the consequence of sin is death. However, if we repent and ask God for forgiveness, we will live.

God shows us compassion every day. Jesus continued His lesson about repentance by sharing a parable about a fig tree that was not producing any fruit. For three years, the tree did nothing, so the master ordered it cut down. However, the gardener urged the master to leave it alone for one more year. He would tend to the plant in hopes that it would bear fruit. If it did not, then he would understand the need to cut it down.

This just reiterates the fact that God loves us and is patient with us when we mess up. He isn't out to destroy us, but in the end, if we choose not to repent and bear fruit for His kingdom, we will be lost. How will we respond to this unfailing love?

—April Espinoza, freshman

The Right Thing

Luke 13:10–17

W e all know the story of Creation and how God created this round rock we call home. He worked for six days creating this masterpiece of a planet for us, and then He did something extraordinary—He created the Sabbath on the seventh day. God gave us this day to rest, reflect on Creation, breathe in the beauty, and spend time with God.

God gave us some guidelines for the Sabbath, instructing us not to work, not to make other people work for us, and not to do anything that directs our attention or other people's attention away from Him as the Creator. Ultimately, God wants us to see the importance of spending time with Him on His holy day. However, like so many other things, some people have taken something good and turned it into something negative.

The Pharisees added a ton of more rules to Sabbath observance than God ever intended. So when Jesus healed a woman on the Sabbath who had been crippled for eighteen years, the religious leaders got riled up, and one of them told Jesus that He had six other days to heal on, but He was breaking the law by healing—working—on the Sabbath (Luke 13:14).

It's pretty ridiculous that they were accusing God, the One who created the day, but they jumped into battle. Jesus replied, "You people are hypocrites! All of you untie your work animals and lead them to drink water every day—even on the Sabbath day. This woman that I healed is a true descendant of Abraham. But Satan has held her for 18 years. Surely it is not wrong for her to be made free from her sickness on a Sabbath day!" (verses 15, 16, ERV).

Jesus showed us by example that it is good to help people and alleviate suffering on the Sabbath. It may feel like it's tricky to know whether something is appropriate for Sabbath or not, but if you're a little hesitant about the activity, pray about it. God will help you if you are seeking to honor Him.

—Megan Epperson, senior

Called to Serve
Galatians 5:13

The door creaked as the five of us filed into the makeshift house in Peru. We had been going door-to-door passing out food all day and were grateful for some shade. A man wearing a soccer jersey and a smile greeted us, gave us plastic stools to sit on, and excitedly introduced us to his son. After the customary greetings and usual questions about his house and his family, we found out that he was a fisherman. Our group perked up, and one of my friends asked, through our translator, "Do you have any interesting stories from your time fishing?"

The man excitedly began telling us of a time he went fishing on the Amazon. "I was out fishing on the Amazon, and the river is very deep. My nets got caught on something in the river, but because the water is so muddy, I could not see what it was stuck on. I jumped into the water to swim down and untangle the net. I was blindly reaching out with my hands to feel what was caught on the net, and my hand brushed up against something. I grabbed hold of it, and it felt like hair. I reached my other hand around to feel it, and it felt like the head of a human. Of course, I dropped the head and swam as fast as I could to the top of the water. Then I got on my boat and left the area."

We all laughed nervously and breathed a sigh of relief that the story was done. We then asked this man more questions about his life as a fisherman and a Peruvian. It was not until later that I realized the powerful lesson I learned from this story. I went on the mission trip in the same way that the man went into the Amazon—totally unaware of what was beneath the surface. I figured I was going to do construction, interact with people, pass out food, provide medical services, build relationships, or even just hold babies, but I experienced the unexpected at times, and I learned about God in ways I wouldn't have if I hadn't gone to another country.

The Bible reminds us repeatedly that our job is to serve others. Galatians 5:13 says, "You, my brothers and sisters, were called to be free. But do not use your freedom to indulge the flesh; rather, serve one another humbly in love" (NIV).

Being called to serve with love means being willing to help others even when you don't know what to expect. That's one lesson God taught me while working in Peru.

I am a witness!

—Amie Shelley, junior

Accepting Him

Matthew 13:1–23; Mark 4:1–20; Luke 8:4–15

The parable of the sower outlines the various ways that people react to the message of the Gospel. As the story goes, a farmer went out to plant his fields. As was the custom back then, he scattered the seeds across the ground as he walked. Some of the seed fell on the path, some fell upon the rocks, some fell in the midst of thorns, and some managed to fall on good soil. The seeds that fell on the path were eaten by birds; the seeds that fell among the rocks grew but were quickly scorched by the sun because they didn't have deep roots; and the seeds that fell among the thorns grew but were choked out by the weeds. Finally, the seeds that fell on the good soil grew well and produced a crop.

After sharing the parable, the disciples asked Jesus why He taught by telling stories. Jesus replied that those who were truly listening and wanting to learn about God would understand but that those who didn't care and were in the crowd for selfish reasons wouldn't understand.

Jesus then quoted from Isaiah:

> "When you see what I do,
>> you will not comprehend.
> For the hearts of these people are hardened,
>> and their ears cannot hear,
> and they have closed their eyes—
>> so their eyes cannot see,
> and their ears cannot hear,
>> and their hearts cannot understand. . . .

> "But blessed are your eyes, because they see; and your ears, because they hear" (Matthew 13:14–16).

Which seed are you? Has Satan taken away the truth that was planted? Did you accept God's Word, but then hard times came, or the things of the world seemed better, and you slipped away? Did you grow a while but then let other things choke out your relationship with God? Or are you seeking a relationship with God and growing in His Word, resulting in the production of a "good crop"?

Are we listening to God's Word? Do we hear Him speaking as He did in this parable, or are our ears closed to the truth like so many people's during Jesus' time on earth?

—Sarah Fisher, junior

The Best Stories
Matthew 13:24–43

There is so much beauty and simplicity in Jesus' parables. The natural symbolism He used provided powerful examples of kingdom truths to His listeners and to us thousands of years later. By preaching in this way, Jesus also fulfilled prophecy: "I will speak to you in parables. I will explain things hidden since the creation of the world" (Matthew 13:35; Psalm 78:2).

Ellen G. White wrote about the effectiveness of Jesus' parables in *Christ's Object Lessons*: "Leading thus from natural to the spiritual kingdom, Christ's parables are links in the chain of truth the unites man with God, and earth with heaven."*

In these parables, Jesus is talking about the kingdom of heaven. In the first story, He shared about a farmer who planted his crop only to discover when the wheat began to grow that there were also weeds growing among the wheat. His workers came to him and asked whether they should pull the weeds. However, the farmer said that would inadvertently pull up the wheat, so he instructed the workers to leave both plants until harvest, at which time they would harvest everything and sort the wheat from the weeds.

The disciples listened to these stories, but even they didn't understand the truths Jesus was trying to teach. In verses 36–43, they asked Jesus to tell them the meaning of the story of the wheat and weeds. Jesus told them that He was the farmer who planted good seed and that Satan is the enemy who sowed the weeds. Both good and evil people will live together until Jesus' second coming, at which time the righteous will be taken to heaven and the wicked will be destroyed.

In between Jesus' story and His explanation, He shared this illustration: "The Kingdom of Heaven is like a mustard seed planted in a field. It is the smallest of all seeds, but it becomes the largest of garden plants; it grows into a tree, and birds come and make nests in its branches" (Matthew 13:31, 32). One way to look at this parable is that we are the mustard seeds. We are very small and insignificant on our own, but when we are connected to God, we play a bigger role in His kingdom. When we allow God to fill us, even our small acts of love and kindness show others who God is and what His kingdom is all about.

—Geoffrey Fowler, senior

* Ellen G. White, *Christ's Object Lessons* (Washington, DC: Review and Herald®, 1941), 17, 18.

Shine Brightly

Mark 4:21–25; Luke 8:16–18

At the beginning of time, God created light. He set the sun in the sky to be a light for our world. Everyone who's ever lived has seen or felt the sun and its effects, from growing plants to heating our earth and sustaining life. The sun is brighter than any light humans have ever invented or experienced. The sun produces light as a by-product of nuclear fusion. God's power is clearly evident in His creation of the sun, which gives us light and so much more.

Jesus is known as the "Light of the world." Just as God created light to sustain life, He sent Light to this world to save our lives. God sent His Son into the world to be lifted up on a cross where everyone could see Him, which literally changed everything in our world. Wars, inventions, religions, countries, exploration, medicine—everything we think of as history is somehow connected to the movement Jesus started when He came here to earth. Jesus took our shame, our sins, and our filth and converted our feeble lives of sin and suffering into lives of freedom. He was able to do that because of the connection He had with God. He took the energy from God and channeled that power to our world.

This whole concept of being lifted up and exalted is a reoccurring theme in the Bible. In today's verses, Jesus talks about how a lamp isn't lit and then covered up or stuck under a bed. That would be ridiculous! No, a lamp is lit and placed on a stand so that it spreads its light around the room. God is calling us to be lights in this world. As teenagers, we can be a positive influence on our world if we simply let God's love shine out of us. Just like the physical sun and God's Son, we can make the world around us a better place through the power of God. We just have to be connected to the Source.

—Jared Freeman, junior

Meeting With Jesus

You have turned my mourning into joyful dancing.
You have taken away my clothes of mourning and
clothed me with joy,
that I might sing praises to you and not be silent.
O LORD my God, I will give you thanks forever!
(Psalm 30:11, 12).

What did you learn about God from this passage?

How can you apply these verses to your own life?

What can you share with others from these verses?

Growing in Faith

Matthew 13:31, 32; Mark 4:26–32; Luke 13:18, 19

B asketball has always been a big part of my life. I believe that I would not be the same person I am today without it. I remember playing as a kid when I was around seven or eight. My dad helped me practice shooting, dribbling, and rebounding, and then he told me something that stuck with me. Dad said that he would always help me practice and that I would get better and better as I kept playing; it didn't matter how good or bad I was at that moment.

As I got older, I spent more time outside, often playing basketball on weekends with friends. Almost every Sunday I had a game, and my dad showed up and cheered me on. Some days I played awfully, and some days I played really well, but my dad always said the same thing. He always reminded me that he would keep helping me practice and that I would get better and better as time went on.

My dad believed in me. He knew I could become good at basketball if I practiced and dedicated myself to the sport. He didn't care if I had a bad game. He didn't care about how many points I scored. My dad simply cared about me. He accepted me for who I was, not for the results I produced on the court.

This reminds me of the parable of the mustard seed. God says we are His children. He tells us He loves us. He says He will help us do great things if we just have faith in Him. Our faith starts out small, like the mustard seed, but as we believe in what God says about us, it grows until it becomes a strong tree.

When I started playing basketball, I wasn't that good, but I kept remembering that my dad was there to help me and that I would get better the more I practiced. When we first believe in God, our faith is small, but God is right there, reminding us that He loves us and that He is there to help us. As we exercise our faith, it begins to grow until it is so big that we share the good news of the kingdom of heaven with other people.

—Jakob Furness, senior

Hidden Treasure
Matthew 13:44–46

E arly explorers risked their lives to cross the ocean and travel to foreign lands in search of treasure—gold, silver, spices, silk, and more. They were willing to endure hardships and not see their families for months or years. The dream of fame and fortune drove them to great lengths.

Of course, that happened back in the day when there were new lands to discover. What about today? It's pretty safe to say that today's treasures still revolve around money. People want to get rich, so they sacrifice family time to work crazy hours and get to the top of their professional game. Other people want material treasures, such as boats, cars, or electronics, so they sacrifice their bank accounts and get strapped with debt so they can have everything they've ever wanted. You get the idea.

Although we often equate "treasure" with "things," Jesus talked about the kingdom of heaven being like a treasure. "The kingdom of heaven is like treasure hidden in a field, which a man found and covered up. Then in his joy he goes and sells all that he has and buys that field" (Matthew 13:44, ESV). In the story, the man was willing to give up everything he had in order to buy the field with the hidden treasure.

"Again, the kingdom of heaven is like a merchant in search of fine pearls, who, on finding one pearl of great value, went and sold all that he had and bought it" (verses 45, 46, ESV). Once again, we find someone giving all he had to obtain treasure.

Are we willing to give all we have to obtain heaven? We know that we can go to heaven by believing in Jesus and accepting His gift of salvation. However, that means we need to surrender to Him and give Him our lives.

It's hard for us to realize, but trading the things of this earth for heaven is more than a good deal. It's hard to imagine heaven being better than the best things we already know, but it will be so much greater!

What treasure are you seeking after? And what are you willing to do to get it?

—Nicolas Galindo, junior

Disaster Averted
Titus 2:6–8

I spent my high school years attending a public school in rural Michigan. As a former Adventist, my father would not allow, or help fund, Adventist education. Most days after school, I worked at a grocery store stocking shelves and bagging groceries. Of all the adult or assistant managers, one stood out as an incredible example of someone I admired.

Dave took a very active interest in my life. We often talked and laughed together. I think I worked more responsibly because of Dave and the way he treated me. I looked forward to working when I knew Dave was in charge. Dave built a relationship with me by asking questions, listening, encouraging, and sharing himself, which drew me to him. Dave was a deeply committed Christian whose dependence upon God had grown steadfast during the years he spent as a young man in Vietnam. We often spoke of spiritual matters, and Dave's witness to me strengthened my faith in God.

Cindy also worked at the grocery store. About three years older than me, she was strikingly attractive. She was one of the cashiers. The other cashiers seemed to be about seventy years old, and I felt sure they had all taken vows to never be pleasant. Cindy was a flower among the thorns. She was very worldly. She was old enough to drink. Tales of her weekend escapades were captivating to this teenage boy. That, and her relationships with different young men, made up some of the stories she told and the rumors that others told about her. To me, as a high school junior or senior, she was mesmerizing—for all the wrong reasons.

One day she asked me whether I would be her date for a day of fun that would involve boating on a nearby lake. I don't remember my response except that the request took me by surprise. I was flattered and flabbergasted that she would see something in me. I have no idea how Dave knew of Cindy's overture, but to this day, I remember Dave taking me aside, away from the shoppers and other workers, looking into my eyes, and saying, "You know you can't do this. You have nothing in common with her, and she can ruin you." Dave spoke deeply into my life, and because of the strength of the relationship, I accepted the truth I did not want to hear. I declined Cindy's offer, and that took care of that relationship. God used Dave, and many others throughout my lifetime, to head off disaster in my life.

I am a witness!

—Greg Gerard, principal

Final Spring Cleaning
Matthew 13:47–50

How good are you at sorting through your closet and cleaning your room? Some people do a deep clean in the spring when they sort their closets and drawers and tidy things up. If you go to a boarding school, you deep clean at the end of the school year when you're clearing out your dorm room. At GCA, the girls' dean collects everything that we don't want and gives it to a refugee community outside Atlanta. You should see the piles of stuff right before everyone moves out! Whatever doesn't fit in a box or in the family car seems to end up down in the rec room for the refugees. Seniors seem to sort and purge even more than the rest of us.

For some people, sorting and cleaning is pure torture. They hate it. They dislike the whole process, whether it's because they are attached to their stuff or because they don't like cleaning in general.

The Bible tells us that there is going to be a time of sorting when Jesus comes back. Check out the parable of the fishing net in Matthew 13: "Again, the Kingdom of Heaven is like a fishing net that was thrown into the water and caught fish of every kind. When the net was full, they dragged it up onto the shore, sat down, and sorted the good fish into crates, but threw the bad ones away. That is the way it will be at the end of the world. The angels will come and separate the wicked people from the righteous, throwing the wicked into the fiery furnace, where there will be weeping and gnashing of teeth" (verses 47–50).

When God finally decides that it is time to come get His children, there will be a final sorting, Jesus' followers will be taken to heaven, and the wicked will be destroyed. Just like it is hard for some people to sort and clean, I imagine it's going to be hard for God to sort His children. Peter wrote, "The Lord isn't really being slow about his promise, as some people think. No, he is being patient for your sake. He does not want anyone to be destroyed, but wants everyone to repent" (2 Peter 3:9).

God loves us so much, but there will come a day when our actions will be judged, and we will be sorted according to whose side we've chosen.

—Lauren Gerath, freshman

Teachers and Treasures
Matthew 13:51, 52

I have a huge amount of respect for teachers. I wouldn't want to be stuck in school from kindergarten to retirement. I personally couldn't take it. The hours of work they put in to teach students, only to have a lot of them complain about homework and projects, show how much teachers care. They also have a very important duty to the world. Teachers are the ones who help shape the next generation into productive citizens who are knowledgeable and hardworking. That puts a lot of responsibility on their shoulders.

A Christian teacher has an even bigger task of not only teaching the basic subjects but also of being an example of God's character to those they teach. Of course, to do so effectively requires understanding of who God is and what His Word says.

Today's passage comes at the end of a series of parables that Jesus shared about the kingdom of heaven. The parables help paint a picture of what the kingdom of heaven will be like and who will be there. " 'Have you understood all these things?' Jesus asked. 'Yes,' they replied. He said to them, 'Therefore every teacher of the law who has become a disciple in the kingdom of heaven is like the owner of a house who brings out of his storeroom new treasures as well as old' " (Matthew 13:51, 52, NIV).

Knowledge is treasure, and Jesus compares the work of a teacher to that of someone bringing treasures out of a storeroom. A teacher who is Jesus' disciple will have new and old insights to share with their students because they are learning from the master Teacher.

Although you and I may never become teachers, we can share with others what we're learning from God's Word. He has asked each of us to tell others about Him. No matter how big or small, whatever knowledge we have of God is like a treasure to be shared with others.

—Dakota Futcher, senior

Beyond Awesome
Psalm 33

When I was a kid, I often sat on the couch with the TV remote and channel surfed, flipping from one station to the next in search of something interesting to watch while avoiding any commercials. I guess we still do the same thing today, but we just have different media formats. It still might be cable TV, but now we have Netflix and Hulu and YouTube, not to mention our social media feeds. There are more options for entertainment today, but getting sucked into watching stuff is the same.

Of course, the beauty of sites such as YouTube is that if you're interested in a certain subject or theme—funny cat videos—you can watch hours of similar content. One popular topic on YouTube is "People Are Awesome" videos. My husband likes to watch them occasionally, and when he does, I usually sit there with my mouth open because I'm literally amazed at what human beings can do. My mind is blown at their athleticism, flexibility, and sheer talent.

Is my mind as blown when I think about God? Psalm 33 tells us that we should "stand in awe of Him" (verse 8, NKJV). Why? Here is a reminder:

By the word of the LORD the heavens were made,
And all the host of them by the breath of His mouth.
He gathers the waters of the sea together as a heap;
He lays up the deep in storehouses.

Let all the earth fear the LORD;
Let all the inhabitants of the world stand in awe of Him.
For He spoke, and it was done;
He commanded, and it stood fast (verses 6–9, NKJV).

We are creative beings, which is evident on YouTube, but there isn't a single person alive who can speak and make something appear or be done. God alone has this power! He speaks, and stuff happens! It doesn't get any more awesome than that. He deserves our love and respect and praise. I hope your prayer is this:

Our soul waits for the LORD;
He is our help and our shield.
For our heart shall rejoice in Him,
Because we have trusted in His holy name.
Let Your mercy, O LORD, be upon us,
Just as we hope in You (verses 20–22, NKJV).

—Chaplain Kalie

Meeting With Jesus
1 John 5:14, 15

Y ou're home alone, and you're hungry! It would be so much better if your
mom was there and could make you lunch, but as she would tell you: "You
have two hands and know how to cook. You can make yourself something to
eat."

You head to the kitchen and open the pantry. Spaghetti. Burritos. Burgers.
You debate how much time you want to spend cooking, and you settle on an
old-fashioned classic—PB&J. You grab the ingredients and slap together a
sandwich. You find an apple in the refrigerator and grab a bag of chips from the
cupboard.

It's definitely not gourmet, but it will work. It's food, and you're hungry!

Just as you sit down at the table, the doorbell rings.

Who could that be? you wonder as you push your chair back and head to the
front door.

You open it to find Jesus standing there. "May I come in?" He asks.

You smile as Revelation 3:20 pops into your mind. "Good timing! I was just
sitting down to eat. Do you want a sandwich?"

"Sounds great."

You walk back to the kitchen and begin making another sandwich for your
unexpected Guest. As you work, Jesus asks you about your week and how things
are going. You fall into a comfortable conversation that lasts for the next hour
as you eat together.

Jesus helps you clean up the kitchen, and then He tells you He needs to go.
"Thanks for lunch," He says. "It was great catching up. Before I leave, let's have
prayer together. What can I pray about as you start this new week?"

Take some time to talk to Jesus or write down your response to His question.

**Read the passage for the day and think about the promise it offers or what
it tells you about God.**

**If you were to talk about this reading with Jesus, what would you say?
What would you ask Him?**

Sacrifice
Matthew 8:18–22; Luke 9:57–62

The US celebrates Memorial Day at the end of this month. It's a day dedicated to paying our respects to the men and women who have died while serving our country. They gave their lives for our freedom. They sacrificed time with their families to protect you and me and our families. They served our country selflessly, ultimately losing their lives in the process.

Jesus sacrificed His life on our behalf as well. However, His death has eternal implications. The death of our country's service members gives us temporary freedom; Jesus' death gives us ultimate freedom through the promise of eternal life.

John wrote the following: "We know what real love is because Jesus gave up his life for us. So we also ought to give up our lives for our brothers and sisters" (1 John 3:16).

When we choose to follow Jesus, we are choosing to sacrifice our needs and desires to serve other people and love them as Jesus loves us.

In Matthew 8 and Luke 9, we find a story of a man coming to Jesus and telling Him that he would follow Him wherever He went. Jesus wanted to make sure this man understood what it meant to follow Him. He replied, "Foxes have dens and birds have nests, but the Son of Man has no place to lay his head" (Matthew 8:20, NIV). Jesus was saying, "My life isn't about comfort and all the things most people want to have in life."

Jesus then turned to another man and said, " 'Follow me.' But he replied, 'Lord, first let me go and bury my father.' Jesus said to him, 'Let the dead bury their own dead, but you go and proclaim the kingdom of God.' Still another said, 'I will follow you, Lord; but first let me go back and say goodbye to my family.' Jesus replied, 'No one who puts a hand to the plow and looks back is fit for service in the kingdom of God' " (Luke 9:59–62, NIV).

It might be easy to assume that Jesus is hard-hearted and unreasonable, but in both of these cases, it seems like the men are making excuses for not following Jesus. Following Jesus requires sacrifice but has great rewards. Are you willing to join His ranks? What are you willing to sacrifice? What excuses pop into your mind when you think about His call to follow Him?

—Robby Gill, sophomore

Braving the Storm
Matthew 8:23–27; Mark 4:35–41; Luke 8:22–25

There are two stories in the Bible of the disciples being caught in a storm: in one, Jesus is with them; in the other, He walks across the water, and they think He is a ghost. The common denominator in both is that the disciples are terrified. These are fishermen who were used to being out on the water and going through storms, so both of these storms must have been very bad for them to be so scared.

The storm documented in these verses is the one in which Jesus is with the disciples, but He's not exactly helping them in the middle of their crisis. What was He doing? He was utterly exhausted and sleeping—of all the times to take a nap! His followers were struggling to keep the boat afloat because the "waves were breaking into the boat" and it was "already filling" with water (Mark 4:37, ESV). Jesus was doing nothing except sleeping.

Did He not care about what was going on? Did He not even notice that a storm was raging around Him? The difference between the disciples and Jesus was that He had faith. Jesus wasn't panicking because He knew He was in His Father's hands. The disciples seemed a bit frustrated when they woke up Jesus. "Teacher, do you not care that we are perishing?" (verse 38, ESV).

Of course Jesus cared! This was a perfect moment to teach the disciples about faith. Jesus stood up and said, " 'Peace! Be still!' And the wind ceased, and there was a great calm. He said to them, 'Why are you so afraid? Have you still no faith?' " (verses 39, 40, ESV).

Jesus was right there with the disciples as they were going through the storm. He hadn't left them. He still cared about them. They just needed to trust in His protection.

When we put our trust in God, He will see us through, so we don't need to fret about our circumstances. He created the world, so He has authority over everything that happens in it. Whether it's a physical storm or an emotional storm—maybe you're moving to a new school or a family member has cancer or your best friend betrayed you—Jesus is there with you in the storm, and He wants to give you peace. What storm are you going through right now? Talk to God about it, and trust in His timing.

—Gabby Fowler, senior

A Refuge for Refugees
Psalm 9:7–10

I saw the top of her head before I saw anything else about her. She might have known that my class wasn't for her, but she said she heard something interesting, so she shyly peeked her head around the corner of the door. When her eyes finally creeped over the threshold, I smiled and invited her in. I could tell she was much too old for my Sabbath School class, but I had a policy of never turning away anyone who walked through my door.

To my surprise, four other girls followed her in. None of them were as tall or as old. The last one carried a very small child on her back, even smaller than the kids in my kindergarten class. They stood just inside the door smiling and looking curiously at the project we had laid out on the table. Not knowing whether they spoke English, I welcomed them and used my hands as much as I could, inviting them to sit down and participate. They all did, and they stayed the whole time.

I found out later from one of the other teachers that they were refugees. They had escaped violence in their country and been placed in our town. Someone from the church had brought them. The oldest girl, whom I'll call Sara, was twelve. The rest ranged in age from ten to two.

They came to my room again the next Sabbath and stayed until someone came to help them find their age-appropriate classes. Even then, they came back again, which didn't bother me at all. I was glad they felt comfortable. I got to know them all a little better and found out that while the younger girls were sisters, Sara and her "brother" weren't related. They were orphans, and in order to escape their country, they had been thrown together with a woman who posed as their mother so they could exit the country. I couldn't begin to imagine the horrors they must've experienced!

Several years later, as we prepared to move away from the area, I spoke with Sara about her experience. She said school had been rough but that our church had been an oasis. She felt out of place in public school, but she felt welcome and loved at church. I was moved by her words. As I looked at the world through her eyes, I realized that she was describing exactly what church is supposed to be: a refuge for refugees. After all, aren't we all refugees who find our refuge in God? When we share His love in our churches and schools, we really are a witness.

Because of my experience with Sara, I am a witness!

—Shannon Scott, science/technology/art/journalism teacher

Everyone Has a Story

Matthew 8:28–34; Mark 5:1–20; Luke 8:26–39

There is so much to digest in today's story! Let's take it from the beginning. Jesus and His disciples have just crossed the lake and are now in the region of the Gerasenes, which was mainly inhabited by pagans. This was why they raised pigs, something the Jews would never do since pigs were an unclean animal. This interesting fact plays into the story at the end.

After landing on the shore, everyone gets out of the boat, and a madman comes running down the beach and throws himself at Jesus' feet. We can only imagine how wretched he looks. The Bible tells us that he is so crazy that chains can't hold him and that he spends the day and night "howling and cutting himself with sharp stones" (Mark 5:5). Jesus does what only He can do—He commands the evil spirit to leave the man, which begins this strange conversation between the demons and Jesus. They shriek, "Why are you interfering with me, Jesus, Son of the Most High God? In the name of God, I beg you, don't torture me!" (verse 7).

Jesus then asks the evil spirit its name. The reply? "My name is Legion, because there are many of us inside this man" (verse 9). For reasons I don't understand, the demons ask to be sent into a herd of pigs feeding on a nearby hillside, and Jesus grants their request. The pigs jump off a cliff and drown in the lake below. Understandably, this makes the pigs' owners really mad, and even though they can see that the demon-possessed man is now clothed and acting like a normal human being, they beg Jesus to leave the area (verses 12–17).

Never one to force Himself on people, Jesus heads back to the boat. Unlike everyone else, who keep Jesus at arm's length out of fear, the man who has been freed from the evil spirits pleads with Jesus to go with Him. Instead of agreeing to this request, Jesus instructs the man to stay where he is, go home to his family, and share the story of his miraculous healing with everyone he meets.

The man didn't go to school to be a preacher or a Bible teacher, but he had an encounter with Jesus and walked away a new person. That's what he shared. He shared about meeting Jesus, and that made all the difference in the world. When Jesus returned to the area later, the people were receptive to Him, which was likely a direct result of one man's story (Mark 7:31–37). What is your story? How has God worked in your life?

—Chaplain Kalie

Don't Tell

Matthew 9:18, 19, 23–26; Mark 5:21–24, 35–43; Luke 8:40–42, 49–56

T his is one of my favorite miracle stories in the Gospels. Although I'm not a parent yet, I can't imagine losing a child to death. It has to be one of the most heart-wrenching things. The death of a child is a life unlived—a future unseen.

I'm sure you know the story. A man by the name of Jairus, who is a ruler in the synagogue, comes to Jesus and begs Him to come heal his twelve-year-old daughter, who is dying. While he is conversing with Jesus, a messenger shows up and says that his daughter has already died and there isn't a point in bothering Jesus. Jesus replies,

> "Do not fear; only believe, and she will be well." And when he came to the house, he allowed no one to enter with him, except Peter and John and James, and the father and mother of the child. And all were weeping and mourning for her, but he said, "Do not weep, for she is not dead but sleeping." And they laughed at him, knowing that she was dead. But taking her by the hand he called, saying, "Child, arise." And her spirit returned, and she got up at once. And he directed that something should be given her to eat. And her parents were amazed, but he charged them to tell no one what had happened (Luke 8:50–56, ESV).

One thing I found interesting is how Jesus tells the parents not to talk about the miracle. Isn't one of the main purposes in our lives to tell everyone about God and all He has done for us? I believe there are two reasons for His request. One, Jesus wasn't ready to have His divinity revealed, at least not completely. He naturally wanted people to follow Him, but at this point, it was early in His ministry, and He was trying to avoid the attention of the Pharisees. Once He caught their attention, it was the beginning of the end of His missionary career. Secondly, Jesus didn't want the people He helped to talk about the miracle as if it were a magic trick and He was a magician. This would only serve to bring attention to the deed and Jesus, not to God and His glory. Jesus was trying to turn the spotlight away from Himself and have people see God.

We often don't see God's miracles in our lives for what they are. We take them for granted, or we wrongly attribute the result to good luck or earthly things instead of pointing to God. The great things that happen to us are gifts from God, and we should give Him thanks every day.

—Aleyra Gonzalez, junior

Sick? Here's the Cure
Matthew 9:20–22; Mark 5:24–34

I magine that you have been sick for twelve years (nausea, vomiting, aches, and pains; you name it, you have it), but the doctors can't figure out what's wrong with you. Your social life has dwindled to next to none. All of your money has gone to the 507 times you've stayed in the hospital. Your family has more or less abandoned you because they don't know how to deal with your illness. You spend your days pondering why God has abandoned you while you "worship" the porcelain throne (the toilet) more times than you care to admit in a day. One doctor finally diagnoses you with sempiternal (eternal) influenza—the forever flu. Long story short, there is no cure, and no one even wants to try for fear they will catch it too. You are living a life of pain, weakness, suffering, and endless bouts of temporary insanity caused by continual coughing.

Although this story is fictional, it mirrors the Bible story of the woman who couldn't stop bleeding. As a last resort to find peace and happiness, the woman makes her way through the crowd, which broke Jewish law, in search of Jesus. There are so many people, but she manages to touch His cloak, and immediately she is healed. Jesus calls her out and has these parting words: "Daughter, your faith has healed you. Go in peace and be freed from your suffering" (Mark 5:34, NIV).

Sometimes life feels like God has abandoned us and we are trapped in a never-ending cycle of guilt, pain, and fear. If you've ever felt like this, you aren't alone because all of us suffer from a disease called sempiternal sinning. We are born sinful. We have a disease that separates us from our heavenly Father. Thankfully, we don't have to be sick forever.

Jesus physically healed the woman who couldn't stop bleeding, but He also spiritually healed her. Once she touched Jesus, she couldn't go back to the way things used to be. He freed her from sin and all of its effects. Jesus offers us that same radical treatment plan. Will you reach out in faith and grab hold of Jesus' robe of righteousness? It isn't easy, and sometimes people might think you are crazy, but Jesus promises that He will never leave us nor forsake us (Deuteronomy 31:6).

—Emily Freeman, freshman

Meeting With Jesus

"And because we are his children, God has sent the Spirit of his Son into our hearts, prompting us to call out, 'Abba, Father.' Now you are no longer a slave but God's own child. And since you are his child, God has made you his heir" (Galatians 4:6, 7).

How should we relate to others based on this passage?

What spiritual principle can you take from this passage?

What stuck out to you in this reading?

Faith Is Key
Matthew 9:27–30

O ne day, two blind men came to Jesus and cried out, "Son of David, have mercy on us!" (Matthew 9:27, NKJV). They approached Jesus and asked Him to heal them. Jesus simply asked them whether they believed that He could perform a miracle and do what they were asking. They replied, " 'Yes, Lord.' Then He touched their eyes, saying, 'According to your faith let it be to you.' And their eyes were opened" (verses 28–30, NKJV).

They believed. They had faith that Jesus had the power to heal them. Does faith really work? Here's an example. Do you have faith that when you turn on the light switch in your bedroom the light will come on? Do you understand how the electric current works to turn on the light? Or do you simply believe that it will work when you flip the switch?

The same can be said about our relationship with God. Do you believe that God is in heaven and that He loves you? Do you believe that He hears your prayers? If the answer to those questions is yes, then you have enough faith to believe that when you come to Him with a problem, He'll be there to help you fix it however He sees best to do so.

In the story of the blind men, we see once again how merciful and kind Jesus is to those who are hurting. They followed Jesus, crying to be healed. We don't know how long they walked after Jesus, because the passage says that they followed Him to a house, and once Jesus had entered the house, the blind men came up to Him (verses 27, 28). When they approached Him, Jesus asked them if they believed He could heal them. Jesus wants us to exercise our faith and to keep pursuing Him for what we need, just as the blind men followed Jesus.

When we use our faith, it grows stronger and causes us to want to tell people about Jesus, which is what the men did who received their sight. Even though Jesus told them not to say anything, they "spread the news about Him in all that country" (verse 31, NKJV). They couldn't stay silent about Jesus' power and kindness.

In which area of your life do you need to exercise faith in God and His plans for you?

—Edgar Garcia, senior

Rejection Versus Submission

Matthew 13:53–58; Mark 6:1–6

S ince the beginning of the earth, people have been rejecting God and His life-changing message of love. It's amazing to think about how God would send His only Son to come to this earth and die for people who would reject His perfect gift—a gift that ensures each one of us eternal life if we will simply accept it.

In Matthew 13:53–58 and Mark 6:1–6, Jesus went to His own hometown and spoke to His own people, but they did not believe Him or His message. The Bible actually says that "they took offense at him" (Matthew 13:57, ESV).

Because they had the written prophecies, the Jews should have been ready for Jesus to come, and they should have recognized Him as their Savior. Yet they were ignorant to His coming, which is what Paul warned the Ephesians about: "They are darkened in their understanding, alienated from the life of God because of the ignorance that is in them, due to their hardness of heart" (Ephesians 4:18, ESV). The townspeople of Nazareth hardened their hearts against the truth that Jesus was the Messiah, and they missed getting to know the greatest Man to ever walk the earth.

When I was about nine years old, I spent some time in Egypt. While I was there, I adopted the Muslim faith, and I spent about a year studying and growing in my new faith. When I came back to the US to live with my grandparents, I refused to have anything to do with Christianity and Jesus in particular. I was ignorant of the truth, and I rejected Jesus because of it. I stayed closed off to what my grandparents were trying to tell me, but when I eventually acknowledged Jesus' existence, I began studying about Him.

When I finally stopped rejecting God and let Him come into my heart, I felt like a new person. Now I want to do good things because I love God and want to reflect Him. Christianity is based on the love of God for us and our sharing that love with other people. God doesn't need us to spread the gospel. He could do it on His own or through another method, but He wants us to partner with Him. We can reject Him as much as we want, but the truth of the matter is that He will still love us, and He will continue to knock on our hearts whether we choose to open the door or not. Are you rejecting God, or have you given Him your life?

—Nathan Griswold, sophomore

Choices

Isaiah 30:21

Choices—big, small, right, wrong—we make them all the time, and they're always impacting our lives. Sometimes the choice seems obvious, like picking up the phone when your mom calls. Others, like where to go for lunch, take some thought. And others still, such as what career path you decide to follow, require more careful consideration. We hear it all the time: ask God for help, and He'll answer you. In my experience, He does!

My eighth-grade year was coming to a close, and I was ready to go to the same school as most of my friends. But at the beginning of April, my mom mentioned that we should check out GCA, so I agreed to attend Academy Days. I arrived for the weekend already convinced that there was no way I was going to attend a boarding school in the middle of the woods. However, while I was on campus, I experienced God in a whole new way. I could feel His presence in the surroundings, and I knew that I wanted to be a part of the school.

When we got back to Florida, I had a difficult choice to make. All of my friends were going to the school near my home, but I'd felt such a spiritual connection at GCA. I didn't know what to do. I needed help. Throughout my whole life, my teachers, pastors, and parents had told me to rely on God, so I did. I poured my heart out in prayer, asking for guidance in this decision I faced. I gave the problem to God because I knew He was the only one who could give me unbiased advice. After I finished praying, I simply sat in silence and waited for God's response. I thought about the direction each school could take me. And then, right on cue, God talked back to me, almost like we were having a conversation or something. He told me that being at GCA would expand my horizons and teach me new things about Him.

God leads each of us down different paths. It isn't about one school or another, or one job or another. He places us where He wants us and where we can grow. If we listen, He will let us know where He wants us. So, when making choices, remember to ask God for His opinion and then wait for His response.

I am a witness!

—Anderson Mills, freshman

Farmhands
Matthew 9:35–38

Last year our school went on a mission trip to Iquitos, Peru. I was lucky enough to raise the necessary money to go, but I have to warn you, this is not another one of those mission stories that show how powerful and amazing God is. Even though God is both of those things and more, I had a different mission experience in Peru.

This was my first mission trip, and I had very high expectations for it. I had heard many stories of people who experienced radical personal transformation after going on a mission trip, so I expected the same to be true for me. Yet, to be honest, I was not impacted in the way I wanted to be. I did what I was instructed to do and served where I was told to serve, but I didn't feel like I was making a difference.

Then I remembered something I had heard from a prayer conference I had attended earlier that year. I had been a leader, which meant I got to co-lead a small group to discuss topics that are challenging for modern Christian youth. The director had told us that we would get discouraged because being a leader isn't easy. He warned us that the students in our groups might not talk or communicate or even show the slightest interest in being there. But then he told us this: "You may not see the harvest, but you can rest assured that you are planting a seed in each and every one of your group members' lives."

I thought about his words and how I was doing the same thing on this mission trip. I probably wouldn't see the harvest during the trip, but I was planting a seed. As we met new people each day on the trip, as we learned about their culture and lives, I had to remind myself that I was making a difference, even if I couldn't see it. Maybe another student on a future mission trip will get to see the harvest.

Jesus clearly needs workers who will plant, tend, and harvest. He told the disciples in Matthew 9:37: "The harvest is great, but the workers are few." He's calling us to love others and share His message of truth with them. Whether it is by going on a mission trip, giving someone food on the side of the road, or leading a small group Bible study, we are planting seeds. We are affecting lives. We are His disciples.

So what are you waiting for? Go and put your faith into action. Go work for God.

—Annabelle Harper, senior

Nothing to Fear
Matthew 10:1–42

Freshman year can be really scary. High school is a big step after elementary school. There are definitely more responsibilities—more homework, harder classes, work in addition to school, and more. When I came to GCA, I was nervous. I didn't know what to expect or how to react to all the new activities and people I was meeting. I decided that the only constant in my life was God, so I simply held on to Him throughout that first year as I learned the ropes. As a senior, I can say He's been with me each step of the way, guiding me to completion of my high school education. Now I'm getting ready to start college and a completely new adventure that feels just as scary as high school.

I wonder how the disciples felt when Jesus sent them out on their first missionary journey. We read about it in Matthew 10. Jesus gives them a bunch of instructions and warnings, including this piece of advice:

"Look, I am sending you out as sheep among wolves. So be as shrewd as snakes and harmless as doves. But beware! For you will be handed over to the courts and will be flogged with whips in the synagogues. You will stand trial before governors and kings because you are my followers. But this will be your opportunity to tell the rulers and other unbelievers about me. When you are arrested, don't worry about how to respond or what to say. God will give you the right words at the right time. For it is not you who will be speaking—it will be the Spirit of your Father speaking through you" (verses 16–20).

Jesus is honest with the disciples and tells them that they will face trials as they are working for Him, but Jesus includes a promise at the end. He promises that God will be with them and tell them what to say. Again and again throughout this passage, Jesus tells the disciples not to be afraid.

King Solomon wrote these wise words in Proverbs 27:19: "As a face is reflected in water, so the heart reflects the real person." When we face new situations, what does our heart say about whom we trust? Do we trust in ourselves or our friends? Or do we trust in God? The disciples chose to trust Jesus as they went out on their missionary journey, and they came back with amazing stories. Whom are you trusting with your life?

—Carlos Gonzalez, senior

Stories for Life

Psalm 44:1–8

A s a kid, I used to listen to audio stories every night as I went to sleep. My parents would turn on *The Bible in Living Sound*, which is a dramatized recording of 450 Bible stories from Genesis to Acts. I would lie in the dark and listen to stories about David, Moses, Ruth, Esther, Jesus, and Paul. I learned so much about the Bible by listening to stories, and it helped build the foundation for me to fall in love with Jesus.

In Bible times, people didn't have books or electronic devices to listen to audio stories. Sure, they had scrolls with God's Word written on them, but the common people didn't have access to Scripture. They relied on oral communication and the passage of stories from generation to generation. Psalm 44 starts with these words:

God, we have heard about you.
>Our fathers told us what you did in their lifetime.
>They told us what you did long ago.
With your great power you took this land from other people,
>and you gave it to us. . . .
It was not our fathers' swords that took the land.
>It was not their strong arms that brought them victory.
It was your power.
>It was because you accepted them and smiled down on them.
God, you are my king. . . .
You are the one who saved us from our enemies.
>You are the one who put our enemies to shame.
We have praised you all day long,
>and we will praise your name forever (verses 1–4, 7, 8, ERV).

Jesus grew up hearing these stories from Mary and Joseph. He learned about God by hearing stories of how He had worked in the past. And as He learned, Jesus fell in love with God the Father for all He was in the past, for all He is in the present, and for all He promises us in the future.

Sure, times have changed. The culture from Bible times was very different from ours now. Yet what remains the same is that we learn by hearing. We absorb God's truths by listening to stories or reading them, and as we get to know Him and all He stands for and promises, we fall in love with Him and want to follow in His footsteps. Are you listening to or reading God's Word? If not, what's holding you back from learning about the Creator of the universe and the Savior of the world?

—Chaplain Kalie

Meeting With Jesus

"See how very much our Father loves us, for he calls us his children, and that is what we are! But the people who belong to this world don't recognize that we are God's children because they don't know him. Dear friends, we are already God's children, but he has not yet shown us what we will be like when Christ appears. But we do know that we will be like him, for we will see him as he really is" (1 John 3:1, 2).

How should we relate to others based on this passage?

What can you share with others from these verses?

What truth is God sharing in this passage?

Faithful to the End

Matthew 14:1–12; Mark 6:14–29; Luke 9:7–9

Herod Antipas imprisoned John the Baptist for condemning his marriage to Herodias, his brother Philip's wife. John had called Herod out for his unlawful behavior, which infuriated Herodias so much that she wanted John killed. However, Herod was afraid to have the prophet put to death because he was so popular among the people. So John sat in prison until one fateful night.

It was Herod's birthday, and he had thrown a banquet and invited a bunch of guests. As part of the entertainment, Herodias's daughter came in and danced for the guests. Because Herod enjoyed her show, he offered her anything she wanted, "up to half [his] kingdom" (Mark 6:23, NIV). Not knowing what to ask for, she ran back to her mother. Herodias seized the opportunity and told her daughter to ask for John the Baptist's head on a platter. The girl did what her mother requested, and although disturbed by the request, Herod didn't want to lose face in front of his guests, so he gave the order for John to be beheaded.

This certainly isn't a G-rated story. It's gory and despicable, but it made me think. Many times we think that following God should be all roses and waterfalls. It should be perfect and beautiful, and we shouldn't have any hardships because we are following Him. That isn't what He promises us. He doesn't promise us a life of luxury when we say yes to being His disciples. He says that we will be treated as He was treated. We will be ridiculed, harassed, falsely accused, and maybe even killed.

John lived a life devoted to God. He fulfilled his mission of sharing the good news about Jesus' coming with everyone he met. He did what was right. But he still died.

We want to see the good guys win. Most movie plots have the hero, who represents good, triumph over the evil villain by the end of the movie. That's how it should be, right? So when stuff goes down like John the Baptist being beheaded or other bad things happening to good people, it's easy to blame God and say that life should be different for His followers.

Here's the thing—it will be. We just have to wait for it. Things will never be perfect on earth. Sure, God will send us blessings, and we'll have amazing days and amazing things happen in our lives. However, when the bad stuff does come, we can remember that a day is coming when everything will be made new (Revelation 21:1–8).

—Josh Hendrix, senior

Resting in Jesus

Matthew 14:12, 13; Mark 6:30–33; Luke 9:10, 11; John 6:1–3

What do you like to do to take a break from the busyness and stress in your life? What would be your ideal day of rest? Would it involve spending time outside? Playing your favorite sport? Exercising? Reading a book? Watching Netflix? Hanging out with friends? Playing games on your phone? Surfing social media?

Maybe your ideal day of rest includes spending time with God, but I think most of us leave Him out of the everyday picture. However, when the disciples returned from their missionary journey and needed rest from their travels, Jesus took them off to a deserted place to spend time with Him. I can only imagine that they spent time talking about and sharing the ups and downs of sharing the gospel in the towns they visited. I'm guessing they asked Jesus questions and told Him about the challenges they experienced and how they should do things differently the next time. I'm sure they asked questions about why this or that happened.

Of course, their rest was short-lived because the crowds saw the disciples and Jesus depart by boat, and the crowds ran on foot to the other shore where they thought Jesus and the disciples would land. It is after this rest that we find the story of Jesus feeding the five thousand. But that passage will be covered another day.

Coming back to the idea of rest, what would happen if you included God in your life when you need a break from all the stress? What could you do to spend time with Him? Being in His presence certainly refreshed the disciples and gave them energy to keep serving and working. What would happen if we followed the disciples' lead and included Jesus in every aspect of our lives?

—Emily Harrison, sophomore

My Real Boyfriend
Romans 6:12–14

As I hung up the phone, a mixture of confusion, embarrassment, and rising panic washed over me. My boyfriend was coming to visit me at the summer camp where I was working. That should have been a good thing. My boyfriend was a great guy and a really good friend. But . . . I had gotten another boyfriend at camp!

For several weeks I had managed to ignore the fact that I had a real boyfriend while pursuing a relationship with another guy—my camp boyfriend. Somehow in my mind the real universe and the summer camp universe had not actually collided until the moment my real boyfriend announced that he was coming to visit. At that moment, I had to confront the truth: I was a cheater and a liar.

Despite my Christian accomplishments—growing up in a Christian home, being baptized when I was eleven, attending Christian schools, being in Pathfinders, serving as Student Association pastor at my academy my sophomore year, participating in choir and drama, planning church services and Sabbath School programs, writing spiritual editorials in the school paper—I was a mess.

I honestly cannot remember the few days of my life when my boyfriend came to visit. I had to tell him the truth. I think I blocked that time out of my memory! I know I was miserable, and I know he broke up with me (as he should have). My relationship with my camp boyfriend fizzled out as the summer ended, and I was left facing the undeniable evidence of my own moral failure. I was such a loser.

I wish I could change the fact that my failure hurt a good friend, but I will always be grateful that my failure reminded me that I am nothing without Jesus. I need Jesus to connect me with God. I need Him to forgive me. I need Him to make up for my failures. On my own, I'm a mess, but with God, I'm a new creation. I'm His child, and I'm loved more than anything.

I am a witness!

—LeAnn Gariepy, English/Bible/drama teacher

Say the Blessing

Matthew 14:14–23; Mark 6:34–46; Luke 9:11–17; John 6:2–17

Besides raising people from the dead, feeding the five thousand has to be one of Jesus' best-known miracles. Jesus and the disciples have just crossed the lake by boat to get away from the crowds and talk about their recent missionary journeys. However, the crowds saw which way they went, and they followed them around the shore on foot.

As the people show up, a compassionate Jesus teaches them and heals the sick. He doesn't get upset that they interrupted His private time with the disciples. Instead, He puts His own interests aside and takes care of those around Him. The Bible says that late in the afternoon the disciples came to Jesus and urged Him to send the crowds away so that they could go eat. Jesus simply says, "You feed them" (Mark 6:37).

I'm sure I would have said the same thing as the disciples. "What? Are you crazy! There is no way we can feed all these people! Even if we could find a place that has enough food for sale, we don't have enough money to pay for food for thousands of people!" (verse 37).

I don't know how much it would've cost back then, but let's just say you gave each person five bucks for Taco Bell; it would cost fifty thousand dollars to feed ten thousand people. (Remember, there were five thousand men. That didn't include the women and children who came with the men.)

Instead of arguing with the disciples about the impossibility of feeding everyone, Jesus tells them to go into the crowd and find out how much food there is. The report comes back that they have found five loaves of bread and two fish. Jesus instructs the disciples to have everyone sit down in groups of fifty. He then looks up to heaven and blesses the food. After that, Jesus starts breaking the bread into pieces and placing the food in baskets for the disciples to go distribute to the people. The original loaves of bread and fish don't run out until everyone is fed!

It must've taken the disciples a long time to feed that many people, but they worked right alongside Jesus until the job was done. They played a part in helping Jesus do the impossible. We have that same privilege. God's plans might seem crazy to us at first, but when we give Him what little we have and allow Him to work with it, we are blessed, just as the disciples and the multitude of people were blessed.

—Kevin Guzman, senior

What Is Filling You?
Matthew 14:23–27; Mark 6:47–50; John 6:17–21

Tired. Exhausted. Worn-out. Beat. Drained. Sleep deprived. Based on how many times I've heard these words in the last few weeks, it seems that both students and staff are in need of a break. We're barreling toward the end of the year, which brings with it projects, tests, grading, home shows, trips, and countless other events. Everyone and everything are vying for our attention as we race toward the finish line—graduation.

As I was thinking about how busy and tired everyone seems, my mind wandered to Jesus and His three years of ministry. Did He feel drained after spending a day healing or preaching to the crowds that clamored for His attention? Was He sleep deprived after working all day and then spending the evening in prayer? Did He ever crash from exhaustion and take a nap in the middle of the day? (He did; remember how He slept through the storm on the boat?)

I think we often place Jesus in a different category, assuming that He had superhuman strength and abilities. However, Hebrews 4:15 reminds us that Jesus was tempted in all the ways that we are. That means He experienced life just as we do, which includes being tired.

So, what do we do when we're tired and worn down? We can take our cue from Jesus and spend time with God to recharge our batteries and gain perspective on His plan for our lives. I imagine that Jesus was tired after spending the day healing the sick, preaching, and feeding five thousand people. At the end of such a crazy day, the Bible tells us that Jesus went to the hills to pray and spend time with God after He dismissed the crowds.

Busyness and tiredness are inevitable in the world we live in. But if we are fulfilling God's purposes for our lives, He will give us the strength and energy we need to keep going. The question is, are we seeking His will and allowing Him to fill us?

—Chaplain Kalie

Don't Let Go

Matthew 14:28–33; Mark 6:51–52

I figured it was going to be a good day. I was with my brother's Pathfinder group, and we were going rock climbing. We entered the climbing gym, and I surveyed the walls. At first glance, I told myself this was going to be fun and easy. Wrong!

We got all of our gear and listened to the safety instructions before getting started. I headed straight for the tallest and hardest climb for my age. I figured I had it. The first part wasn't that difficult, but about a foot or so from the top my muscles began to cramp, and I felt as if I couldn't move any further. I was stuck. Then a voice from below shouted up, "Don't look down!" Of course, my natural instinct was to look down. Bad idea! I suddenly realized how high I was, and the only thought that ran through my mind was, *If I fall, I will die! I have to hold on to this rock for dear life!* I clung to the rock and didn't move for at least ten minutes. My muscles were aching, but I couldn't move up. I didn't want to let go, either, because I thought I would fall and die.

Then I heard a voice encouraging me to move just a few more feet. It was my dad. I wanted to believe him, but I was scared. He continued to tell me I could do it, and with each passing moment, I mustered up enough courage to reach for the next handhold. I went for it, but I slipped and began falling. For a split second, I thought I was going to die, but then the rope tightened, and I was lowered gently to the ground. As I descended, I thought about how I had let my fear paralyze me when all that time I had the rope attached to me to keep me safe.

The same thing can happen with our relationship with Jesus. He is always there, but sometimes we forget and take our eyes off Him. It is in those moments that we begin the fall. Fortunately, Jesus is always there to catch us and help us back up. Think about Peter when he walked on water. He was so confident and excited when he stepped out of the boat. He walked without any problems—until he took his eyes off Jesus and let fear overtake him. Then he began to sink. The moment Peter called out for help, Jesus was right there to save him.

Remember, God is your lifeline. Don't take your eyes off Him.

—Carlos Hernandez, junior

Meeting With Jesus

"For the Lord himself will come down from heaven with a commanding shout, with the voice of the archangel, and with the trumpet call of God. First, the believers who have died will rise from their graves" (1 Thessalonians 4:16).

What did you learn about God from this verse?

_____

_____

_____

_____

_____

What stuck out to you in this reading?

_____

_____

_____

_____

_____

What question would you like to ask God about this verse?

_____

_____

_____

_____

_____

An Empty Heart
John 6:22–40

A s a busy high school student, I am literally going from one class or activity to another all day long, which means I'm tired all the time. Taking the time to scavenge up a nap or pray to God seems impossible. However, I'm here to tell you that John 6 puts everything into perspective and reminds us of all that's valuable in life.

The crowd finds Jesus on the other side of the lake the day after He fed the five thousand. Someone approaches Jesus and asks Him where He went after dismissing the crowd. Jesus completely ignores the question and says, "I tell you the truth, you want to be with me because I fed you, not because you understood the miraculous signs. But don't be so concerned about perishable things like food. Spend your energy seeking the eternal life that the Son of Man can give you" (John 6:26, 27).

We each have an empty heart that needs to be filled. Unfortunately, we often try to fill it with friend groups, music, movies, books, food, exercise, and other distractions. However, Jesus is straightforward when He says that only He can give us the life we want.

The people in the story act as if they're committed to Jesus. They say they want to do great things as He did, and they ask what they should do. Jesus tells them to believe in Him. Instead of taking Jesus at face value and letting Him fill the empty hole in their hearts, they turn around and ask for proof that He is sent from God. They just don't seem to get it!

Jesus then says, "I am the bread of life. Whoever comes to me will never be hungry again. Whoever believes in me will never be thirsty" (verse 35). If we go to Him, we will never thirst for things that ultimately suck the life out of us. The promise for living a fulfilling life is there; however, in the next verse, the unfortunate truth smacks them in the face: "But you haven't believed in me even though you have seen me" (verse 36).

Our lives on earth are short compared to the eternal bliss of heaven. Don't waste your absolute happiness on pursuing the enjoyments of the world. Don't be in the group of people who Jesus won't recognize at the end of time because you didn't spend time with Him. Live for God because He is the only One who can fill your heart.

—Sydney Hoffman, sophomore

It Doesn't Matter

John 6:41–49

A painting of daffodils that my mother purchased at a friend's garage sale hangs on the wall in my dining room. It was a pretty piece, and I liked it. My mom is not the type to pick up art (or anything for that matter) from a garage sale, so I asked her why she chose it.

"I painted it," she replied. I was speechless. I knew my mom had done some art in college, but I had no idea she was that talented and that she'd painted pictures for other people. Sure enough, she showed me her signature in the bottom corner of the painting.

Just as I had no real understanding of my mom's abilities, the Jews couldn't seem to believe that Jesus was the Son of God. They knew His parents were poor, working-class people, so they reasoned that He couldn't have come from heaven.

Here's the thing: it didn't matter what the Jews thought about Jesus. He was confident in His connection with God the Father and His mission. "No one can come to me unless the Father who sent me draws them" (John 6:44, NIV). Jesus knew He had the ability to save the world through His Father. It didn't matter what other people thought, only what God said, and God said Jesus was His beloved Son.

The sad thing is that because the Jews were so closed-minded, they missed out on the greatest gift ever. They held on to their preconceived ideas and traditions, and they failed to connect with the God of the universe who was standing right in front of them. Jesus went on to tell them, "No one has seen the Father except the one who is from God; only he has seen the Father. Very truly I tell you, the one who believes has eternal life" (verses 46, 47, NIV).

We need to take a cue from Jesus—don't worry about what others think and just share the good news. He showed the world who God is despite being rejected and misunderstood and ridiculed. You don't have to be a millionaire to spread the gospel. You don't have to travel to a far-off country or get up front and give a long sermon. There are so many ways to serve the Lord. God gave each of us talents and abilities to use for His glory. Remember, it doesn't matter what others think; it only matters what God thinks.

—Aimee Hunt, senior

Japan or Bust
1 Peter 5:7

I had just finished my sophomore year of college, and I decided I wanted to spend the next year as a student missionary. I prayed about it and felt God leading me to spend a year abroad. After applying to be a student missionary and looking at my options, I settled on a position in Japan.

Before I could leave, I had to raise enough money to purchase a plane ticket to Japan. I prayed about it and watched God's mighty hand smooth out the obstacles. A few friends agreed to help me plan a benefit concert in an effort to raise the necessary funds for the ticket.

After the concert, we counted the money, and I began searching for airfare that fit my budget. The route was less than direct, but it was affordable! The plan was for me to leave Milwaukee, Wisconsin, and fly to St. Louis, Missouri. From there I would head to New York City and then to Anchorage, Alaska. I would then cross the Pacific Ocean and land in Seoul, Korea, where I would catch one more flight to Tokyo, Japan. This circuitous route was not very time efficient, but God had provided enough money from the concert for me to pay for my airfare to Japan.

I started on this wonderful adventure with much enthusiasm, but by the time I landed in New York City, I was beginning to feel the effects of all the connecting flights. I had a lengthy layover in New York, which gave me plenty of time to think about how I already missed my family. I sat in the airport and talked to God about how tired and lonely I was feeling. It was not long after that prayer that I looked up to see a familiar face walking among the crowds of people in the airport. It was a classmate from college! I asked him what he was doing in the airport, and he told me he worked there and was on his lunch break. He spent some time with me and then headed back to work. That brief time together was enough to remind me that God cares about every aspect of our lives—He even cares about a college-age guy who was tired and missing his family.

What are the cares of your heart? Have you given them to God?

I am a witness!

—Derrick Collins, Bible teacher/guidance counselor

Stay or Go
John 6:60–71

W hy am I a Christian? If God really exists, then why is He allowing this to happen to me?" If you're like me, you've asked this question or something similar many times. I know personally that it can be difficult to trust when life gets tough. As I watched my family fall apart at the seams, I sank into a deep depression. I even had some suicidal thoughts. When bad things happen, it's easy to give up and run away, but it's possible to handle all of life's hardships and disappointments. Rather than blaming God for the bad things that happen, we should turn to Him for help. Practically speaking, how do we do this?

In John 6:60, the disciples voice their concern amongst themselves over a statement Jesus made about being the bread of life and saving those who eat the bread. "This is a hard saying; who can listen to it?" (ESV). Jesus turns around and asks them directly: "Do you take offense at this?" (verse 61, ESV). Some of the men who followed Jesus didn't come to Him with teachable hearts (most notably Judas), but that's the kind of heart we need in order to walk with God. Jesus presents us with hard truths sometimes, and it's our job to accept them, even if they are difficult to understand. This is why we must be born of the Spirit of God. In verse 63, Jesus says to His followers, "It is the Spirit who gives life; the flesh is no help at all. The words that I have spoken to you are spirit and life" (ESV). Staying true to God and trusting Him mean being open to the prompting of His Holy Spirit.

Following God can sometimes be difficult. Life doesn't always make sense, but what's the alternative? After this exchange, John records that many disciples stopped following Jesus, which prompted Him to turn to the twelve and ask, "Do you want to go away as well?" (verse 67, ESV).

Peter answered, "Lord, to whom shall we go? You have the words of eternal life" (verse 68, ESV). Like Peter, we have a choice to go or stay. We aren't always going to understand. We are going to have questions. That's okay. But will we hold our ground and cling to God? Or will we let the devil sidetrack us with our doubts?

—Lance Hoffman, senior

Kiss-Ups

Matthew 15:1–20; Mark 7:1–23

D o you have any classmates who kiss up to the teacher? Or maybe you've seen a politician or celebrity who kisses up to whomever they are with at the time, trying to look like they are that person's best friend, but then the media catches them talking bad about the person behind their back? It's so fake, and everyone seems to be able to see it except for the person kissing up.

Well, the Pharisees were the same way. Jesus quotes from Isaiah when He says,

"These people draw near to Me with their mouth,
And honor Me with their lips,
But their heart is far from Me.
And in vain they worship Me,
Teaching as doctrines the commandments of men" (Matthew 15:8, 9,
NKJV).

The Jewish leaders swore that they were honoring God and worshiping Him. Instead, they were kissing up to the God of the universe by enforcing burdensome adherence to thousands of laws they had made up. Jesus called them out on this, reminding them that their obedience was in vain because they had made up the laws.

The disciples try to tone Jesus down and ask Him whether He realizes that He's offended the religious leaders, but Jesus doesn't answer the question. Instead, He drives home the point. Whatever comes out of a person's mouth condemns them or acquits them. It doesn't take long to identify someone who is being disingenuous for personal gain, and it didn't take Jesus long to identify the true character of the religious leaders. They didn't want to get to know Jesus or learn the truth. They liked doing things their way. They wanted to be in charge. They didn't want to change. All of these feelings were in their hearts, and hatred for Jesus spewed out of their mouths because of all their negative thoughts.

Stop and take a minute to think about what comes out of your mouth. Write down the things you think and say. Jesus says that what comes out of our mouths shows what is going on in our hearts. What is your heart saying?

—Evan Hyde, junior

Don't Just Exist
Psalm 92

The Biltmore Estate in Asheville, North Carolina, was built in 1895 by George Vanderbilt. The mansion took six years to build, and when it was completed, it featured 250 rooms, including 34 bedrooms, 43 bathrooms, 65 fireplaces, and an indoor pool and bowling alley. In addition to the grand home, the grounds that surround the home are some of the most beautiful gardens I have ever visited. You can walk for hours on the paths that wind through the acres of gardens on the property, including the Italian Garden and the Rose Garden, which features more than 250 different types of roses. The gardens at the Biltmore Estate thrive under the care of the many horticulturalists who keep the property in pristine condition.*

In Psalm 92, we see a picture of God as the Master Gardener.

> But the godly will flourish like palm trees
>> and grow strong like the cedars of Lebanon.
> For they are transplanted to the LORD's own house.
>> They flourish in the courts of our God.
> Even in old age they will still produce fruit;
>> they will remain vital and green (verses 12–14).

"Existing" and "flourishing" are two very different things. I have a hydrangea bush in my yard that is existing. It's planted and growing, but it isn't thriving. It's small and kind of looks straggly. On the other hand, the hydrangea bushes in the Biltmore Gardens flourish. The gardeners take time to prune the plant and make sure it is getting the right nourishment from the soil, adding minerals as needed to ensure it has the ideal growing environment.

Similarly, we can exist on this earth. We can live and breathe and go about our days. Or we can flourish. We can grow stronger and produce more fruit if we are connected to the Master Gardener. Part of this process means that we must allow the Master Gardener to prune us, water us, and maybe even transplant us. All of this takes surrender and trust in our heavenly Father, believing that He has our best interests in mind. When we take that step, we will begin to live our best lives, and as this psalm says, we "will flourish like palm trees." Do you want to exist, or do you want to flourish?

—Chaplain Kalie

---

* *Encyclopedia Britannica Online*, s.v. "Biltmore Estate," by Amy Tikkanen, last modified April 12, 2018, https://www.britannica.com/place/Biltmore.

Meeting With Jesus

"All praise to God, the Father of our Lord Jesus Christ. God is our merciful Father and the source of all comfort. He comforts us in all our troubles so that we can comfort others. When they are troubled, we will be able to give them the same comfort God has given us" (2 Corinthians 1:3, 4).

What did you learn about God from these verses?

What spiritual principle can you take from this passage?

How can you apply these verses to your own life?

Holding on Tightly
Matthew 15:21–28; Mark 7:24–30

Tenacious. Determined. Persistent. Unwavering. Resolute. Unshakable. These are desirable qualities to possess if used in the right way. A21 is an organization created to abolish slavery in the twenty-first century. You might be thinking, "What? Slavery ended years ago with the Civil War." Unfortunately, it has not. There are millions of slaves around the world today. Human trafficking is a $150 billion industry. The different types of slavery include sex trafficking, forced labor, bonded labor, involuntary domestic servitude, and child soldiers. A21 operates in fourteen countries around the world with resource centers, rescue homes, and recovery sites to save and help victims of modern slavery.*

Organizations are not the only ones to inspire us with their resolve to make the world a better place. My mom has a friend who lost her leg in a motorcycle accident. She said that while she was lying in the hospital bed, she made a conscious decision that she was not going to let this slow her down or destroy her. She chose to have a positive attitude and fight through the pain and the bad days. She demonstrated tenacity, and it inspired those around her.

As Jesus was traveling through the region of Tyre and Sidon, He met a tenacious woman who ultimately inspired Him. This Canaanite woman approached Jesus and His disciples and asked Him to heal her demon-possessed daughter. At first, Jesus appears to ignore her request because the disciples say to Him, "Send her away, for she is crying out after us" (Matthew 15:23, ESV). Jesus then says that He was sent to Israel and that because she is a Gentile it wouldn't be right to help her—it wouldn't be "right to take the children's bread and throw it to the dogs" (verse 26, ESV). This sounds so unlike the compassionate Jesus we know, but He was obviously testing her and driving home a point for the disciples. Her response demonstrates an unwavering resolve and belief in Jesus' authority. "Yes, Lord, yet even the dogs eat the crumbs that fall from their masters' table" (verse 27, ESV).

This is what inspires Jesus. He says, " 'O woman, great is your faith! Be it done for you as you desire.' And her daughter was healed instantly" (verse 28, ESV).

What would it look like for you to live a tenacious life for Jesus?

—Chaplain Kalie

---

* "Human Trafficking," A21, accessed May 8, 2019, https://www.a21.org/content /human-trafficking/gnjb89.

Physical and Spiritual Healing
Matthew 15:29–31; Mark 7:31–37

I had the opportunity to go on a mission trip to Iquitos, Peru, over spring break. A few days after we arrived, we were assigned to work groups. Some of us helped with maintenance around the facility while others assisted at the medical and dental clinic. Still others distributed food to needy families in the community while others led a Vacation Bible School program for the local children.

I helped distribute food and assisted in the clinic. As we were distributing food, we spent time getting to know the families. We asked them questions and encouraged them to visit the clinic if they had any medical or dental needs. Many people accepted our invitation. Day after day, we helped the people in the area by passing out food and inviting them to the clinic.

Jesus spent His whole life helping people. He gave of Himself in all that He did. Not only did He provide physical food and healing to the lame, blind, mute, and disabled, but He also provided spiritual healing through a connection with God. "So the multitude marveled when they saw the mute speaking, the maimed made whole, the lame walking, and the blind seeing; and they glorified the God of Israel" (Matthew 15:31, NKJV).

The food and medical services we provided to the community in Peru were good, but of greater importance were the relationships formed. We hope the people saw something different in us that would cause them to want to know more about the God we serve.

Healing is all about getting better. As sinners, we need healing from the sickness of sin. Jesus is the only person who can heal us from this disease. Just as the lame and blind people came to Jesus and asked for physical healing, we have to come to Him and ask for spiritual healing. Just as He gladly healed those who were sick, He will gladly heal us and help us to become who He wants us to be.

—Joshua Holland, senior

Moving Struggles
Jeremiah 29:11

I moved to Boonsboro, Maryland, when I was a year old, so when my parents announced that we were moving away, I wasn't sure what to think. I had lived in the same house for nine years of my life. I was just getting ready to turn ten, and the idea of moving sounded a bit scary. I liked my house and my friends and my church, but all of that would change when we moved. What I didn't realize at the time was how God was working behind the scenes.

My parents put our house on the market during the time when houses were hard to sell. They were praying about whether we should move, so they asked God to make it clear whether we should leave Maryland or not. It only took two weeks to sell the house, so it seemed like God was telling us it was time to go. My parents wanted to be close to an academy, so they planned a trip to look at the towns near Highland Academy, Madison Academy, Georgia-Cumberland Academy, and Mount Pisgah Academy. We started our whirlwind tour in Calhoun, on the campus of GCA, and we never left. My parents both felt completely at peace and as if God was telling them to put down roots and not look anywhere else.

We sold our house in February, but we didn't want to move to Georgia until June, so we needed a place to live for a few months. God orchestrated everything perfectly. My mom's cousin and her husband moved out of their home one week before we needed a place to stay. They had decided not to sell their home, so they agreed to rent it to us for the three months we needed before moving to Georgia.

God continued to provide after our move. The whole adventure had seemed exciting until we loaded the truck and drove away from the town and people I had known and loved my whole life. God helped me adjust to my new surroundings, and He sent me friends, a new home, and a wonderful church family. At the time, I didn't understand everything, but looking back, I can clearly see how He led our family to Georgia. Even though I didn't know what God was doing at the time, He had everything under control, just as He always does. It isn't our job to understand—it's our job to trust.

I am a witness!

—Katelyn Kelch, freshman

Doing It Again

Matthew 15:32–39; Mark 8:1–10

Someone coined a new word a few years ago to describe someone who is so hungry that it makes them cranky or angry—*hangry*. I wonder whether the crowd of four thousand people was hangry. The Bible tells us that they had been with Jesus for three days listening to Him preach. They might have brought food with them, but it was long gone. Jesus didn't want to send them away hungry; He worried they might faint as they traveled home, especially since some had come a long distance (Mark 8:1–3).

His disciples listened to His concerns, and they immediately assumed it would be impossible to solve the problem. "How can one feed these people with bread here in this desolate place?" (verse 4, ESV). The absurd thing is they had seen Jesus feed even more people with less just a short while before! Still, they seem to have forgotten that episode, and they went with the "this isn't possible" mind-set.

I wonder whether Jesus was thinking, *Really, guys? You don't think God can feed them?* Yet He didn't respond in a snarky tone. He simply asked them how much bread was available. They had seven loaves and a few small fish. Jesus then went through a similar routine as He did with the crowd of five thousand. He had the crowd sit down, and then He gave thanks for the bread and began breaking it into pieces to be distributed to the people.

Once again, everyone ate their fill, and there were leftovers. It's easy to criticize the disciples for their lack of faith, especially since they had witnessed Jesus feeding a large crowd before, but are we any different? God is constantly working in our lives and providing for our needs, but the minute we hit a new snag in the fabric of our lives, we doubt His providence. We ask how it will all end and how we will make it through this new crisis, forgetting how God has led in the past. This is one of the biggest dangers we face. Ellen G. White warns about this very thing: "We have nothing to fear for the future, except as we shall forget the way the Lord has led us, and his teaching in our past history."*

How has God led in your life? Hold on to that knowledge as you navigate whatever is in front of you.

—Chaplain Kalie

---

* Ellen G. White, *Life Sketches of Ellen White* (Mountain View, CA: Pacific Press®, 1943), 196.

Need a Sign?

Matthew 16:1–12; Mark 8:11–21

Most people don't like tests. In fact, most people would say that they would rather have their knowledge tested through experience rather than by a series of questions on paper. We dislike it even more when people question us or doubt our abilities in an area where we feel proficient. The irony emerges, however, when we begin to test God.

Growing up I remember hearing stories in church about crazy miracles God had done for people when they asked for His help. I wondered why something so radical had never happened to me. We often want proof of God's presence through big miracles, but other times we go the route of looking for signs.

We make demands such as, "God, if this is what You want me to do, show me a sign!" Sometimes our expectations of a sign include driving on a dark road and seeing a bright neon sign with our exact answer to prayer written on it. We expect a message in a bottle that says, "Here is your sign; go this direction," to float up to our toes on a shore. Unfortunately, when these things don't happen, we often doubt God and lose faith in Him.

Sometimes God sends us messages through simple things, such as a sunset, a smile from a stranger, or a compliment from a friend. However, sometimes God sends us exactly what we ask for at exactly the right time, and we marvel at how gracious He is. The point is, God always answers our prayers, and He wants to reveal Himself to us, but He isn't a genie who is here to grant our whims. He wants a relationship with us.

The Pharisees and Sadducees saw or heard of Jesus' miracles. These were enormous, visible signs of the goodness of God. He fed thousands of people, gave sight to the blind, healed the sick, cleansed lepers, and transformed lives. Yet even after all of this, they still tested Jesus and refused to believe that He was from God. I can't fathom how one could see all of these things and still doubt God. But am I really any different? God answers my prayers in a billion ways, yet sometimes I still doubt His providence. It's a struggle to remember at times, but I have learned that God will give us what we ask for in His own way and in His own time. He's already given us the biggest sign of His love—His Son. We can trust Him with all the details of our lives.

—Shelby Huse, senior

Different Every Time

Mark 8:22–26

S top reading and close your eyes for a few moments. Imagine only seeing darkness for the rest of your life. It would be rough if you couldn't see, wouldn't it? You would have to learn a completely new way of getting around and functioning. Easy tasks, such as making a sandwich, would become much more difficult.

In Mark 8:22–26, we find the story of Jesus healing a blind man in the town of Bethsaida. Some of the man's friends brought him to Jesus and begged Him to heal the man. For some reason, Jesus takes the blind man by the hand and leads him outside of the town. Jesus is never predictable in the way He heals someone. The only constant is that He cares and that He wants to make the person better.

After taking the man outside the village, Jesus spits on the man's eyes. Talk about gross! I bet the guy was thinking, *What just happened?* After Jesus spits on his eyes, He places His hands over the man's eyes and asks him, "Do you see anything?" (verse 23, NIV). The man responds, "I see people; they look like trees walking around" (verse 24, NIV). So Jesus puts His hands over the man's eyes again; this time his eyes are fully restored, and he can see clearly.

Strange, right? I mean, why did it take two times for the man to be able to see? Why didn't it work the first time? Why did Jesus lead the man outside of the village to perform the miracle? These are all good questions to think about as we explore this story and try to understand more about Jesus, but we don't have any concrete answers because the Bible doesn't provide us with all the behind-the-scenes details.

We know one thing for sure. We can confidently come to Jesus to solve our problems. It won't look the same as how He works in our friends' lives. It may not even look the same from one situation to the next in our own lives. Regardless, we can come to Him, as Hebrews 4:16 tells us: "Let us then approach God's throne of grace with confidence, so that we may receive mercy and find grace to help us in our time of need" (NIV).

—Jordan Hyde, junior

Meeting With Jesus
Romans 8:38, 39

A light breeze swirls around you and the soft sand squishes through your toes as you walk in the surf along the deserted beach. It's nearing sundown, and most of the beachgoers have packed up their blankets, chairs, and umbrellas and headed in after a long day in the sun. The sky is ablaze in fiery colors—red, orange, purple, and pink. You marvel at God's artistry.

The ocean is calm, giving no hint of the storm that blew through the area the day before. You watched the fury from the safety of your condo. The waves pounded the beach, and the rain and wind splattered against the windows. Today brought a much different picture. The fury of yesterday gave way to the calm of today.

You can't escape storms in life. How do you find peace? Is it as simple as trusting God to bring you through and replace the howling wind with a gentle breeze?

The sun has set, so you decide to head back to the condo while it's still light. You turn around and almost bump into someone.

"I'm so sorry. I didn't see you," you quickly blurt out, not truly looking at the person you almost ran into.

"That's OK," comes the response.

You recognize Jesus' voice, and you feel your body relax, going from flustered to calm in a matter of seconds. "Where did You come from?" you ask.

"I've been walking right behind you the whole time," Jesus says. "Would you like to walk back together? I'd love to talk about what you were mulling over, about finding peace in the storm. I'd love to know what storms you're going through right now. Even more than that, I'd like to bring you peace. So how about it?"

Take some time to talk to Jesus or write down your response to His question.

Read the passage for the day and think about the promise it offers. What does it tell you about God?

If you were to talk about this reading with Jesus, what would you say? What would you ask Him?

Combating Fear

Matthew 16:13–23; Mark 8:27–33; Luke 9:18–22

I often have days when I allow my problems to consume me and stress clouds my vision of the future. My troubles tower over me, and I feel as though I am in this alone. It's a scary feeling that we have all felt before: the feeling of helplessness. It comes when we allow our fear of what's ahead be stronger than our faith in God.

As a kid, I was deathly afraid of tornadoes because I had convinced myself that a tornado followed every rainstorm. This was an absurd conclusion for my third-grade mind to make, but it was my reality. So when my mom suggested that I visit my grandparents in Tennessee for the weekend, I immediately ran to the computer to check the weather. Much to my dismay, I discovered that there was an 80 percent chance of rain on Sabbath. Despite my tears and begging to stay home and not go visit my grandparents, my mom made me go. She assured me that there wouldn't be any storms and that I would be fine. Boy, was she wrong! That Saturday night was the first time in my life that I saw the sky turn green and look angry. The wind was more powerful than anything I had ever witnessed. I was freaking out, pacing the room like a lunatic. Then my grandpa said something that has always stuck with me, and it went something like this: "You know, we serve such a powerful God who is Lord of lords. He is bigger than this storm or any problems we may face."

The disciples recognized Jesus as the Messiah, but they didn't fully understand His mission, so when Jesus told them He had to die, they were scared. They loved Jesus, and I'm sure they couldn't imagine life without Him. The unknown frightened them, and they let fear take over. After all this talk about death, "

> Peter took Jesus away from the other followers to talk to him alone. He began to criticize him. He said, "God save you from those sufferings, Lord! That will never happen to you!"
>
> Then Jesus said to Peter, "Get away from me, Satan! You are not helping me! You don't care about the same things God does. You care only about things that people think are important" (Matthew 16:22, 23, ERV).

Peter spoke out of fear, which Jesus recognized as coming from Satan. When fear tries to derail your thinking, turn to the One who is bigger than anything we face.

—Jordan Jablonski, senior

Submitting

Matthew 16:24–28; Mark 8:34–39; 9:1; Luke 9:23–27

As a junior in high school, I often catch myself thinking about the pressure of future decisions and college plans. Like many other young people with their whole lives ahead of them, I have ambitions and expectations for the things to come. I have imagined many things for myself: going to a good college, working at a rewarding job, traveling around the world, and having a family—the list goes on. Although seeking these things is not bad, God makes it clear in His Word that we need to seek after Him and heavenly things and not get caught up in the things of this world.

Jesus told the disciples, "If any of you wants to be my follower, you must give up your own way, take up your cross, and follow me. If you try to hang on to your life, you will lose it. But if you give up your life for my sake, you will save it" (Matthew 16:24, 25).

When I first thought about this passage, I had to pause for a moment and consider it carefully. I don't want to give up my future. I want to succeed in life. I want to experience it and reach my full potential. Does denying myself mean I have to hand over all my plans and only serve God? As I've studied this verse, I've concluded that it isn't a call for me to give up all material things and my dreams and live a solitary life. Rather, it's a call to stop making myself the center of my life and the object of my thoughts and actions. It's a call to shift the focus from myself to God. I could live my life looking for things that would make me feel good, such as achieving success and taking on the world, but if those things cost me the eternal life that God has offered, they're worth nothing.

"And what do you benefit if you gain the whole world but lose your own soul? Is anything worth more than your soul?" (verse 26). Nothing in this world can equal what God has planned for us, so the only thing I need to do is submit myself to His plan, and He will satisfy the desires of my heart.

—Namie Imayuki, junior

Night Light

Psalm 119:105

I don't know why I started. I don't remember an event that caused me to make this decision. But the resolution was made. In the middle of my junior year at Ozark Adventist Academy, I decided I was going to start reading the Bible.

I had grown up in church, attending Pathfinders, Christian schools, and evangelistic meetings. I had earned prizes for memorizing Bible verses. (I remember a homemade, stuffed frog filled with dried beans made by my incredible Sabbath School teachers. They loved all of us kids!) This commitment was different. This was me taking things more seriously. This was me deciding on my own to discover more about Jesus.

And so it began. Each evening after my roommate had gone to bed, and after lights out in the dorm, I read my Bible. I turned on the light in the closet, cracked open the closet door, and opened my Bible under that narrow sliver of illumination. As I read, just two or three pages a night, I always looked for at least one verse I could underline, one thing I felt was relevant to me, one area of life where I could see God leading me.

As I read, I found what I was looking for! I found stories of a God who created me, of a Savior who died for me, of a Friend who is coming back soon. I found words of hope and wisdom and comfort.

I still read my Bible almost every day. (Unfortunately, I have missed some days.) I still look for ways that God is speaking to me and leading in my life. Just like everyone who walks this planet, I have amazing days and very challenging days. Through it all, I know that God is leading and guiding.

I am a witness!

—Greg Hudson, senior pastor, GCA Church

Ultimate Glory

Matthew 17:1–13; Mark 9:2–13; Luke 9:28–36

In today's passages of Scripture, we read about the Transfiguration. Peter, James, and John accompanied Jesus up to the top of a mountain. Suddenly, "Jesus' appearance was transformed, and his clothes became dazzling white, far whiter than any earthly bleach could ever make them. Then Elijah and Moses appeared and began talking with Jesus" (Mark 9:2–4).

In amazement, Peter, James, and John watched Elijah and Moses talking to Jesus, and then a cloud enveloped them, and from deep in the cloud, a Voice said, "This is my dearly loved Son. Listen to him" (verse 7). The cloud went away, and the disciples were left wondering what had just happened. As they descended the mountain, Jesus told them not to tell anyone about this experience until He had risen from the dead. Of course, this left the three even more confused because they weren't sure what He meant about "rising from the dead" (verses 9, 10). The Transfiguration had reaffirmed who Jesus was and demonstrated His glory, but the disciples had plenty of unanswered questions. What did they do with those questions?

When we have questions, we sometimes begin to doubt. Because we can't find an answer, we get frustrated and back away from God, figuring that if we can't figure things out with Him, then there isn't any hope.

When I was in middle school, I put on a mask and acted like I was a good Christian, but on the inside, I didn't really want to know Jesus. This feeling stuck with me through my freshman year of high school. Anytime I went to church, I blocked out what the preacher or anyone said because I had no desire for a connection with Jesus. Then the summer before my sophomore year, something shifted in my head, and I began to want to know Jesus more. Now I'm attending GCA, and I appreciate being in God's presence.

I certainly don't understand all there is about God, but I choose to follow Him and get to know Him more, just as the disciples did.

—Nathan Jacobs, sophomore

Exercising Our Faith

Matthew 17:14–21; Mark 9:14–29; Luke 9:37–43

Jesus, Peter, James, and John have just come off the mountain. A man comes out of the crowd and kneels down before Jesus. " 'Lord, have mercy on my son,' he said. 'He has seizures and is suffering greatly. He often falls into the fire or into the water. I brought him to your disciples, but they could not heal him' " (Matthew 17:15, 16, NIV).

In response, Jesus seems angered that the disciples were unable to heal the boy. He even rebukes their entire generation because of it. " 'You unbelieving and perverse generation,' Jesus replied, 'how long shall I stay with you? How long shall I put up with you?' " (verse 17, NIV).

However, the more I read the passage, I began to sense His disappointment instead of His anger because after casting out the demon from the boy, Jesus gives the disciples a lesson about faith. They asked, "Why couldn't we drive it out?" (verse 19).

Jesus replied, "Because you have so little faith. Truly I tell you, if you have faith as small as a mustard seed, you can say to this mountain, 'Move from here to there,' and it will move. Nothing will be impossible for you" (verse 20).

A mustard seed is tiny, but the disciples lacked even that much faith. How much more do we lack today? This is all pretty sad when you think about it. God has given us plenty of examples of His faithfulness, but somehow we doubt and wonder whether He really is as powerful as the Bible says He is. So how does faith grow? Just like a mustard seed grows from a seed into a tree by water and sunshine, we grow by reading the Bible, praying, and going through experiences that test our faith.

Think about it another way. If I want to run a half marathon, I don't just suddenly wake up one day and decide to run 13.1 miles. I need to start training by running one mile, then two, then three, and so on. My muscles will protest at first, but over time, a few miles will seem like nothing, especially compared to when I first started training. When my muscles work often, they become strong.

The same principle applies to our faith. It grows when we use it, and we use it by hanging out with God and trusting Him to guide us each day.

—Elijah Hooker, senior

Comparison Versus Contentment
Psalm 49

Have you ever wanted to yell at someone to listen to you because you knew the right answer, or how to fix something, or what to do, but they were too busy doing their own thing to pay attention to you? Maybe this has even happened with your parents. What seems obvious to you is anything but clear to them, but they won't listen to you because you're a teenager and they are adults. I can only imagine that Jesus was frustrated and discouraged by the sheer number of people who wouldn't listen and didn't understand His ministry.

One of the principles that Jesus taught was to not get caught up in acquiring earthly possessions. The quest for more stuff often comes with a level of competition over who has more. We look at what our cousins or neighbors or classmates own, and we want what they have. If we are really competitive, we want the model above what they purchased so that we can brag about our new, better toy.

The danger of comparing ourselves to others is that we lose sight of who God has created us to be and of the blessings that He has given to us. Paul warns of this in Galatians 6:4–8:

Pay careful attention to your own work, for then you will get the satis-faction of a job well done, and you won't need to compare yourself to anyone else. For we are each responsible for our own conduct. . . . Don't be misled—you cannot mock the justice of God. You will always harvest what you plant.

Those who live only to satisfy their own sinful nature will harvest decay and death from that sinful nature. But those who live to please the Spirit will harvest everlasting life from the Spirit.

We need to keep our eyes focused on Jesus instead of on those around us because He has given us exactly what we need. If we plant a crop of comparison, we will reap jealousy, resentment, and discontentment, but if we plant a crop of contentment, we will reap joy, happiness, and fulfillment.

—Chaplain Kalie

Meeting With Jesus

"I tell you the truth, those who listen to my message and believe in God who sent me have eternal life. They will never be condemned for their sins, but they have already passed from death into life" (John 5:24).

What spiritual principle can you take from this reading?

_____

_____

_____

_____

What stuck out to you in this reading?

_____

_____

_____

_____

What question would you like to ask God about this verse?

_____

_____

_____

_____

_____

Just Let It Go
Matthew 17:24–27

Have you ever heard the phrase "be the bigger person"? Personally, I find it to be one of the most maddening dictums humans have created. With our sinful human natures, it's hard just to walk away from an argument or a fight. Of course, there's a time and a place for everything because sometimes we need to stand up for what we believe in, but most times we should probably just keep our mouths shut.

Even though I dislike that phrase, it honestly can feel good to let things go. It's way better than beating yourself up and keeping anger in your heart, which is about as fun as semester exams on Christmas. Letting go doesn't mean forgetting or dismissing the other person's behavior. It means protecting yourself from the ugly effects of staying stuck in bitterness.

Jesus was the best person in the history of the world at knowing when to speak and when not to speak. There were definitely times when He spoke His mind and told the Pharisees to go fly a kite, but then there were other times where He followed the law of the land, such as in today's story.

Have you ever heard the phrase about money growing on trees? Sure. How about money growing in fish? Not so much. In this little snippet of a story in Matthew, Peter gets cornered by some tax collectors who ask whether Jesus pays His taxes. Peter says yes because he doesn't want to get into trouble with the law. When Peter enters the house where Jesus is staying, Jesus asks him a question. "From whom do the kings of the earth collect duty and taxes—from their own children or from others?" (Matthew 17:25, NIV). Peter says, "From others" (verse 26, NIV).

Jesus says, "Then the children are exempt" (verse 26, NIV). This makes it sound like Jesus is saying we don't have to pay taxes, but here's the part where being the bigger person comes in. Jesus starts His next sentence with this point: "But so that we may not cause offense, go to the lake and throw out your line. Take the first fish you catch; open its mouth and you will find a four-drachma coin. Take it and give it to them for my tax and yours" (verse 27, NIV).

Sometimes you have to let things go and do things out of respect in an effort to keep the peace. Be the bigger person. Be like Jesus.

—Becky James, freshman

Be a Child
Matthew 18:1–6; Mark 9:33–41

Ever since I was a small child, I remember learning about Jesus and His love for children. When I could talk, I learned to sing "Let the Little Children Come" and "Jesus Loves the Little Children." Of course, I was little, so I didn't stop to think about the lyrics. I just enjoyed the tunes and singing with the rest of my class. Now that I am older, I can look back at those songs and really understand what I learned from such a young age about God and His love.

In Matthew 18, Jesus said, "Assuredly, I say to you, unless you are converted and become as little children, you will by no means enter the kingdom of heaven. Therefore whoever humbles himself as this little child is the greatest in the kingdom of heaven" (verses 3, 4, NKJV).

Jesus loves adults just as much as He loves children, but what sets children apart from adults is their state of mind. Children rely on other people, mostly their parents, for assistance to complete all kinds of tasks they can't do on their own, such as cooking a meal or driving to a location. They are quick to ask for help when they can't do something, such as reaching the light switch. As we grow up and become more capable, we start to fend for ourselves and rely on our own abilities and intuition.

We should all practice being like children and relying fully on God for all of our needs. We need to remember that we don't know how to do things on our own and that we need our loving heavenly Father to guide us.

Jesus went on to talk about cutting sin out of our lives: "If your hand or foot causes you to sin, cut it off and cast it from you. It is better for you to enter into life lame or maimed, rather than having two hands or two feet, to be cast into the everlasting fire" (verse 8, NKJV).

It may seem hard to get rid of the things we know are bad for us, but is it worth losing our salvation for a few moments of pleasure? Just as a dad gladly helps his son tie his shoes because he can't do it on his own, God will gladly help us deal with whatever sin is holding us back.

—Gage Hufstetler, senior

Battles of the Spirit
Ephesians 6:12

I lived in the jungle of a developing country for five years. During that time, I learned that almost nothing scared me, except for the one thing that modern culture seems to idealize—the spirit world. My father is a nurse practitioner and a pilot, and my mother is a medical technician and a biologist. While living and working in the jungle, they taught the natives about the Bible. The struggle was that most natives were very strong believers in animism, the belief that all objects have a soul.

We lived in a two-story house that was split into two—my family lived upstairs, and a native family lived downstairs. I had befriended the oldest daughter in the family, whom I will call Buttercup. One day she came home from high school early, complaining that she had a bad headache. We heard her crying downstairs, saying, "Take it away, Mommy! Take it away!" My father told my mother to take her some ibuprofen, which she did.

About thirty minutes later, my father asked me to check on her. I went downstairs, but she didn't seem well, so I convinced her to come upstairs and talk to my father. We sat down on the couch, and Dad asked her a series of questions to rule out any serious medical conditions. While he was talking to her, she lay down on her side and put her hands to her head again and said, "Take it away, Mommy. Take it away." Dad continued asking her some questions, and then, all of a sudden, she started saying, "Stay away!" repeatedly.

At this point, my parents realized that this was not just a headache, but devil harassment. Mom took the lead and started praying. She asked God to send His angels and to make the demon leave. She also told the devil that Christ had died for Buttercup and that she was His. My dad prayed a similar prayer. Buttercup leaned over against my mother, grabbed her arm, wrapped it around herself, and said, "Fight for me, sister! Fight for me!" Then she pulled her feet up and started to kick at the air.

A few minutes later, Buttercup fell asleep. My father checked her pulse and breathing; both were normal. He let her rest for a few minutes and then he said, "Open your eyes, Buttercup," and immediately she opened them and sat up. She acted very confused, as if she didn't know what had just happened, but she wasn't fighting like before.

I am a witness!

—Anonymous

Regret Bites

Matthew 18:7–9; Mark 9:42–50

I have a big regret from when I was in the fifth grade. I'm from Korea, and the public school system had school on the Sabbath, which is God's day. It wasn't a full day of school, just an orchestra class first thing in the morning, so my mom made the decision that I should go to class and then come to church right after it was finished. If I left right after class, I would make it in time for the church service.

However, one day my friend tempted me to skip church and go to his house to play video games. I knew I should say no, but I didn't want to stand out, so I agreed to his invitation. I figured that I could go to his house and play games until 11:50 A.M. Then I could quickly run over to the church and be there as soon as the service let out.

I carried out my plan, but I didn't think about having to lie to my mom. She found me after church and asked me where I had been. I told her that I had come straight from school when class had ended. She didn't say anything else, but I felt like she knew I was lying. I felt bad about skipping church and lying to my mom. However, I did the same thing the next Sabbath and every Sabbath after that for quite a while. This decision drastically changed my relationship with God. I felt very distant from Him, and I really didn't care about Him anymore.

One Sabbath I got to church after the service ended, and my mom caught me in the middle of my lie. She was angry with me for lying. She told me that if my tongue caused me to lie, I should cut my tongue out so that I couldn't lie again. Jesus said something similar: "If your eye causes you to stumble, gouge it out and throw it away. It is better for you to enter life with one eye than to have two eyes and be thrown into the fire of hell" (Matthew 18:9, NIV).

We discussed this verse in my religion class, and some students think that God is mean and ruthless to say such a thing. On the other hand, I think it's the right thing to say. He isn't really saying that people should poke out their own eyes. He is just emphasizing that we should get rid of anything that causes us to sin or tempts us to go against God. He said this because He loves us and He wants to protect us from sin. I would rather choose to lose my eye and go to heaven than to have full sight and be lost for eternity.

—Eujin Jeon, sophomore

Exclusive or Inclusive?
Mark 9:38–41; Luke 9:49, 50

John's words in today's passages may not seem so absurd in a world that is all about exclusivity. Countless magazines, newspapers, websites, and stores require exclusive membership in order to access content and services. Like John, most of us agree that Jesus' followers deserve to be treated exclusively and have the right to claim certain privileges.

John and the other disciples saw Jesus turn water into wine, multiply loaves of bread, heal the sick, give sight to the blind, cast out demons, and raise the dead. In addition to witnessing miracles, they were given the ability to do similar works in Jesus' name. They had special access to the Son of God, which may have gone to their heads. When they saw another person who was not from their group cast out demons in the name of Jesus, they strongly reprimanded him. Confident that Jesus would approve, John might have been surprised at Christ's response.

Jesus was not only disappointed with their action, but He uttered this eye-opening truth: "Do not stop him, for no one who does a mighty work in my name will be able soon afterward to speak evil of me. For the one who is not against us is for us" (Mark 9:39, 40, ESV).

With these words, Jesus demonstrates a broader and more inclusive view of discipleship than the discriminating perspective of the disciples. Discipleship is about professing His name faithfully and acting according to His principles. Even if someone is from a different Christian denomination, that does not make him or her against us or God.

Christ's statement was a warning to the disciples, as well as to us, to prevent exclusivism in the church. Instead of looking at denomination or upbringing, we should measure someone's actions according to Scripture. If they are showing God's love and working in His name, they are partakers of the same divine grace that we partake of. May we not fall into the trap that the disciples did. May we love and work for Jesus. Period.

—Narumi Imayuki, senior

Setting the Record Straight
Matthew 18:15–20

D ealing with challenging people in the church can be a sensitive topic. The Bible offers counsel on the best way to speak to individuals who are acting inappropriately. Jesus said, "Moreover if your brother sins against you, go and tell him his fault between you and him alone. If he hears you, you have gained your brother. But if he will not hear, take with you one or two more, that 'by the mouth of two or three witnesses every word may be established.' And if he refuses to hear them, tell it to the church. But if he refuses even to hear the church, let him be to you like a heathen and a tax collector" (Matthew 18:15–17, NKJV).

The first step that Jesus highlights is to have a private conversation with the individual. It is not everyone's business or right to know unless the offending actions are blatantly committed against the entire church. When matters are addressed privately, the individual is most likely going to respond to the person in a positive manner, correcting the issue at hand. In the end, though, not every private meeting will go according to plan. If the person continues to be problematic, the situation becomes a little less private.

The next step is to take people with you to address the situation and try to correct the problem. At this point, the Bible speaks of the possibility of the individual completely disregarding the meeting, at which point the local church should get involved. If the person continues to behave badly and won't listen to the church, steps must be taken to protect the church family.

All of this must be done in love and with the intention of helping the individual, not shaming them. The church is supposed to be a family and a safe environment, not a circus to drag others into the limelight for all to see. In all of this, one of the key elements to resolving conflict is talking to the person instead of going behind their back. Too often we run around and talk bad about people without ever discussing our problems with the person who hurt us. The model that Jesus outlined would save us a lot of heartache if we followed it and communicated in love with those around us.

—Sassy Mura, junior

Meeting With Jesus

"The LORD is my shepherd; I have all that I need. He lets me rest in green meadows; he leads me beside peaceful streams. He renews my strength. He guides me along right paths, bringing honor to his name. Even when I walk through the darkest valley, I will not be afraid, for you are close beside me. Your rod and your staff protect and comfort me. You prepare a feast for me in the presence of my enemies. You honor me by anointing my head with oil. My cup overflows with blessings. Surely your goodness and unfailing love will pursue me all the days of my life, and I will live in the house of the LORD forever" (Psalm 23).

What did you learn about God from this psalm?

How can you apply this chapter to your own life?

What can you share with others from this chapter?

Endless Forgiveness
Matthew 18:21–35

Lord, how often should I forgive someone who sins against me? Seven times?" (Matthew 18:21). Peter was proud of himself, thinking that he was going beyond the call of duty to forgive someone seven times. However, Jesus upped the ante.

" 'No, not seven times,' Jesus replied, 'but seventy times seven!' " (verse 22). Jesus then told a parable about a king who called in one of his servants who owed him a large sum of money, equivalent to millions of dollars in today's money. He was getting ready to sell the servant, along with his wife and children, in order to pay for the debt, but the servant begged the master to have compassion on him and give him more time to pay off the debt.

The master was "filled with pity for him, and he released him and forgave his debt" (verse 27). The servant had only asked for an extension on the due date, but the master completely wiped out the debt and told him not to worry about it. Talk about a generous gift! I'd be jumping for joy if I owed millions of dollars and then suddenly I didn't.

The servant left the master and ran into someone who owed him money, but instead of showing the man the same compassion he had received, he demanded immediate payment. When the man begged for mercy, the servant who had just been forgiven everything had this guy thrown in prison for not being able to pay him back. The king heard about this and called the servant back in. "You evil servant! I forgave you that tremendous debt because you pleaded with me. Shouldn't you have mercy on your fellow servant, just as I had mercy on you?" (verses 32, 33). Then the king threw the ungrateful and unmerciful servant in prison.

God has bestowed mercy on all of us Christians by sending His Son to die for our sins. Like the servant, we don't deserve the grace that has been given to us. Based on our sinful lives, we deserve death, but Christ pardoned us and wiped our slates clean.

Even though we have been forgiven, we often choose to act like the first servant and refuse to extend grace to our family or friends. However, God has called us to be compassionate and forgiving to those around us because that is how Christ treats us.

—Brandon Hudson, senior

Patience Is the Key
John 7:2–13

Jesus illustrated humility and patience throughout His life, but in John 7:2–13 we see a direct example of these qualities at work when Jesus' brothers urged Him to attend an upcoming Jewish festival to show off His miracles (verses 2–4). Jesus didn't play into their attempt to seek fame and notoriety. If He had done so, it would have been for selfish reasons and not because God had told Him to do so. Jesus' time had not yet come, so He patiently waited on God to direct Him instead of running after His own plans or the desires of others.

When I was twelve years old, I was in a string ensemble. One day my teacher announced that there would be auditions to determine who would play the solo in the next big concert. There was a part of me that wanted to audition, but I was also scared that I wouldn't do well. Mrs. Johnson, my teacher, began handing out the music to anyone who wanted to try out. In a burst of adrenaline and "I can do it" gumption, I raised my hand. Little did I know that the solo was a Mozart piece.

When I looked at the music, I started to freak out because I had only been playing for three years, and the music was way beyond my skill level. My teacher saw my frightened face and whispered in my ear, "It's OK. I know you can do it." Those eight little words boosted my confidence through the roof. I practiced and practiced and practiced. However, the more I practiced, the more I got frustrated because I couldn't master one little measure. My mother could feel my frustration rising, and she said, "Ngady, patience is key." I repeated the mantra, "patience is key," over and over in my head, and I kept practicing.

The auditions finally came, and before I played the piece for my teacher, I whispered a prayer and reminded myself that patience was key. I played the piece as best as I could, and then I walked out of the room, relieved that I hadn't messed up. After everyone had played, Mrs. Johnson gathered us together to announce the winner of the audition. "The soloist for the next concert is Ngady Kabia." At first, it didn't register that I had been selected, but then I jumped for joy because all the practice and hard work had paid off.

Whatever it is you're facing, patience is key. God's timing is not our timing, but He is faithful, and we can trust Him to fulfill His promises.

—Ngady Kabia, junior

Teaching Moments
Psalm 71:17

When I was in college, I spent my summers working at Cohutta Springs Youth Camp as a mountain biking instructor. The camp is beside a lake and surrounded by hills, which makes for some great mountain bike riding.

One day I had taken my campers up the road that led to the cabins when I saw a flock of geese down by the lake. In the moment, it seemed like a fantastic idea to ride down the hill leading toward the lake and the geese and scare them. Of course, the campers were up for the adventure, so we took off down the hill. I was almost to the bottom when I realized that if we didn't stop before we came to the road, we'd hit the ditch, which was a pretty big drop off. I slammed on my brakes before I reached the bottom, and I waved my arms and yelled at my campers to stop. All of them listened—except for one.

I watched in horror as he came flying down the hill at top speed, hit the ditch, flew over his handlebars, and slid across the pavement. My first thought was that I was going to get fired for being irresponsible and hurting a camper. I ran over to him, and although his bike helmet was cracked and he was pretty scraped up, he jumped up with a smile on his face and exclaimed, "That was awesome!"

As I thought about this experience later on, God brought this lesson to my mind. Matthew 6:33 reminds us to seek the kingdom of God above all else. However, we sometimes get sidetracked, even though the things we focus on are good things. I had a plan that morning for my mountain bike class, but I got sidetracked by the geese, and I didn't think about the safety of my campers or the end result of a wild goose chase down the hill. God knows that there are many things in this world that can distract us from our real purpose, which is loving God and others. That's why He gave us the instruction to stay focused on His kingdom.

God teaches us lessons in the most unexpected ways. We just have to be tuned in to His voice and pay attention to His instruction.

I am a witness!

—Josh Woods, chaplain

Heart of the Matter

John 7:14–26

What motivates you? What compels you to do the things you do? Do you do the right thing because it's the right thing or because you expect something in return? We're often nice to people so they will be nice to us, or we help someone out so they will one day return the favor. On the other hand, if someone is rude to us, we are often rude back because we believe that they deserve it. Human beings expect to receive what they give, but if Jesus followed this rule, the human race would've been doomed. Jesus saved us in spite of our behavior.

Jesus' way of thinking baffled the religious leaders of His day because it was countercultural. (It still confuses people today.) He talked about loving your neighbor, including your enemies. He talked about forgiveness and acceptance. He talked about oneness with God. Jesus reminded those who questioned Him that His ideas were coming straight from God. "My teaching is not mine, but his who sent me. If anyone's will is to do God's will, he will know whether the teaching is from God or whether I am speaking on my own authority. The one who speaks on his own authority seeks his own glory; but the one who seeks the glory of him who sent him is true, and in him there is no falsehood" (John 7:16–18, ESV).

The Pharisees thought they had it right. They lived by the rule that doing the right thing resulted in rewards for themselves. The Pharisees truly believed they were doing good and that Jesus was doing wrong because He was breaking their laws. They judged others while thinking they were blameless. They were in denial about the true state of their hearts and souls. They thought they were doing God's will, but if they truly had been, they would've recognized who Jesus was. They had a heart issue, and it showed in their words and actions.

Jesus looks at our heart. He cares deeply about why we do what we do. So why do you act the way you do? What motivates you? Jesus calls us to a fuller understanding of what it means to be a Christian. He asks us to live for Him and others, not ourselves. He cares about the heart of the matter, and He asks us to do the same.

—Hannah Johnson, senior

The First Step
John 7:37–52

I was born and raised in Korea, and until high school, I attended public school in my home country. I grew up in a Christian home, but in the seventh grade, I began to question God's existence. I was learning about evolution and many other things in school that contradicted what the Bible taught, and I began to believe in what I was learning in school more than what I had been taught at home.

As my interest in God waned, I refused to go to church with my parents. Naturally, my parents were concerned about my skepticism about the Bible, so they introduced me to a student pastor and encouraged me to meet with him and share my concerns. I agreed to meet with him, and we ended up having a long discussion. His logical and meaningful explanation of the Bible changed my heart. At the end of our conversation, I realized that I had never really tried to believe or learn more about God. Whenever I had a question about the Bible, I doubted instead of looking for answers in the Bible. I didn't have faith in God. After I accepted Jesus into my heart, I wanted to learn more about Him, and I began sharing what I had learned from the Bible with other people.

It all comes down to whether we choose to believe or not. Jesus said, "Whoever is thirsty may come to me and drink. If anyone believes in me, rivers of living water will flow out from their heart. That is what the Scriptures say" (John 7:37, 38, ERV). Jesus has always been present in my life, but I finally became thirsty, and I accepted Him after meeting with the student pastor. It was then that I began to value Scripture and to spend time with God.

Although the religious leaders seemed to know everything about the holy writings they had, they didn't accept Jesus due to their lack of faith. Knowing the Bible and going to church are very important, but I wasn't a Christian until I chose to have faith in Jesus. I wasn't a true Christian until I accepted Jesus with my whole heart and gave my life to Him. Accepting Christ through faith is the first step to becoming a real Christian.

—Junhyuk Jeon, senior

Churning Seas
Psalm 69

I'm much more of a mountains and lakes kind of girl, but growing up in Florida meant that I went to the beach instead of the mountains. The state is flat and covered with sand! I was a strong swimmer, so the ocean didn't scare me—well, except for the idea of sharks and jellyfish and other creatures I couldn't see in the murky water. I remember one time when I thought I was going to die.

I was about chest-deep in the water, and I was jumping waves. They were rolling in pretty strongly, and I was laughing as they crashed into my back and pushed me forward. Each time I found my footing, moved out a few feet, and waited for the next one. All of a sudden, a bigger wave came in that caught me off guard. I jumped, but it swept my feet out from under me and slammed me to the the ocean floor. My body scraped against the coarse sand, and I fought to get my feet under me so I could shoot back up to the surface and get a breath. Panic welled up instead of me as I tried to orient myself in the surging water. It was only a matter of seconds, but it felt like an eternity before I surfaced and inhaled a breath of air.

There are days when life feels like a swirling ocean of challenges, but in those moments when we're gasping for air, we can bring our fears before God and lay them at His feet as David did:

Save me, O God,
　　for the floodwaters are up to my neck.
Deeper and deeper I sink into the mire;
　　I can't find a foothold.
I am in deep water,
　　and the floods overwhelm me.
I am exhausted from crying for help;
　　my throat is parched. . . .
Answer my prayers, O Lord,
　　for your unfailing love is wonderful.
Take care of me,
　　for your mercy is so plentiful.
Don't hide from your servant;
　　answer me quickly, for I am in deep trouble! (Psalm 69:1–3, 16, 17).

What are you facing today that seems as if it will overwhelm you? Don't give up. Don't stop praying. God is faithful. He is merciful. He hears you, and He won't let you drown.

—Chaplain Kalie

Meeting With Jesus

"Let us hold tightly without wavering to the hope we affirm, for God can be trusted to keep his promise" (Hebrews 10:23).

What stuck out to you in this reading?

What question would you like to ask God about this verse?

How can you apply this verse to your own life?

Redeeming Grace
John 7:53–8:11

T here she was on the ground, surrounded by her accusers. She had sinned—of that, there was no doubt. Those around wanted only to condemn her. They were ready to stone her. One Man stood between her and the mob of angry people. He slowly bent down and started writing in the dirt with His finger. One by one, her accusers dropped their stones and left the circle surrounding them until it was just the woman and the Man, Jesus, remaining.

"Woman, where are they? Has no one condemned you?"

"No one, sir," she said.

"Then neither do I condemn you," Jesus declared. "Go now and leave your life of sin" (John 8:10, 11, NIV).

Jesus was different from the rest of the people. He saw past her sins and forgave her for what she had done. Unlike her accusers, who only wanted to punish her, Jesus wanted to lift her up out of her sins. Jesus did not excuse her sin. He wanted her to have a better life, so He told her to leave her life of sin, but He didn't beat her up over her past choices.

In this story, Jesus teaches us how we should act toward others who have made mistakes or poor choices. Instead of judging others, we should help them with their problems. It can be hard not to judge when we see people suffering the consequences of their own poor choices, but shame and gossip don't help anyone. Instead, we should be loving, understanding, and kind. Like Jesus, we should show compassion to others. We aren't perfect, either, and Jesus shows us compassion again and again when we mess up.

Perhaps someone has wronged you or someone you know. You don't know why they did the things they did. Instead of giving hate or resentment space in your heart, forgive them. Before you judge, think of all the times you have made mistakes and how upset you would be if people wouldn't forgive you. Next time someone makes a mistake, remember how Jesus treated the woman caught in adultery.

—Gracie Jenkins, sophomore

Unwarranted Aggression

John 8:12–30

G rowing up, I decided that I wouldn't play with or talk to anyone who was ugly or whom I didn't like. I ignored them or treated them poorly because I thought they were less than me. This was a horrible way to act, but I did not grow up in a Christian environment, so I didn't know any better.

When I was seven years old, I remember going to school and throwing a pair of scissors at a boy I didn't like. The scissors hit him in the stomach, but I didn't feel bad because I figured I could do whatever I wanted if I didn't like someone. I judged this boy, whom I really didn't know, based on his looks. I didn't even take the time to get to know him. I just made an assumption about him because of his appearance.

The religious leaders and many others falsely judged Jesus based on where He grew up, how He acted, and what He preached about. Their preconceived ideas clouded their minds, and they were not open to anything He said.

In John 8, Jesus calls them out on this fact. "You judge according to the flesh; I judge no one" (verse 15, NKJV). They looked at the outward appearance of people to decide whether they liked them or not. Jesus looked at the hearts of people to determine their true identity. Jesus went on: "And yet if I do judge, My judgment is true; for I am not alone, but I am with the Father who sent Me. It is also written in your law that the testimony of two men is true. I am One who bears witness of Myself, and the Father who sent Me bears witness of Me" (verses 16–18, NKJV).

Because we are sinners, it's easy to fall into the trap of judging others based on how they look or behave. However, we have no idea why people act the way they do. I wasn't taught that it was wrong to treat my classmates the way I did, but people can change if they are loved and taught what is right and wrong.

Jesus is the only one who can judge people. He is the Creator and Savior of the world. Who are you judging? What would happen if you looked at them as Jesus does?

—Bobby Jeong, senior

A Sweet Surprise
Philippians 4:19

Last summer was my third summer working as a colporteur. It's a hard job, but I enjoy meeting new people and sharing Jesus' love with others. One of my favorite places to canvass is at gas stations because there are so many people to talk to. I had just finished talking to someone at a gas station and was moving on to a nearby strip of businesses. I made my way from door to door and eventually came to a chocolate business. I checked the door, and it was open. I didn't see anyone in the shop, so I knocked and called out, "Hello!" No one answered, but I heard music, so I knew someone was inside. I walked inside and kept calling but still got no response.

I checked the bathroom and kept knocking and calling. I typically wouldn't have stayed so long in one place without any response, but I believe the Lord impressed me not to give up. I saw a door leading toward the back, so I made my way over there. As I got closer, the music got louder. I peeked around the corner and saw a woman. Her back was toward me, and the loud music must've drowned me out. I didn't want to scare her, so I backed away and kept calling "Hello!" and knocking loudly until she turned around and acknowledged me. She was a bit surprised because she always locks the door when she is alone in the store.

I told her that I had heard the music, and then I shared with her what I was doing. I told her that I was spending my summer encouraging people with inspiring books and that the money I raised helped to pay for my school bill. She looked at my books and asked me some questions. As we talked, she started to open up. She shared that she, too, was a Christian and that her son had strayed away from God.

Before I left, she gave me fifty dollars for a copy of Steps to Christ. She said she was impressed by the ministry and encouraged by what I was doing, and she wanted to help me reach other people. We prayed for each other, and I continued on my way. That encounter, and so many others, reminded me of God's faithfulness to provide for His children.

I am a witness!

—Calvin Scott, junior

Be the Best You Can Be

John 8:31–59

Have you ever gotten into a heated discussion with someone? Maybe it was one-on-one, or maybe it was a class discussion. Maybe you were debating politics or a Bible verse and its interpretation. Whatever the case, intense conversations don't go well when both sides dig in their heels and refuse to see the other side. Productive discussions happen only when both sides are willing to hear each other out and learn from each other.

John 8 documents a passionate dialogue between Jesus and a group of Jews. The conversation starts with Jesus saying, "If you abide in my word, you are truly my disciples, and you will know the truth, and the truth will set you free" (verses 31, 32, ESV). The Jews take offense at His comment because it implies that they are enslaved to someone or something. They pull their relationship to Abraham into the discussion, as if to suggest that they are justified because of their lineage. Jesus reminds them that anyone who sins is a slave to sin, and He calls them out on the fact that they are trying to kill Him, which does not match up with the character of Abraham, whom they claim as their father.

They fire back at Him, and then Jesus drives the point home:

> "If God were your Father, you would love me, for I came from God and I am here. I came not of my own accord, but he sent me. Why do you not understand what I say? It is because you cannot bear to hear my word. You are of your father the devil, and your will is to do your father's desires. He was a murderer from the beginning, and does not stand in the truth, because there is no truth in him. When he lies, he speaks out of his own character, for he is a liar and the father of lies. But because I tell the truth, you do not believe me. Which one of you convicts me of sin? If I tell the truth, why do you not believe me? Whoever is of God hears the words of God. The reason why you do not hear them is that you are not of God" (verses 42–47, ESV).

Our actions and words reveal our true character. The Jews were not open to the truth because it went against their own ideas and selfish desires. It's easy to judge them, but are we any different? Are we truly open to God's Word and His instruction in our lives?

—Alex Klischies, sophomore

Lost in Darkness
John 9:1–41

W hen bad things happen, we want someone to blame, and back in Jesus' day, the Jews thought that if anything bad happened, it must mean that the person had sinned and God was punishing them for their bad behavior. This theory is evident in the story of the man who had been blind since birth. When Jesus and the disciples passed the man, the disciples asked Jesus who had sinned, the man or his parents. Jesus set the record straight and told them that neither had sinned. It had to do with the fact that the man lived in a world of sin and bad things happen, but God has the final say.

"It was not that this man sinned, or his parents, but that the works of God might be displayed in him. We must work the works of him who sent me while it is day; night is coming, when no one can work. As long as I am in the world, I am the light of the world" (John 9:3–5, ESV). Then Jesus spit on the ground, made some mud, stuck it on the man eyes, and told him to go wash in the pool of Siloam (verses 6, 7, ESV).

The blind man did as he was told, and his vision was restored, which was a great cause for celebration! However, not everyone was pleased. The Pharisees found out about the miracle, which Jesus performed on the Sabbath, and they were mad. They questioned him on how he had received his sight and who had healed him, and the man told his story.

Later, Jesus found the man and told him who He really was. The man worshiped Jesus and told Him he believed in Him. Then Jesus said, "For judgment I came into this world, that those who do not see may see, and those who see may become blind" (verse 39, ESV). It sounds cryptic, but Jesus was talking about how He came not only to open people's eyes physically but also to open their eyes spiritually.

Are you blind? Or can you see?

—Allen Lee, sophomore

Tuning in to God's Voice
John 10:1–18

Once upon a time, there was a princess. She was kind and often rode through the village helping anyone in need. Her father, the king, sat with her in the evenings and told her stories about people who stood up for their faith in God. He instructed her on how to become like those people and to follow God with all her heart.

One day the princess was sitting in a meadow with her younger siblings when she noticed a flash of light down the road. She squinted and saw a knight riding up the lane. As he drew near, the children scampered back to the princess. He greeted them with kind, soothing words.

"Good day, your Highness. You are looking quite beautiful today. Your dress makes the blue in your eyes look like inviting pools of water." He bowed. "I am riding to the castle. Would you like to come with me?"

She blushed. No one had ever spoken to her this way. In the back of her mind, she remembered her father's voice warning her never to listen to young men who are flirtatious and flatter her beauty. They are selfish and only want their way, he had warned. She looked him in the eyes and said, "I'm sorry, but I cannot do so."

"Well then, I am sorry," he said soothingly. "You are certainly missing out. You are a young, independent woman who deserves the world."

There was a piece of her that was intrigued, but her father's words echoed in her mind, and she determined to listen to his voice.

This illustration is similar to the parable Jesus shares of the good shepherd whose sheep listened to his voice instead of to the enemy's. Jesus is the Good Shepherd, and we are the sheep. Knights battling for our attention can easily overwhelm our lives. We need to listen to God's voice to ward off the voices that try to sway us off track. He is the only one who can give us the strength to get through each day.

—Katelyn Kelch, freshman

Meeting With Jesus
Psalm 102:1, 2

Imagine that you left your favorite Bible at church last Sabbath. You really want to find it. Your grandparents gave it to you on your thirteenth birthday with your name engraved on the front, so it's extra special. You say hi to the church secretary and head toward the sanctuary. You're sure it's in the fifth pew where your family normally sits.

The lights are off in the sanctuary, but it's still bright because of all the windows. The sun is streaming through the stained-glass window at the front of room, casting patches of red, yellow, blue, green, and purple light all over the stage.

You locate your Bible right where you thought you would, and then you make your way to the front pew and sit down. You can't explain it, but you're mesmerized by the shimmering colors on the platform. You look up from the floor and focus on the image that is throwing the light around—it illustrates the Second Coming. You've seen it since you were a kid, but somehow today it looks different.

As you stare at Jesus riding on the clouds, surrounded by angels with trumpets, you feel a hand on your shoulder, and a voice says, "It won't be long. I'm coming back soon. I can't wait to take you and everyone else who loves Me home forever. Are you ready?"

Take some time to talk to Jesus or write down your response to His question.

Read the verses for the day and think about the promise it offers or what it tells you about God.

If you were to talk about this passage with Jesus, what would you say? What would you ask Him?

197

The Unbreakable Connection
Luke 9:51–56

Among stories of feeding the five thousand, healing a demon-possessed boy, and settling arguments between the disciples about who is greatest, we find a story buried at the end of Luke 9 about an encounter Jesus had with a Samaritan village. It may seem insignificant, but it drives home the very character of Jesus.

Jesus makes the decision to head back to Jerusalem, so He heads out with His disciples. Planning ahead for where they will stay along the way, Jesus sends a messenger to a Samaritan village and asks them to prepare a place for Him and His disciples.

At this time, Jesus is a superstar, and everyone knows who He is. He is not an unfamiliar face. In fact, one can guess that this village had heard about Jesus' interaction with the Samaritan woman at the well. However, the disciples soon find out that they are not welcome in the village. The villagers seem to be upset that He is on His way to Jerusalem and isn't really there for them. The disciples are mad at this snub, so they ask Jesus an out-of-the-blue, weird question. "Lord, should we call down fire from heaven to burn them up?" (Luke 9:54).

I understand that the disciples were angry, but their response seems over the top. Jesus immediately rebuked them for having such thoughts.

We see God's love in the smallest of stories like this one. An entire village appears to be set against Jesus, and yet He still loves them and cares about them. Jesus isn't put off by their rejection; He loves them regardless. Jesus isn't angered at their hatred toward Him but is disgusted by the hatred His disciples return to these villagers. Throughout His ministry, Jesus presented one simple message—love others as yourself. This concept is what separates Christians from the rest of the world. Love strengthens us while hatred tears us apart. Love connects us to our Savior while hatred drives a wedge between us.

—Zach Kirstein, junior

Entitled or Grateful?

Luke 17:11–19

There are some spoiled kids on this planet. Just type in "kids opening Christmas presents" on YouTube, and you'll be amazed at the stash of stuff that some kids haul in on Christmas Day. Maybe they're truly grateful for all the money their parents spent on them, but maybe they just feel entitled. They probably don't realize how much they've been given or what it's worth, and they already have a lot of junk sitting in their rooms collecting dust.

When I was a kid, there were many times that I wanted something and then begged and begged until I got it. Of course, there were other times when I didn't get anything at all. However, I learned that the more I begged for it, the more I lost appreciation for it once it was mine. I started to expect to receive stuff if I begged enough. I lost the concept of being thankful for what I had and what I received.

I hope that the people Jesus healed were grateful, but I'm guessing that not everyone recognized the magnitude of the gift He gave them when He restored their health or forgave their sins. In fact, Luke shares one such story with us.

As Jesus was on His way to Jerusalem, traveling from Galilee to Samaria, He was nearing a small town when ten lepers caught His attention. They were yelling, "Jesus, Master, have pity on us!" (Luke 17:13, NIV). Moved with compassion, Jesus simply tells them to go show themselves to the priests, and "as they went, they were cleansed" (verse 14, NIV). Only one of the men ran back to Jesus when he saw that he had been healed. "He threw himself at Jesus' feet and thanked him—and he was a Samaritan" (verse 16, NIV).

One of the men grasped the magnitude of the gift he received. Maybe it was because he was a Samaritan and understood that, according to Jewish culture, he was less worthy than the other men. Whatever it was, he expressed his gratitude and didn't take it for granted that Jesus had healed him. As the man was kneeling before Jesus and praising God, Jesus asked, "Were not all ten cleansed? Where are the other nine? Has no one returned to give praise to God except this foreigner?" (verses 17, 18, NIV).

Just as we want to be appreciated when we give a gift to someone, so does God. We are not entitled to any of the good things He gives us. Let's thank Him for His goodness.

—Nya Lucas, freshman

Saving Diane
Philippians 4:13

My dad grew up on a farm in New Mexico. He was the oldest of four, with three younger sisters. One day when he was about ten, my grandma asked him to go pull weeds in the garden. He begrudgingly made his way to the garden, opened the gate through the six-foot-high chicken wire fence, and latched it behind him. The fence helped keep critters away from their precious food source. My dad hated pulling weeds, but he was extra annoyed that day because his sister Diane was lounging on the drag behind the tractor as my grandpa worked to smooth out the field and prepare it for planting.

My dad tried to focus on the job at hand, but he kept glancing up at Diane, wishing he could relax instead of work. One time when he looked up, she wasn't there. He scanned the horizon to see whether she was walking back to the house, but he didn't see her. He kept looking, and that's when he saw her hair sticking out from under the drag! She had obviously fallen off and gotten caught under the drag, but my grandpa didn't know it. My dad's heart raced, and he sprang into action. He had to save his sister!

He ran toward the tractor and signaled for my grandpa to stop. As soon as the machine came to a halt, my dad grabbed the drag with one hand and took ahold of Diane's hair with the other, lifted, and pulled. Diane emerged, scared and dirty, but after a thorough assessment, they praised God that nothing was broken. They took her to the house to get cleaned up, and then my dad walked back to the field with his dad. They first stopped at the garden, where they discovered that the gate was still latched, and then they went to the drag and tried to lift it. Together my dad and grandpa tried to lift the drag, but they couldn't make it budge. It was then that they realized an angel had helped my dad jump the fence and lift the drag with one hand to rescue Diane. They couldn't wait to head back to the house to tell Diane and my grandma about the miracle!

I am a witness!

—Randy Kelch, IT director

Not Enough Workers
Luke 10:1–20

Many people think that Jesus only had twelve disciples, but that is not the case. Jesus had many people who were devoted to Him. In Luke 10, we read about Jesus sending out seventy other disciples in pairs to prepare the people for Him to visit later.

Before they left, Jesus gave the group instructions. He said, "The harvest is great, but the workers are few. So pray to the Lord who is in charge of the harvest; ask him to send more workers into his fields. Now go, and remember that I am sending you out as lambs among wolves" (verses 2, 3). He tells them what to, and not to, take with them. He instructs them to heal the sick and announce that God's kingdom is near. Then Jesus tells them what to do if they are ignored or rejected. If the town did not accept their message, they were to shake the dust off their feet and move on (verses 10–12).

This reminds me of a time I went canvassing in a nearby neighborhood. It was a school assignment, and I wasn't too gung ho about it, but I didn't exactly have a choice. I was with my best friend, and we made an agreement that we would take turns knocking and speaking at every other house. He made me go first, which was a disaster. I felt like the words that came out of my mouth were alphabet soup. Even worse than the fact that I couldn't seem to speak, I dropped at least two books. The lady kindly turned us away, which made me super upset. It didn't help that at the next house my friend got a donation even though they did not buy a book.

I got better throughout the day, but it seemed that I was always turned away and he always got a donation. The day ended, and although we had received some donations, we hadn't sold any books. I was crushed. I had always heard stories of how powerful canvassing could be. When we got back to the school, the leader reminded us that even if we didn't sell anything or get any donations, we still had made an impact on the people, which is exactly what I needed to hear.

When Jesus sent the disciples on their missionary journeys, He warned them that it wouldn't be easy. He encouraged them to go anyway, because "the harvest is great." There are many people searching for God, but there are few out there sharing Him. Are you willing to work? Are you willing to share Jesus with someone? It might not be easy, but it will be worth it.

—Sydney Lopez, junior

Living Peacefully
Matthew 11:28–30

S in is a heavy burden to carry. We cannot defeat it on our own, nor can we carry it. We are in desperate need of a Savior to help us along the way. The overwhelming stress that people endure on a daily basis breaks people's lives apart. It is because of sin that stress weighs down our lives, but we have only ourselves to blame because Jesus offers to carry that burden for us.

Matthew 11:28–30 says, "Come to Me, all you who labor and are heavy laden, and I will give you rest. Take My yoke upon you and learn from Me, for I am gentle and lowly in heart, and you will find rest for your souls. For My yoke is easy and My burden is light" (NKJV).

This illustration isn't as familiar to most of us because we don't live on farms, but the listeners to whom Jesus was talking understood how a yoke worked. You see, it attaches around the necks of two oxen so they can pull a plow or cart together, thus lightening the load a bit instead of having one animal doing all the work.

If you think about it in this context, Jesus wants to team up with us to help us go through life. He doesn't say that He will do all the work for us, but He says that He will stand right beside us and help us pull through whatever challenges we face.

Jesus tells us that we can lay our burdens on Him. He says this because He cares about all our worries, even the ones that seem tiny compared to others. Jesus cares about every issue we have, whether it's not having enough money, studying for a test, or even losing something valuable. He loves us so much that He died for our sins. He wants to be part of our daily lives. Imagine having someone so supportive in your life that, with Him, all your problems seem to disappear! Jesus is that supportive Friend whom everyone needs in life—He is the best of the best. He is waiting for you to turn to Him and ask for His help in dealing with the cares of this life. In return, He promises to give you rest because, as you will discover, you are no longer pulling the cart on your own; now you have a Partner.

—Amber Maddox, senior

A Strong Shelter
Psalm 91

During my first year of college, I was exploring the great outdoors near my new home. Signal Mountain is a popular hiking spot outside of downtown Chattanooga, Tennessee, and that's where I found myself one Sabbath afternoon with a group of friends. The view of the Tennessee River and the surrounding valley was spectacular. We hiked for a while before we stopped to take a break and enjoy the view.

We sat and talked for quite a while, and then someone noticed a storm on the horizon. As it got closer, we could see a wall of water moving across the valley toward us. Although it looked cool, we decided it was time to hightail it off the mountain. Of course, we had waited too long to beat the storm. Huge raindrops started to pelt us, but we spotted what looked like a good shelter just up the trail. We sprinted to a huge rock that we could sit under if we crouched down low. We all waited out the storm, nice and dry.

David describes God as our shelter from the storms of life.

> Those who live in the shelter of the Most High
> > will find rest in the shadow of the Almighty.
> This I declare about the LORD:
> He alone is my refuge, my place of safety;
> > he is my God, and I trust him. . . .
> If you make the LORD your refuge,
> > if you make the Most High your shelter,
> no evil will conquer you;
> > no plague will come near your home.
> For he will order his angels
> > to protect you wherever you go (Psalm 91:1, 2, 9–11).

What do you understand about God and His love for you after reading this psalm? What stands out to you the most?

—Chaplain Kalie

Meeting With Jesus

"For the angel of the LORD is a guard; he surrounds and defends all who fear him" (Psalm 34:7).

What truth is God sharing in this passage?

_____

_____

_____

_____

_____

What can you share with others from this verse?

_____

_____

_____

_____

_____

What did you learn about God from this reading?

_____

_____

_____

_____

_____

To Love Them
Luke 10:25–37

What is the most important commandment? " 'You must love the LORD your God with all your heart, all your soul, all your strength, and all your mind.' And, 'Love your neighbor as yourself' " (Luke 10:27).

To demonstrate what this looks like, Jesus told a story about a Jewish man who was attacked by robbers and left for dead on the side of the road. Two of his own fellow citizens walked past him, but a Samaritan—whom the Jews hated because the Samaritans were descendants of conquered Jews who had intermarried with other nations that worshiped pagan gods—stopped to help him. In other words, the Good Samaritan was merciful to someone who despised him and counted him worse than a Gentile. How could he do that? Simply because God said to love them—your neighbor.

We hear our parents and teachers tell us to love our neighbors and to be like the Good Samaritan. However, too often we are more like the priest and the Levite who ignored the injured man. Repeatedly, I've chosen to ignore others in need and any responsibility I might have toward them. In this parable, Jesus explains that to show mercy to others is a fulfillment of the law.

Mercy is more than doing something for someone who doesn't deserve it; it is showing mercy out of love. Without this love, our acts of kindness are empty and meaningless. This love is also impossible for any of us to show on our own. The love we need comes from God. If we allow God's love to fill us, then it flows over into our actions toward others. This means the pressure is off us, whether someone brushes us off or accepts the offer for help, because either way, the person is accepting or rejecting God's love, which is simply being reflected through us.

In 1 John 4:19, we are reminded why we should love them. "We love each other because he loved us first." I encourage you to read verses 16–21 too. The catch is that if we don't allow God's love to fill us and don't accept His gift, we won't be able to love others. Our mission, should we choose to accept it, is to accept God's love and let it fill us and then turn around and love others.

—Noelle Lucas, junior

The One Necessity

Luke 10:38–42

When I was younger, my parents frequently invited church members and friends over to our house for lunch after church. My mom often spent Friday running through the house cleaning, making sure everything was put away and picture perfect. When Sabbath arrived, she ran around making sure the food, table settings, and atmosphere of the dining room were just right. The focus was on everything being perfect for her guests.

One Sabbath the pastor invited us over for lunch. It was clear that it was a last-minute invitation because when we arrived, there were other guests and not enough chairs to accommodate everyone at the table. The pastor's wife seemed surprised at our arrival and the fact that she had even more guests. Our hosts quickly added a piano bench and lawn chair to the table, and everyone sat and enjoyed the meal together. It turned out to be a blessing because my mom was feeling a little lonely since we were relatively new to the area.

After this experience, my mom decided that the beauty of hospitality is not in the preparation or perfection of presentation but is in enjoying each other's company. What makes a meal meaningful is not the food or the atmosphere but the fellowship.

When Jesus arrived at Martha and Mary's home, Martha focused on everything being perfect for the Messiah. She cared more about the details than the relationship. Jesus gently reminded her of what is truly important: "Martha, Martha, you are worried and troubled about many things. But one thing is needed, and Mary has chosen that good part, which will not be taken away from her" (Luke 10:41, 42, NKJV).

Sometimes in our personal walk with Jesus, we set Him aside and focus more on the details of our busy lives. Many of us, like Martha, cling to our to-do list. We are pulled away by demands and deadlines; however, most of these urgencies are not going to matter in the long haul. We often forget to just sit and rest in Jesus' presence. Spending time with Him is the most important necessity of life. Like Mary, we should keep our focus on Jesus and our relationship with Him. The rest will fall into place if we keep our priorities straight.

—Caroline Markoff, senior

Time With God

Psalm 71:17

I dislike weeds, and I dislike weeding, but I have a large vegetable garden, so I have to go out and pull weeds regularly if I want to be able to see the plants that I'm actually trying to grow. In addition to getting rid of the weeds, I use the time to talk to God in the quiet of the outdoors.

One week I had neglected to weed the garden, and it was becoming overrun with weeds. While I was working, I talked with God and grumbled a bit about all the nasty weeds. It was in that moment that I thought about the different kinds of weeds around me. Some actually look nice, with small flowers on them. I was tempted to leave them alone, but then I reminded myself of the time I did that; they quickly took over my garden and tried to choke everything else out. There are weeds with short roots that pull out quite easily. The weeds with a spreading root system are more bothersome. The bigger they grow, the more branches they shoot out and the more the root system digs in. There are weeds with thorns, and they seem to fight back as you try to pull them up. Then there are the mega-weeds with roots that are deep; these require a shovel to be extracted from the ground.

As I thought about the different kinds of weeds in my garden, I realized that my life is not much different. God wants my life to be weed free and beautiful. My sins are much like the weeds in my garden. There are some that look pretty and harmless at first, but when I leave them alone, they eventually spread and try to choke out God. There are sins that are easy to overcome, like the weeds with short roots. Other sins spread and lead to more sins, just like the weeds that have spreading root systems. Then there are the sins that dig down deep and fight back. Satan doesn't want us to give up any of these sins because they separate us from God. Just as I have to keep up with the weeding in my garden, I have to ask God continually to get rid of the weeds in my life and to help me overcome the sins that try to overtake me.

When we spend time talking with God, He has a way of showing us truth. He helped me to look at sin in a different way as I worked in the garden. This isn't the first time that He's taught me something, and I know it won't be the last. The key to learning from Him is to spend time with Him. That's when we grow. I am a witness!

—Sue Hullquist, ASSIST director

Our Father
Luke 11:1–4

A simple request to teach the disciples to pray resulted in what we call the Lord's Prayer, and it begins like this: "Our Father" (Luke 11:2, NKJV).

A lot can be said about this prayer, but I want to focus on the first two words. Why? Because this phrase was a milestone in the disciples' understanding of their relationship with God and one another.

All of them had heard God referred to as a Father. They were familiar with the close relationship Jesus had with His Dad; when He spoke about God, He often used the phrase "the Father." Although spoken about in somewhat general terms, they were well aware that God was His Father. But Jesus replaced "the" with "our" in His prayer. God was their Father too! Taking it a step further, if God was their Father, as well as Jesus', that meant Jesus was their Brother.

The disciples revered Jesus as their Teacher and Lord. Even at the Last Supper, it was hard for Peter to let his Master wash his feet. Yet with this one phrase, Jesus was reminding the disciples that they were related and that their relationship went much deeper than Teacher and student. The use of the word "our" also reinforced the idea that they were all equal. Like many of us, the disciples battled over who would be Jesus' most important helper in the coming kingdom. Jesus was subtly reminding them that they could all claim God as their Father.

Of course, these words were not meant just for the disciples. They are true for us as well. We are God's children. "See how very much our Father loves us, for he calls us his children, and that is what we are!" (1 John 3:1). He's as much your Dad as mine. That means we have many siblings. Just remember, God chose us, despite all the bratty, annoying things we do. He loves us so much that He sent Jesus to die for us—His sisters and brothers. As Jesus loves us, may we love our brothers and sisters who have been adopted through Jesus. May we model to everyone the powerful and eternal love Jesus has freely given to us.

—Charis McRoy, freshman

Just Ask
Luke 11:5–13

After teaching His disciples the Lord's Prayer, Jesus tells them an interesting parable about prayer. He describes a scene in which a friend goes to another friend's house at midnight, wakes him up, and asks for bread because he had some guests just show up and he's all out of bread. The guy who was asleep is pretty perturbed, but the friend who needs the bread keeps knocking and won't go away. Finally, the guy who was trying to sleep gets up and gives his friend some bread to make him go away.

Then Jesus says, "Ask and it will be given to you; seek and you will find; knock and the door will be opened to you. For everyone who asks receives; the one who seeks finds; and to the one who knocks, the door will be opened" (Luke 11:9, 10, NIV).

Jesus isn't done yet. He asks a ridiculous question. "Which of you fathers, if your son asks for a fish, will give him a snake instead? Or if he asks for an egg, will give him a scorpion?" (verses 11, 12, NIV). These questions tie into the parable. If we believe that God is trustworthy, then when we ask Him for things, we can trust that He will give us good things. If a friend who is annoyed at your presence at midnight still gets up and helps you, how much more will God, who loves you, help you?

I remember praying for another friend when I was in the third grade. Sure, I had friends, but something was missing, so I told God I wanted a friend. A few weeks after that prayer, my parents announced to my sister and me that my mother was pregnant. I remember getting really upset at first because I loved being the baby of the family. However, as my mother's belly grew, so did my affection for my new sibling. When she gave birth to my baby brother, I was really excited and happy. God didn't answer my prayer the way I thought He would, but He gave me something better than I could've imagined.

We serve a loving God who cares for us and wants to give us good gifts. We just have to trust Him and keep praying for His will to be done in our lives.

—Darrby Marshall, junior

False Accusations

John 10:22–39

Have you ever been misunderstood for your actions or words? Let's say a classmate tells you that you talk about God too much, you are too Christian, and your faith is too much a part of your life. Or maybe your parents overhear you talking to a friend about sex, and they jump to conclusions and accuse you of going too far when you were just advising a friend not to have sex. I'm sure you can think of a time where someone incorrectly judged you based on what they thought you said or did.

If this hasn't happened to you, congratulations. If it has, then you're in good company because Jesus experienced this all the time with the religious leaders. In John 10:22–39, we find Jesus cornered by a group of Jews in the temple. They ask Him to tell them whether He is the Messiah. Jesus doesn't flat-out say yes because He knows they are trying to trap Him. Instead, He answers the question by pointing to what He's already done, much to their frustration.

He says, "I told you, and you do not believe. The works that I do in My Father's name, they bear witness of Me. But you do not believe, because you are not of My sheep, as I said to you. My sheep hear My voice, and I know them, and they follow Me" (verses 25–27, NKJV). Jesus has given them plenty of evidence to believe, but they refuse. He reminds them that His followers—His sheep—know who He is.

This just makes the Jews angrier. So mad, in fact, that they accuse Him of blasphemy, which is speaking sacrilegiously about God, and they pick up rocks to stone Him. Blasphemy is a crime worthy of death in their laws, so they attempt to kill Him right there in the temple. But God protects Jesus, and He escapes.

Jesus didn't back down from telling the truth, even when He knew He would be misunderstood and persecuted for what He said and did. This is a powerful lesson for us—even if everyone is against us and the consequences seem too great for us to bear, we can rest assured that God is with us when we stand up for what is right and speak the truth in love.

—Austin Manning, freshman

Meeting With Jesus

"The LORD is my rock, my fortress, and my savior;
   my God is my rock, in whom I find protection.
He is my shield, the power that saves me,
   and my place of safety.
He is my refuge, my savior,
   the one who saves me from violence.
I called on the LORD, who is worthy of praise,
   and he saved me from my enemies" (2 Samuel 22:2–4).

What spiritual principle can you take from this verse?

What stuck out to you in this reading?

What can you share with others from this verse?

Narrow Doors

Luke 13:22–30

W hen you come to a door, there is a decision to be made. You can either enter the door or turn around and go a different direction. We walk through a bunch of physical doors each day as we go in and out of our houses, schools, or stores. What about metaphorical doors? Doors to opportunities or experiences also require decisions.

Jesus used the example of a door in relation to entering the kingdom of heaven. He said, "Work hard to enter the narrow door to God's Kingdom, for many will try to enter but will fail. When the master of the house has locked the door, it will be too late. You will stand outside knocking and pleading, 'Lord, open the door for us!' But he will reply, 'I don't know you or where you come from' " (Luke 13:24, 25).

Jesus is inviting us to come through the open door and enter the kingdom, but we have a choice to make. We can go through the door or turn away. As Jesus explained, there will come a time when the door will shut, and if we're not on the inside, we will be lost. Jesus shared this with the people to express the importance of not wasting time in making a decision about following Him. The people portrayed in this story who were left on the outside of the door ate and drank with Jesus, but they did not commit to following Him and to having a relationship with Him. They simply traveled in the same circles.

This example is very similar to what happened to the people who died in the Flood. Noah invited them into the ark. The door was open for 120 years, but they chose to stay outside. It wasn't until the rain started to fall that they panicked and wished they had listened. Banging on the door didn't help because an angel had shut it.

Just as Noah preached about the Flood and invited people to be saved in the ark, Jesus warns in this passage about the end of the world and the way of salvation. Jesus doesn't want to exclude anyone, but eventually the door will close. The Bible is full of verses that talk about this important decision. God is inviting us in to a relationship with Him through the open door of the death of His Son. Will we go through the door? Or will we hang out outside?

—Elysse Mastrapa, junior

The Love of a Mother
Luke 13:31–35

Mother hen? It seems odd that Jesus would refer to Himself this way, doesn't it? We are familiar with likening God to a king or a warrior. It would even seem appropriate to compare Him to a majestic eagle or mighty hawk—but to a chicken?

Here's the context in which Jesus shares this analogy. He has been traveling through various towns and villages, preaching. He's headed toward Jerusalem, but He hasn't arrived yet. Some Pharisees approach Him on the way and tell Him that Herod is out to kill Him. Jesus seems unfazed by this threat. In fact, He calls Herod a fox and tells the Pharisees that He won't die outside of Jerusalem, so He isn't worried. Then Jesus has this to say about the city of David: "O Jerusalem, Jerusalem, the city that kills the prophets and stones those who are sent to it! How often would I have gathered your children together as a hen gathers her brood under her wings, and you were not willing!" (Luke 13:34, ESV).

To a mother hen, her chicks are very valuable. She will protect them at all cost. When a predator is near, she calls her chicks. When they come running, she hides them under her wings, shielding them from danger.

Satan is our predator, and just as the mother hen literally uses her body to protect her chicks, Christ literally used His body to save His children from spiritual destruction. His death means that we don't have to die. His life means that, when this world is finished, we can live with Him in heaven if we simply accept His gift of salvation. But we have to accept it. We have to run to Jesus. Baby chicks obey by instinct. They come to their mother when she calls. Without delay and without question, they run to the safety that is found only under their mother's wings. We instinctively have an emptiness in us that only Jesus can fill, but we also have the baggage of sin that tries to pull us away from God.

The beauty of the hen metaphor is that it goes beyond language, allowing us to simply feel Christ's love for us. Like a hen who watches gently over her chicks, Christ is always there. He knows us, and He loves us! We can trust Jesus' purpose for us and rest in the promise of His care because our Heavenly Father knows what we need before we even ask Him.

—Aspen Dain Meadows, sophomore

Heaven's Bank Account
Matthew 6:25–34

When I was six or seven, my family bought a big poultry farm on fifty acres. There were eight big chicken barns on the property that could hold thousands of chickens. For us as kids, the best part was how much land there was to roam around on, plus there was a pool and a pond. It was definitely a great place to grow up.

The unfortunate part about our move is that we bought the farm in 2008 in the middle of the economic downturn, which made it harder to run a business and bring in a profit. On top of that, the farm was old and rundown. This was a bad combination. My parents worked hard. They poured hours into working the farm and running the business, but after a few years of hanging on, they filed for bankruptcy, and we moved.

About this time, my older sister, Kylie, was getting ready to go to GCA. My parents managed to scrounge up enough money to send her, but we still weren't that financially stable after the ordeal with the farm. Somehow, they made it work. Fast-forward two years after that and my twin brother, Kevin, and I were graduating from eighth grade and getting ready to enter high school. We had spent the last two years listening to Kylie talk about all the fun she had at GCA, so naturally we wanted to go. However, all summer long my parents kept telling Kevin and me that they didn't think they could afford to send all three of us to a boarding school, so we needed to be prepared to go to the local public school.

Then, about a month before school started, my parents got a letter in the mail saying that there had been a mix-up and the bank had received more money than they needed when the bankruptcy was settled. A check was included in the letter that was enough to pay the necessary down payment for all three of us to attend GCA.

This letter came years after the bankruptcy. It was so out of the blue, but it wasn't random to God. He knew we needed the money, and He provided. This was definitely a turning point in my life. Looking back on my time at GCA now that I'm an upperclassman, I know that God wanted me here, and He provided the funds necessary to get me where He wanted me.

I am a witness!

—Kristin Burgess, junior

Doing Good
Luke 14:1–6

E very October, my Pathfinder club collects cans to help make Thanksgiving food baskets for people in need in our community. We go door-to-door for one or two Sabbaths asking for donations of canned goods or nonperishable foods that we can take to our church's food bank. Then, after all the food has been collected, we spend another Sabbath delivering it to the homes of the people who need it most. It's such a blessing to see the smiles on the faces of the families as we share food with them! It might not seem like much, but we're following Jesus' example and helping one person at a time. Of course, if we lived in Jesus' day, the Pharisees would be scolding us for working on the Sabbath, just as they got after Jesus.

Luke 14 contains a story of a miracle that Jesus performed on the Sabbath.

Now it happened, as He went into the house of one of the rulers of the Pharisees to eat bread on the Sabbath, that they watched Him closely. And behold, there was a certain man before Him who had dropsy. And Jesus, answering, spoke to the lawyers and Pharisees, saying, "Is it lawful to heal on the Sabbath?"

But they kept silent. And He took him and healed him, and let him go. Then He answered them, saying, "Which of you, having a donkey or an ox that has fallen into a pit, will not immediately pull him out on the Sabbath day?" And they could not answer Him regarding these things (verses 1–6, NKJV).

Jesus was getting ready to eat lunch with some of the religious leaders when He noticed a man who was suffering from dropsy, which is a term for the swelling of the soft tissues in the body. Naturally, Jesus helped the man, but He first asked the Pharisees whether it was lawful to heal on the Sabbath. I don't know whether they were stumped or afraid to take a stand, but they didn't say anything. Jesus healed the man and sent him on his way. Then He turned back to the Pharisees and asked whether they would save one of their animals if it fell into a pit on the Sabbath. Once again, they kept their mouths shut, which proves that they would've saved their animal but not met the needs of a human being. They were more concerned about themselves than others. God wants us to be the exact opposite of the Pharisees. He wants us to be concerned about others instead of ourselves.

—Josh Martinez, freshman

Knocked Down a Notch

Luke 14:7–14

It was July 6, 2013, and the Ultimate Fighting Championship's main event was about to commence. Reigning middleweight champion Anderson Silva was about to take on the undefeated champion, Chris Weidman. The match attracted much publicity because a feud broke out between the two fighters. Both believed it was their fight to take, but one was louder than the other. Silva had a reputation of trash talking and taunting his opponents before and during fights, and this fight was no different. When both fighters entered the ring, Silva taunted his opponent between jabs and hooks. However, his arrogance proved to be his downfall. In the second round, he lost the match and his title.*

Humility is a hard lesson to learn. We see arrogance and pride often displayed in athletes and celebrities, but we are certainly not immune to the quest for power and dominance. We all need to learn to be humble.

Jesus was having dinner with a group of Pharisees when He noticed the leaders bickering about who deserved the seat of honor. Astounded by their lack of humility, Jesus went on to tell the leaders not to think so highly of themselves. He said it is best to humble oneself and to sit in the last seat and not clamor for the seat of honor. If deserved, the host will call upon the guest and ask him to take a seat of honor. "For whoever exalts himself will be humbled, and he who humbles himself will be exalted" (Luke 14:11, NKJV).

God specifies the importance of humility many times throughout the Bible. King Solomon highlighted this topic a lot in Proverbs. Those who are wise realize that everything they have is from God, not from themselves. Selfishly passing off accomplishments as our own gives no honor to our Creator, to whom the credit is actually due. May we act like Jesus and be humble in all that we do and say!

—Bryan Melo, sophomore

---

* Mike Chiapetta, "UFC 162 Results: Chris Weidman Knocks Out Anderson Silva to End Legend's Title Reign," MMA Fighting, July 7, 2013, https://www.mmafighting .com/2013/7/7/4499496/ufc-162-results-chris-weidman-knocks-out-anderson-silva -to-end.

Togetherness
Psalm 111

The church I attended as I grew up often ended the Sabbath with a vespers program, and my family usually attended. Sometimes there was music and sometimes just a short devotional thought. I don't remember much about the programs other than the fact that I had to sit through another service, but I do remember the fun I had after the service as my friends and I played outside. We'd run around playing tag or whatever other game we made up while our parents talked and talked and talked. Then we'd bug them to invite our friends over so that we could spend even more time together.

Don't get me wrong; church is about spending time with God and getting to know Him better. But church is also about friendship and fellowship. In Psalm 111, we read,

> Praise the Lord!
> I will thank the Lord with all my heart
>   as I meet with his godly people.
> How amazing are the deeds of the Lord!
>   All who delight in him should ponder them (verses 1, 2).

Our job as a church family should be to encourage one another and point each other to Jesus. The psalmist celebrates this concept in these first few verses. I don't know whether during David's reign people would share their personal testimonies, as we like to call it, but we need to communicate with each other about how God is working in our lives. When we do that, we bring life to the church through our stories, and more people get excited about God. They see Him not as an abstract deity but as a real person who lives and moves in our daily lives.

That's why the writer of Hebrews counseled the church to be vigilant in meeting together. "And let us not neglect our meeting together, as some people do, but encourage one another, especially now that the day of his return is drawing near" (Hebrews 10:25). We find strength and encouragement in each other's stories as we think about God's goodness.

"Everything he does reveals his glory and majesty. His righteousness never fails. He causes us to remember his wonderful works. How gracious and merciful is our Lord!" (Psalm 111:3, 4).

What is God doing in your life? Whom can you share it with today? We are the church, and we need to lift each other up and point each other to Jesus.

—Chaplain Kalie

Meeting With Jesus

"LORD, you know the hopes of the helpless. Surely you will hear their cries and comfort them" (Psalm 10:17).

How can you apply this verse to your own life?

_____

_____

_____

_____

_____

What can you share with others from this verse?

_____

_____

_____

_____

_____

What did you learn about God from this reading?

_____

_____

_____

_____

_____

The Invitation
Luke 14:15–24

J esus loved to tell stories, and this passage includes one of His many parables. A man threw a big party, and he invited a bunch of people whom he knew. He apparently didn't list a specific time on the invitation; it was more of an announcement. When everything was ready, he sent one of his workers to tell the invitees to come on over because the party was about to start. However, all the people who had once been excited about the party began to make excuses why they couldn't come. They were too busy with business engagements or family commitments.

The worker came back and told his boss that no one could come. The man was frustrated that his invitation had been rejected, so he sent his worker back out with these instructions: "Go quickly into the streets and alleys of the town and invite the poor, the crippled, the blind, and the lame" (Luke 14:21). Essentially, instead of the first batch of ungrateful invitees, the rich man invited all the people who would truly appreciate the gesture. The worker must have thought his boss had gone crazy, but he did what he was told. Naturally, the poor and handicapped people jumped at the chance to do something fun. They gladly accepted the invitation.

When the worker showed up with the new guests, he discovered that there was plenty more room in the house for more guests, so he went back out to find even more people.

In this story, Jesus was shining a big spotlight on how heaven works. Going to heaven is the ultimate party invitation. However, there are people who get excited when they hear about it but in the end decide that they are too busy with other stuff here on earth to worry about heaven. God doesn't beg and plead for people to accept Him. Instead, He goes and shares the good news with others: those who are struggling and who recognize how amazing the offer is. God invites those people to heaven. God doesn't have a cap on the number of people who can go to heaven. There is plenty of room. The choice of whether we will accept His invitation is ours. What's your response?

—Anthony Melgar, senior

The Ultimate Pledge of Allegiance
Luke 14:25–33

Jesus said some unexpected things, and this passage contains one such statement. Jesus said, "If anyone comes to me and does not hate father and mother, wife and children, brothers and sisters—yes, even their own life—such a person cannot be my disciple. And whoever does not carry their cross and follow me cannot be my disciple" (Luke 14:26, 27, NIV). What? Does Jesus really want us to hate the people we love? That sounds like an oxymoron.

Of course Jesus isn't saying that we should literally hate our families. This goes against what He taught about loving each other, including our enemies. No, there is a much deeper meaning to it than most would think. What Jesus is trying to say is that when we choose to be His disciples, we must be willing to put Him above everyone and everything else. That can be a challenge since most of us are selfish and tend to lose focus on what's important because of the distractions of this world; even the worthwhile things can make us lose focus. But Jesus wasn't kidding. He wants our full devotion. He wants our whole hearts. If we want to be Jesus' disciples, we have to be committed to Him, just like a bride and groom commit to each other on their wedding day.

When I think about someone who modeled this relationship with God, putting Him above everyone else, I think of Daniel. He was devoted to God. He stood up for what he believed in from the time he was a young man first brought into captivity until he was an old man. Daniel faithfully served the rulers he worked under, but he never put their requests above his relationship with God. When the decree was given to worship the king, Daniel counted the cost, picked up his cross, and continued to pray three times a day to God. This earned him an overnight stay in the lions' den.

Like Daniel, we need to commit ourselves to God. Jesus calls us to put Him above all else. If we want to follow Jesus and be His disciple, we need to surrender our ambitions, plans, possessions, and riches to God. Jesus is calling us to be His disciples. The question is, Are we up to the challenge? Are we ready to hand everything over to God and commit ourselves to Him?

—Emely Mendez, sophomore

No More Tears

Psalm 56:8–11

I managed to hold off the tears until I was far enough away from the school that no one would see me cry. I was tired—tired of walking, tired of school, tired of people, tired of crying. I suppose I was angry too. I had cried on my way home from school so many times that it seemed I couldn't remember the last time I had walked home without tears.

I honestly can't remember what the issue was that day. It was my eighth-grade year, and I distinctly remember it as a rough one. There always seemed to be an endless stream of struggles at school. I attended a small bilingual school in the Pacific Northwest (there were only two students in my eighth-grade class), and the students who attended were ones I had known for as long as I could remember. You would think that it would be easy to get along, but I was an easy target. I was sensitive, eager to please, small, and generally happy, and I loved learning, which all seemed to contribute to my vulnerability.

Regardless, I remember feeling a sense of desperation that day. Whether the issue was something big (sometimes the kids were pretty mean) or something small, it was irrelevant to me because I felt lost and alone. So I cried, and in that fit of anger at the fact that I was so often crying, I cried out to God. It wasn't a prayer so much as an accusation and, in every way, a plea for help. God didn't respond in a flash of light or a voice from heaven, but He answered. I suddenly felt that I wasn't alone. With that realization came a sense of calm. I stopped walking for a minute to try to make sense of it. Why should I feel calm, like everything was going to be OK? This time I prayed, asking God whether He was trying to tell me something. As I continued my walk, I let my mind explore the ideas that came to me, such as the fact that maybe I wasn't alone at school and that maybe there were others who needed my friendship. The most important thought in those moments was the one that changed my outlook on life from that day forward—it doesn't matter what others think of me because God knows me best and thinks I'm great.

I never really found my niche in eighth grade, but I found happiness, joy, and a sense of belonging that I could only explain by my newfound understanding of God's love for me. As a result, the loneliness wasn't really a problem any longer, and I never cried on my way home again, even though I probably continued to have rough days, similar to that day. I am a witness!

—Shannon Scott, science/technology/art/journalism teacher

The Lost Blanket
Luke 15:1–7

W hen I was about three years old, I lost my favorite blanket. It had been a gift from a relative when I was a baby. I cherished that blanket dearly. I always had it with me. My family and I were driving back home from my grandparents' house when I realized I didn't have it with me. I know I was little, but I felt empty without it. We searched the car and couldn't find it anywhere. Then we called my grandma and grandpa. They promised that they would look everywhere. They found it! They went out of their way to mail it to me, and I waited, rather impatiently, for my priceless blanket to arrive. When I finally received it in the mail, I was overjoyed that my lost blanket had been found.

My childhood story reminds me of the parable of the lost sheep. The Pharisees accused Jesus of spending time with sinners, and instead of arguing with them, He told this story: "Suppose one of you has 100 sheep, but one of them gets lost. What will you do? You will leave the other 99 sheep there in the field and go out and look for the lost sheep. You will continue to search for it until you find it. And when you find it, you will be very happy. . . . In the same way, I tell you, heaven is a happy place when one sinner decides to change. There is more joy for that one sinner than for 99 good people who don't need to change" (Luke 15:4–7, ERV).

When we are lost and have wandered away from God, He searches for us. Unlike the story in which I lost my blanket, God doesn't lose us—we lose Him. We lose Him by being too busy, neglecting our prayer time and Bible study, making bad choices, or ignoring the prompts of the Holy Spirit. Fortunately, God still loves us, and He comes looking for us. When He finds us, He and all of heaven rejoice.

God's love blows my mind. If I were the only person on earth who ever sinned, He would still have sent Jesus to die for me! That's how much God loves us!

—Carissa Melton, freshman

Lost and Found
Luke 15:8–10

My ID card is one of the most important things I carry with me. I have it with me every day because I use it every day. It gets me into my dorm room. It gets me into the school buildings. It clocks me in and out of work. I use it throughout my day. As you can imagine, if I misplace my ID card, I begin a frantic search to find it. If my roommate or any of my friends are in my room, I tell them about my woes because, let's face it, they can relate because most of them have lost their cards at some point too. After lamenting about it being lost, I proceed to rip my room apart. It usually looks like a tornado has hit it when I'm done, but it always results in the lost being found. Everyone knows when I find my card because I get super happy!

In the parable of the lost coin, Jesus tells the story of a woman who loses one of her silver coins. It may not seem like that big of a deal; however, Bible scholars point out that the loss of this coin was equal to a full day's wages. The woman cannot afford to lose that money. Just as any sensible person would do, the woman begins to search her house. Jesus says that she lights a lamp, sweeps the house, and searches carefully until she finds it. I can't imagine sweeping a dirt floor looking for a small coin. I'm sure it was no easy task, but she doesn't give up until she finds what she has lost. Once she finds the coin, she celebrates by calling her friends and neighbors to come and rejoice with her.

Jesus uses this story to demonstrate just how much He cares for us and how He feels about those who are lost. Just as the woman did all she could to find the coin, Jesus does all He can to lead us back to Him. He goes out of His way to make sure we are safe, sound, and found in Him. Once we are found, Jesus says that there is rejoicing among the angels of God in heaven.

—Gabi Mendonca, junior

Coming Home
Luke 15:11–32

The parable of the prodigal son is the last of three stories Jesus told to illustrate His amazing love for us. We've already read the last two days about the lost sheep and the lost coin. All three stories feature something or someone who is lost, but this story is a bit different because the son chose to be lost. The sheep didn't know any better, and the coin is an object without any reasoning power.

The prodigal son was greedy. He wanted his inheritance before his dad died. Amazingly, his dad agreed to the arrangement, and the son left home. The Bible says he took all of his belongings and moved to a distant land where he spent all of his money on partying and doing whatever he wanted. Unfortunately, a famine struck about the time his money ran out, so he found himself in a bad place. He was far from home, he didn't have any money, and he was starving. He convinced a farmer to hire him to take care of pigs.

"When he finally came to his senses, he said to himself, 'At home even the hired servants have food enough to spare, and here I am dying of hunger! I will go home to my father and say, "Father, I have sinned against both heaven and you, and I am no longer worthy of being called your son. Please take me on as a hired servant" ' " (Luke 15:17–19).

The son returned home, and the father ran to meet him in the road with joyful hugs and kisses. The young man gave his prepared speech, but the father seemed to ignore it. Instead, the father gave the son all new clothes and put the family ring on his finger. If that weren't enough, the father told the servants to prepare a big feast to celebrate the son's return.

This is a picture of how happy God is when we turn from our wicked ways to live the life He wants for us. You might be hesitant to come back to God if you've fallen away because you're afraid God is mad at you for messing up, but when you take one step toward Him in repentance, He will run to you with open arms and forgive your sins. Don't wait, thinking sometime down the road will be a better time to leave sin behind. Repent now and run back to Jesus. He is waiting for you with arms wide open. The choice is yours.

—Nayha Miller, sophomore

Meeting With Jesus
Isaiah 43:1–3

The pressure is mounting. You feel it starting to well up inside of you. It's only Monday morning, but you just found out that two of your teachers scheduled tests for the same day. That means you have two tests on Wednesday, not to mention the major research paper that is due on Friday for English class. Throw in a history quiz on Thursday that's more like a test, and you're fried. Just when you think it can't get worse, you remember that you have intramurals twice this week, and you committed to planning an activity for Sabbath School long before you knew how busy this week would be.

You put your head down on your desk just as the bell rings, and the rest of your classmates leave the room. "How am I going to get through this week?" you ask yourself. You have a free period next, so you decide to sit for a few more minutes before joining the chaos in the hallway. You take a deep breath and sit up. As you turn to grab your backpack, you see Jesus sitting in the seat behind you.

"Rough start to your week?" He asks.

"You could say that. I've got so much to do that I don't know where to start! Plus, I doubt I have enough hours in the day to get it all done!"

"Want some help?"

"How can You help?" you snap back. "I doubt You're going to do my homework for me or magically transport me to next Monday! What good does it do to talk about it when You can't take away the problem!"

"Suit yourself, but I'm here to listen and help you in other ways," He responds. "Sure, I'm not going to do your homework for you, but I will sit with you and help you study. I can help you concentrate and focus on what you're learning. And I can give you peace and help you stay calm. But you have to trust that I can help and come to me when the demands of school get to be too much. The choice is yours. What can I help you with?"

Take some time to talk to Jesus or write down your response to His question.

Read the passage for the day and think about the promise it offers or what it tells you about God.

If you were to talk about these verses with Jesus, what would you say? What would you ask Him?

Honest Living

Luke 16:1–15

S ome people are just plain sneaky and dishonest. They cheat and steal, and even when they're caught, they still manage to work the system. Jesus tells a parable about a rich man who had a manager who oversaw his estate. However, when the master found out that the manager was ineffective at his job, he fired him. The manager made a quick decision before leaving. He called in a few people who owed his master money, and he cut their debt in half. He assumed that now these people would owe him, and he could ask them for a favor once he was without a job and a place to live.

Then Jesus drives home the point with this statement:

"One who is faithful in a very little is also faithful in much, and one who is dishonest in a very little is also dishonest in much. If then you have not been faithful in the unrighteous wealth, who will entrust to you the true riches? And if you have not been faithful in that which is another's, who will give you that which is your own? No servant can serve two masters, for either he will hate the one and love the other, or he will be devoted to the one and despise the other. You cannot serve God and money" (Luke 16:10–13, ESV).

This suggests that people can be measured by their willingness to comply with the truth. If a kid grows up telling little white lies, then there is a good chance that as he or she gets older, the lies will get bigger. Because of how long he's been doing it, it won't seem like a bad thing. The little has grown into much.

In addition to Jesus' main point, I believe the manager saw his position and the perks of working for a rich man as luxuries that he deserved. He took his job and his master's trust for granted. Sometimes I think we do the same thing with God. We take for granted the gifts He gives us. We recognize that _____ (fill in the blank) is from Him, but we fail to give Him honor or praise for what He does in our lives. We begin to expect His blessings, and this gets us into trouble. We let selfishness take over our thoughts, which shifts our focus to ourselves and away from God's goodness.

—Kudzai Mhondiwa, junior

The Least of These

Luke 16:19–31

A few years ago, my family and I were in Boston touring the city. We were walking the 2.5-mile Freedom Trail, which winds around the city and stops at the various historic sites that played a part in the American Revolution. As we walked, we passed a homeless person on the sidewalk who held a sign asking for help. I gave a sideways glance so as not to make eye contact, quickly read the sign, and then looked off down the street, trying not to feel guilty for not stopping to help. I reasoned that I only had two dollars in my wallet, which was barely anything. However, as I walked, my conscience kept bugging me. It didn't matter how much or how little I had; I felt the push to turn around and give the man what I could. The prompt seemed to get louder with every step, so I told my family that I would be right back. I turned around, headed back to the man with the sign, and stuck my dollars in his outstretched cup.

He thanked me, and I headed back to join my family. It wasn't much, but my conscience wouldn't rest until I had given what I had. Needless to say, I felt much better afterwards, and I prayed that God would turn what little I could give into whatever that man needed that day.

Luke 16 features two parables dealing with money. The first one, which you read about yesterday, deals with greed and the quest to take care of oneself through monetary gain. This second parable features a rich man whom Jesus describes as living in the lap of luxury. He wears fine clothes and has whatever he wants. He lives in stark contrast to a poor man who lies at his gate: Lazarus has sores all over his body and is starving. He is clearly in rough shape. Sadly, the rich man doesn't show him any kindness. He doesn't do anything to alleviate his pain and suffering. In fact, Jesus says that the rich man won't even share the scraps of food from his table. This story reminds us of our responsibility to those who have less than us. Jesus calls us to take care of the poor and needy.

The Old and New Testament are full of verses that address the subject of helping the poor, the oppressed, the outcast, and those without families. Micah 6:8 sums up our mission: "He has told you, O man, what is good; and what does the Lord require of you but to do justice, and to love kindness, and to walk humbly with your God?" (ESV).

How is God asking you to serve?

—Chaplain Kalie

Out of My Control
2 Corinthians 1:8

The Christmas of my sophomore year didn't go exactly as planned. Instead of being at home with my family, I was stuck in a hospital bed clinging to life.

A few weeks before, I had developed some pain in my abdomen, but I figured it would go away. It didn't. It just got worse. Because it built up gradually each day, I didn't know how much pain I was in, but my parents finally convinced me that I needed to go to the hospital. This was the Sunday before finals. I checked in at the emergency room, and they ran tests. They discovered that I had appendicitis, so they admitted me to the hospital, and I had an appendectomy the next morning. The doctors discharged me on Tuesday, and I assumed everything would be okay. That's how it's supposed to be. It was a simple laparoscopic procedure and wasn't supposed to be invasive. I had three small incisions, and I was supposed to be back to normal in a week.

However, that didn't happen. I couldn't stop throwing up, and I felt as if I was going to die. I went back to the hospital a few days after getting home, and they opened up my abdomen and found that I had a perforated bowel. My intestine had been accidentally cut during the appendectomy, and it was leaking waste all over my insides. They cleaned me out, stitched me up, and then transported me in an ambulance to the children's hospital in Chattanooga. I had two more surgeries over the next few days, but my body still wasn't happy. My white blood cell count was over fifty thousand, and normally it's supposed to be at ten thousand. Whenever your white blood cell count is high, it means that your body is trying to fight infection. My body was fighting hard, but it was losing. If that weren't bad enough, I developed acute respiratory distress syndrome, meaning that my lungs were filling with fluid. I was in critical condition. The doctors sedated me so that I was in a light sleep and then put me on a ventilator so that a machine could breathe for me.

I couldn't eat. Talk. Think. Walk. Breathe. Pray. But people were praying for me. Earlier in the year, I had prayed that people would see God's power through me. This experience was an answer to that prayer. I began to turn a corner after a few weeks. I woke up. My lungs got better, and my body began to heal. I didn't do anything. God did everything. He made me better. He saved my life.

I am a witness!

—Amie Shelley, junior

No Regrets

Luke 17:20–37

B efore Jesus comes back to save us, there is going to be a lot of information flying around about Him, some true and some false. We sometimes think of false prophets as people who will appear in the distant future right before Jesus returns, but there are false prophets who are spreading lies in our world right now. A few years ago, there was a man in Russia claiming to be the Messiah. He had followers, people who sold everything, lived with him, and hung on his every word. Others have claimed God has spoken to them or that they've seen Him. Don't fall for it! They twist God's Word, and they deceive many people. Stay true to what you know.

Jesus warned about this type of deception and the need to be ready. He then told those listening about two examples from the Old Testament in which people were so caught up in doing their own thing that they missed the signs and weren't prepared for the impending destruction.

Noah tried hard to get people to come into the ark, but no one believed it would flood. They'd always had nice weather. They lived lavishly. They threw banquets, parties, and weddings because they thought they had all the time in the world. By the time they believed—when the first raindrops began to fall—it was too late. Noah and his family were saved because of their faith in God and because they obeyed His command to prepare.

Lot is another example. The people who called Sodom and Gomorrah home were doing what they usually did: partying, getting drunk, and being violent. The citizens chose to party instead of praying. Then one night the whole place went up in flames! Thanks to an angel, Lot, his wife, and his two daughters were taken out of the city, but his wife didn't believe the angels when they warned her to follow them and not look back. She turned back and looked longingly at her city, and instantly she turned into a pillar of salt.

Revelation 16:15 talks about Jesus coming like a thief in the night. "Blessed is the one who stays awake, keeping his garments on, that he may not go about naked and be seen exposed!" (ESV). Jesus is reminding us to be ready and pay attention to the little things so that we are not caught off guard, thus regretting our decisions or actions.

—Anderson Mills, freshman

Keep Asking

Luke 18:1–8

It is easy to doubt God and lose heart in His Word when our prayers are not answered when and how we want, but Jesus reminds us to be persistent and to remember that God's promises are just and true.

> And he told them a parable to the effect that they ought always to pray and not lose heart. He said, "In a certain city there was a judge who neither feared God nor respected man. And there was a widow in that city who kept coming to him and saying, 'Give me justice against my adversary.' For a while he refused, but afterward he said to himself, 'Though I neither fear God nor respect man, yet because this widow keeps bothering me, I will give her justice, so that she will not beat me down by her continual coming.' And the Lord said, 'Hear what the unrighteous judge says. And will not God give justice to his elect, who cry to him day and night? Will he delay long over them?' " (Luke 18:1–7, ESV).

If an unrighteous judge responds to persistent pleas, then God, who loves us, will certainly answer our prayers. The key is that we must be patient and wait for the answer. He knows best, and His timing is perfect. We have to surrender to His plan. Sometimes the Lord tests our faith, just like when He tested Job, but we shouldn't lose heart. We need to simply keep praying because our faithfulness ultimately leads to eternal life.

About four years ago, I started praying for a friend of mine. She didn't have the best home life, and I really wanted her to become closer to God. Day after day, she came to my house in tears telling me how awful things were at her house. I kept praying and begging God to help her and draw her closer to Him. Three months went by and she still kept coming to my house upset and at a loss about what to do.

I decided to start praying with her. We pleaded with God and asked Him why He was not helping her. After a while, we stopped praying because we weren't seeing any results. However, a couple of days later, I felt moved to keep praying for her. About a week later, she came to my house and told me things were getting better. Then, a bit after that, she told me she was thinking about getting baptized. I rejoiced, thanking God that He had heard my prayers.

My friend and I were both baptized the following year. I was so glad that I kept praying. You should never give up on God because He will never give up on you. At the end of the parable, Jesus asks if He will "find faith on earth" (verse 8, ESV). Will He find faith in you?

—Heather Morris, junior

Mystery Solved
Psalm 110

There was a TV show that started when I was a kid called *Unsolved Mysteries*. I never watched it, but the show featured reenactments of unsolved crimes, missing persons cases, and conspiracy theories. In a few cases, viewers actually contacted police after the shows aired and were able to fill in the missing details to bring about justice. Mysteries intrigue us.

The Pharisees faced a mystery regarding Jesus. They didn't want to believe that He was the Messiah, so they kept trying to put the pieces together and figure out where He had come from and what His purpose was. In Matthew 22:41–46, a group of Pharisees surround Jesus, and He asks them this question: "What do you think about the Messiah? Whose son is he?" (verse 42).

They throw out the answer that the Messiah is the son of David. Maybe that was a logical answer because they know that the Messiah was to come from David's lineage. Jesus then quotes from Psalm 110, pressing the Pharisees to look deeper and think logically to answer the question of His origins. Psalm 110:1 says,

The Lord said to my Lord,
"Sit in the place of honor at my right hand
until I humble your enemies,
making them a footstool under your feet."

Jesus then said, "Since David called the Messiah 'my Lord,' how can the Messiah be his son?" (Matthew 22:45).

The Pharisees didn't know how to respond, so they didn't say anything. They didn't ask questions. They didn't dialogue further. They just clammed up; it is likely that they were frustrated and embarrassed that this unschooled preacher had just schooled them. This attitude is what got them into trouble. They were never willing to humble themselves and accept the fact that maybe someone else knew more than they did.

There is nothing mysterious about Jesus—if we choose to believe in what the Bible says. He came. He lived. He died. He was resurrected. And He's coming back again.

—Chaplain Kalie

Meeting With Jesus

Yet I still dare to hope
  when I remember this:

The faithful love of the Lord never ends!
  His mercies never cease.
Great is his faithfulness;
  his mercies begin afresh each morning (Lamentations
    3:21–23).

What question would you like to ask God about this verse?

How can you apply these verses to your own life?

What can you share with others from these verses?

No Better

Luke 18:9–14

D o you compare yourself to other people? Be honest. There are so many areas in which we measure ourselves against others: looks, health, academics, sports, musical talent, and religion. We don't want to compare ourselves to God even though He's the only one we should be looking at. He is perfect, so we look at our peers and measure whether we are somehow better than them. It's kind of crazy when you think about it because our friends and their level of spirituality won't get us to heaven. But this idea of comparison isn't a new topic.

Jesus talks about this very issue in Luke 18. "He spoke this parable to some who trusted in themselves that they were righteous, and despised others" (verse 9, NKJV). Jesus goes on to talk about a tax collector and a Pharisee and how, when the two men went to the temple to pray, the Pharisee exalted himself by comparing himself to sinners, including the tax collector. He boasted about how he fasted and paid tithe. In contrast, the tax collector prayed, "God, be merciful to me, a sinner!" (verse 13, NKJV).

Jesus then says of the tax collector, "I tell you, this man went down to his house justified rather than the other; for everyone who exalts himself will be humbled, and he who humbles himself will be exalted" (verse 14, NKJV). Jesus wants us all to humble ourselves and ask God for forgiveness because we are all sinners and make mistakes. It doesn't matter what position we hold in this world. We aren't supposed to compare ourselves to others. Our salvation is based on our relationship with God, not on how we look compared to others.

God is merciful, and He wants to forgive us our sins, but we have to be honest with Him and recognize that we need a Savior. We will never be good enough on our own to earn salvation. We must come to Jesus and accept His gift of salvation if we want eternal life.

—Caleb Mitchell, sophomore

The Same Gift
Matthew 20:1–16

God is a generous and understanding God who watches over us every day. He truly wants what is best for us, and He will do whatever it takes to save us.

The parable of the workers in the vineyard describes a gracious landowner who goes out in the morning and hires some workers. This landowner offers them a set amount of money, a denarius, which was the usual daily wage for a laborer in Bible times. The men agree and go off to work in the vineyard.

Well, a few hours later the landowner goes back to the marketplace and hires some more workers for his vineyard. Then, right before quitting time, the landowner heads to the marketplace one more time and sees others still standing there waiting to be hired. He asks the men why they are still there, and they tell him that no one gave them a job. The landowner tells them to head to his vineyard.

When the time comes to pay everyone, the workers line up, and the last ones hired get paid first, all the way up to the first ones hired. The men begin to compare their wages and find that everyone was paid for a full day of work.

The men who worked all day are envious and begin to complain. The landowner says to the complainers, "I am not being unfair to you, friend. Didn't you agree to work for a denarius? . . . Don't I have the right to do what I want with my own money? Or are you envious because I am generous?" (Matthew 20:13–15, NIV). Then Jesus adds, "So the last will be first, and the first will be last" (verse 16, NIV).

God wants as many people in heaven as possible. It doesn't matter whether you are the first person or the last person to believe in salvation. God accepts you as long as you accept Him. He is so generous, and He loves us so much! Don't wait until the last minute to say yes to His invitation. If you've already said yes, rejoice with Him when someone says yes to His invitation, and don't be jealous because they get the same reward, even if they came at the last minute.

—Justin Moore, junior

Not Just a Cafeteria Worker
Matthew 5:14–16

L ast summer I worked in the kitchen at Camp Heritage. I had to get up at 6:30 A.M. and be to work by 6:45 A.M. every morning to get breakfast ready for the campers. It was hard work cooking and cleaning. The best part of the day was when the kids came through line. That was the only time that I got to interact with them, so I decided that I was going to be the best kitchen worker there was, and I would smile and help them see Jesus in everything I did.

Camp was going well when one week—Junior 1—the girls' director asked me to serve as a sub-counselor for a few hours one afternoon. I jumped at the chance and showed up at the appointed time to meet the girls I would be watching, but they weren't there. I waited for about twenty minutes, worried that I had lost a bunch of girls I hadn't even met. Finally, I connected with the girls, and we headed off to worship for the evening. We had a great time together, and by the end of the evening, the counselor came up to me and told me the girls wanted to keep me. She asked whether I could hang out with their cabin for the rest of the week when I had free time. In the kitchen, I was serving the kids, but I didn't get to hang out with them, so I jumped at the chance to spend time with the campers.

On one of the last evenings, I was talking to one of the campers, and she told me she didn't want to go home. I asked her what she meant, and she poured out her heart about the struggles in her family. The thought went through my mind that I was just a kitchen worker and wasn't equipped for this type of conversation. It definitely seemed like a counselor-type discussion. My job was to cook and wash pots and pans, not help kids with impossible situations. My mind whirled with what to say and how to say it, but instead of talking, I just listened. By the end of our talk, this camper said, "I know that Jesus loves me and that everything will be okay."

Jesus asks us to be His hands and feet, but that evening I was His ears, and that's exactly what He needed me to be.

I am a witness!

—Angelina Nesmith, freshman

Into the Unknown
John 11:1–16

Mary, Martha, and Lazarus were some of Jesus' closest friends. He cared about them, so when He heard that Lazarus was sick, He made plans to go see them. Jesus stayed where He was for two extra days, and then He told His disciples that they should leave and head for Judea.

Instead of trusting in God for protection, the disciples told Him they thought it was a bad idea to go there because the Jews in Judea had tried to stone Him. Then Jesus said, "Are there not twelve hours in the day? If anyone walks in the day, he does not stumble, because he sees the light of this world. But if anyone walks in the night, he stumbles, because the light is not in him" (John 11:9, 10, ESV). Jesus is the Light of the world, and although heading to Judea was dangerous, He knew He would not stumble because He was following what God the Father was directing Him to do.

I'm sure this statement left the disciples scratching their heads a bit, but the next thing Jesus said also left them confused. Jesus told them that Lazarus was asleep but that they would go wake him up. The disciples told Jesus that if he was sleeping that was a good sign because he was getting the rest he needed to get better. Then Jesus clearly told them that Lazarus had died. "And for your sake I am glad that I was not there, so that you may believe. But let us go to him" (verse 15, ESV).

This part of the story ends with Thomas, the one who was later labeled "doubting Thomas," who says, "Let us also go, that we may die with him" (verse 16, ESV). This was a commitment on Thomas's part, even if he did run for the hills with the rest of the disciples when Jesus was arrested. He was saying that if Jesus was going to head to Judea and face the Jews who wanted to stone and possibly kill Him, Thomas would go with Him.

After reading this, I wonder whether I trust God enough when things seem hopeless. Lazarus was sick, and Jesus didn't go to him immediately. Then Lazarus died. That seems hopeless, but Jesus had a plan. Am I willing to put my life on the line for God? The disciples were walking into a tense situation in Judea, but they were willing to follow Jesus because they loved Him.

—Ephraim Mura, junior

God's Timing

John 11:17–44

S ometimes in your life, you might feel as though time is just passing by. You might feel that you're alive but not really living or thriving. I know I have felt this before. Sometimes I become so accustomed to a routine that I don't even feel alive. It feels like the clock or calendar is slowly creeping by and that there isn't much to this life. This feeling especially strikes when you're stuck in the middle of a rough time that doesn't seem to have an end. You begin to feel hopeless and dead inside.

I'm guessing Mary and Martha felt like time dragged by when their brother died and Jesus was nowhere to be found. Mary and Martha were obviously heartbroken and questioned why Jesus was not there. Little did they know that Jesus would soon demonstrate God's power over death! This wasn't about their timeline. It was God's timeline, and God's timing is always right. In order for Jesus to demonstrate God's dominance over death, He waited until everyone was sure that Lazarus was dead beyond any doubt. His body had begun to decay and they had prepared it for burial.

Jesus' intentional delay does not mean He was insensitive to grief. He was deeply moved by the pain Mary and Martha were experiencing, and He wept with the family and friends gathered at Mary and Martha's home. While people may think He wept because of Lazarus, I think it was deeper than that. Jesus wept because death is still the biggest enemy in our lives. Far from being insensitive to death, Jesus came to take on the curse of death for us. His purpose in all of this was God's glory so that we might believe in God and in His power, through Jesus, to cancel our sin and give us new life forever in His presence.

Standing in front of the tomb with the stone rolled away, Jesus prayed, "Father, I thank you that you have heard me. I knew that you always hear me, but I said this on account of the people standing around, that they may believe that you sent me" (John 11:41, 42, ESV). And then, in a loud voice, He called out, "Lazarus, come out" (verse 43, ESV).

Even though you may feel hopeless inside, remember that God is always with you and His timing is always right on schedule. Trust Him to do the impossible because He is more than capable.

—Cameron Morrison, freshman

Finding Answers

Matthew 19:3–12; Mark 10:2–12

If you want to know all of the prepositions in the English language, you look in an English textbook. If you want to understand how to solve an algebraic formula, you consult a math textbook. If you want to learn about the theory of relativity, you check out a bunch of science books, and then you beat your head against a wall. Just kidding! The point is that we rely on all kinds of books to teach us about science, literature, math, and history, but what do we rely on for life decisions?

We should rely on the Bible, but most of us rely on the advice of our friends and family, past experiences, and our own feelings at the time. Sure, we may pray to God or look at what the Bible says on a certain topic, but then we tend to choose what feels comfortable. We rationalize our decisions and justify our actions when they go against God's Word. I'm not pointing fingers; we all do it. However, if we truly want to know the answers to life's toughest questions, we can find them in the Bible. God spells things out clearly, but He requires us to surrender, put away our selfish thoughts and ideas, and obey, trusting that our loving Father knows what is best.

With all of that said, let's look at the topic of divorce. I come from a divorced home, but Jesus spells out His view of marriage in Matthew 19. Once again, the sneaky Pharisees are trying to trap Jesus with one of their targeted questions. They ask Him whether a man should be allowed to divorce his wife. Jesus responds that the Bible says that when a man leaves his parents and gets married to his wife, the two become one, and no one should separate them. The Pharisees throw back this question, "Then why did Moses say in the law that a man could give his wife a written notice of divorce and send her away?" (verse 7).

To me, this is the kicker. Jesus says, "Moses permitted divorce only as a concession to your hard hearts, but it was not what God had originally intended" (verse 8). God allowed the provision for divorce because of hard, sinful hearts, not because it was what God wants. God works with our stubbornness, but we would be so much better off if we checked our attitude at the door and followed His plan. It may not be easy, but it will be worth it.

—Chaplain Kalie

Meeting With Jesus

" 'For I know the plans I have for you,' says the LORD. 'They are plans for good and not for disaster, to give you a future and a hope. In those days when you pray, I will listen. If you look for me wholeheartedly, you will find me' " (Jeremiah 29:11–13).

What spiritual principle can you take from this verse?

_____

_____

_____

_____

_____

What question would you like to ask God about this verse?

_____

_____

_____

_____

_____

What did you learn about God from this verse?

_____

_____

_____

_____

_____

Waiting to Bless You

Matthew 19:13–15; Mark 10:13–16; Luke 18:15–17

S ome people picture God as a big man dressed in white standing in heaven and glaring down at us, just waiting for us to make a mistake so He can punish us. When you read about Jesus blessing the children, this image seems laughable. What kind of God, who calls for little children to come to Him, would then turn around and punish them for making a mistake?

It was the disciples who were cranky and tried to prevent the kids from seeing Jesus, and the Bible says that Jesus was really unhappy about this. He told them, "Let the little children come to Me, and do not forbid them; for of such is the kingdom of God" (Mark 10:14, NKJV).

Lest we miss it, note that the best thing about this exchange is that God calls all of us His children, regardless of how old we are. He invites us to come to Him, and when we do, He can barely contain His happiness. We are God's children, and there is nothing more that God wants than to give us more than we can imagine. He wants to blow our minds with the kingdom of heaven. If we know this, why don't we run toward Him? The Creator of the universe is sitting there with open arms, ready to move mountains for us. All we have to do is run toward Him as fast as we possibly can.

Not only does Jesus love us, but He sticks up for us. Somehow I've grown up with the idea that Jesus was some soft, quiet man who took things as they came. But if you read this story, you will see a picture of a strong man who wasn't afraid to rebuke His followers for the sake of a bunch of children. He stood up for what was right even when it meant that He was misunderstood. He didn't back down from conflict, but He always spoke the truth in love.

Mark 10:16 says that Jesus "took them up in His arms, laid His hands on them, and blessed them" (NKJV). Jesus blessed the children then, and He blesses us now. What are some ways He showed you His love last week? Take the time to thank Him for His love.

—Alexander Nesmith, senior

Sacrifice

Matthew 19:16–30; Mark 10:17–31; Luke 18:18–30

S acrifice is the act of giving something up that we cherish in order to achieve or receive something else in life. The more you have, the harder it is to give things up. At least, this was the case for the rich young man found in Matthew 19:16–30.

A man comes to Jesus and asks what he needs to do to have eternal life. Jesus tells the man to keep the commandments, and the man asks Him which ones. Jesus lists some of the Ten Commandments, and the man responds that he has obeyed all of those commandments. So he asks, "What do I still lack?" (verse 20, ESV). Then Jesus says, "If you would be perfect, go, sell what you possess and give to the poor, and you will have treasure in heaven; and come, follow me" (verse 21, ESV). At that, the man turns away. The Bible says he was sad because he was rich. Giving all that up would be hard.

This isn't just about money because Abraham and Job were rich. It's more about sacrifice and being willing to obey and follow God even if it means giving up things that are important to you.

It was the summer after my freshman year that my parents asked whether I wanted to go canvassing. My older brother had spent two summers selling books, and they thought it would be good for me to spend a summer doing the same thing. They wanted me to do something productive with my life and share the gospel with other people. However, I wasn't sure I wanted to spend my entire summer walking around telling people about God. I thought about how I'd rather be home sleeping in. Like the rich young man, I faced a decision. Would I do my own thing? Or would I spend my summer working for God? I thought about how this experience could also strengthen my relationship with God. Finally, I surrendered my summer to God and headed off to California to sell books. I chose to serve others rather than waste my summer on my own pleasure.

What Jesus asks me to sacrifice will probably be different than what He asks you to sacrifice, but He does ask us to give Him our lives. Of course, the reward is going to be out of this world. "And everyone who has left houses or brothers or sisters or father or mother or children or lands, for my name's sake, will received a hundredfold and will inherit eternal life. But many who are first will be last, and the last first" (verses 29, 30, ESV).

—Michael Nanbu, junior

Where Are You Looking?

Hebrews 12:1, 2

My wife Joely and I were enjoying a beautiful vacation on the sandy beaches of the Dominican Republic when we decided to go parasailing one afternoon. We found a local company who promised a grand adventure we wouldn't forget. Little did I know what an adventure that would be! The time of our departure arrived, and we headed to the beach where a small motorboat picked us up and took us to a larger boat farther out in the water. We strapped on harnesses and prepared for our ride. As the boat took off, we climbed higher and higher until we were soaring above the clear blue water and coral reefs.

After enjoying our exhilarating adventure and safe landing, we boarded the small motorboat and headed back toward the beach. Joely and I were taking a selfie from the front of the boat, which later revealed the unexpected adventure.

Picture 1: Joely and I are smiling into the camera. The boat driver is visible behind us, gazing at the ocean scenes to his left.

Picture 2: I am smiling into the camera. The boat driver is still looking to his left. Joely is looking ahead of the boat; she is half-standing, half-pointing with a look of concern on her face.

Joely had caught sight of a small kayak with two paddlers in front of our boat. As in, right in the path of our boat. As in, we were about to hit the kayak. She yelled and pointed at the kayakers, and our driver snapped back to attention and turned the boat just in time. We spun around to see that our engine had cut one of their paddles in two pieces and the wake from the boat capsized the kayak. Thankfully, no one was hurt.

That day, God reminded me of the importance of keeping my eyes focused on Him and not getting distracted by the world. It's easy to be caught up in what is happening around us, and much of what goes on is good stuff. However, whatever takes us away from God needs to go. God promises to guide us through life and help us avoid the spiritual dangers that can get in our way.

I am a witness!

—Greg Hudson, senior pastor, GCA Church

It's Going to be OK

Matthew 20:17–19; Mark 10:32–34; Luke 18:31–34

I t's going to be OK," said the nurse as she adjusted my IV tube and taped it back on my arm. The hospital was quiet—too quiet for my liking. Hadn't it been just twenty minutes before when I was with my brothers and their friends playing ultimate tag? The beeping of a monitor across the hall brought me back to the present. I stared at the wall and silently felt the sticky pads placed all over my head. Why was I here? Then I remembered.

I had been playing tag with my brothers, Alex and Calvin, and their best friends, Woody and DW. During the most intense round, I had sprinted to get away from Alex. I slipped and hit my head on the wall. I blacked out. Then I remembered being held and hearing my dad yelling. After that, everything went dark. When I finally woke up, I was in the ER with my mom at one side of the bed and a lady in scrubs standing at the door with a clipboard.

My monitor beeped, and my mom looked at me and started to cry. I wanted her to hug me, fix me, and take me out of this weird place, but she didn't. The lady left, and a man in a big white coat came to my bedside and flashed a light in my eyes. When he did, I blacked out again.

When I finally came to the third time, I saw a nurse standing by me, shooting a clear liquid into my IV tube. My little mind raced, and I asked the question, "Am I going to die?" She jumped, probably because you don't often hear a third-grader ask that.

The nurse said, "No, it's going to be OK." My head ached, and my brain swam laps inside my skull, but right then I knew everything was going to be fine. Since that major concussion, I've broken bones from crazy volleyball saves, gotten sprains from soccer, had surgeries for torn tendons, pulled ligaments, and yes, sustained a couple of less serious concussions. Through it all, since that first concussion, I've always known that God is with me.

I can't imagine what it was like for Jesus to keep talking about how He was going to be killed. Sure, He talked about how He would be raised to life, but that still took a crazy amount of trust in His heavenly Father. I'm just glad Jesus believed God when He said it was going to be OK because if He hadn't gone through with dying on the cross, we'd all be lost, and then nothing would be OK. Whether it's a concussion, a math test, a challenging relationship, or anything else, God says, "It's going to be OK. Let Me help you. I've got this."

—Angelina Nesmith, freshman

Becoming Somebody Great
Matthew 20:20–28; Mark 10:35–45

Going to church both here in America and in my home country of Nigeria, I was taught about how God humbled Himself to give us salvation. This verse in particular was drilled into my head: "But whoever would be great among you must be your servant, and whoever would be first among you must be your slave, even as the Son of Man came not to be served but to serve, and to give his life as a ransom for many" (Matthew 20:26–28, ESV). If I'm honest, it got boring after hearing it for the umpteenth time.

However, a few years ago, as I was memorizing the book of Matthew for Bible Bowl, I came upon this verse once again, and I saw it in a different light. Reading it for myself, for probably the first time, I finally started to understand the meaning behind it, and I was filled with excitement. I realized that Jesus had come to this ragged, desolate earth for me. Me!

For a long time, I had dreamed of moving to America because I had always heard that it was the land of many opportunities. I'd thought to myself, *In America, I will become somebody.* Never had it crossed my mind that I already was somebody—a child of God. God Himself had come down to serve me, but instead of wanting to return the favor, I wanted to make myself great. In my desire for greatness, I hadn't learned to humble myself, to serve others, and to put their needs before mine.

When I read this verse, all of this finally dawned on me. In order for me to accomplish great things and become great, I have to put others before me. I have to stop being proud, and instead I need to seek God and try to please Him. Finally, I grasped the fact that through serving God, I would be great. I don't need to seek greatness here on earth because God has promised me great things in heaven, and that is better than anything I can ever hope to get here on earth.

Since understanding this, I have seen those great promises happen in my life. It's my prayer every day that with God's help I can serve others as Jesus did.

—Chizaram Gift Chiamaka Nnakwu, junior

Look for It

Psalm 118

About ten years ago, I convinced my husband that we should build a desk for our office. Neither one of us had done any woodworking, but I had found a plan online that had step-by-step instructions, so I figured, *How hard can it be?* Since completing that project, we've gone on to build a bookshelf, a bench, a laundry room storage system, an entertainment center with an electric fireplace, and two queen-sized beds. We've learned a lot since that first project, including the importance of picking good wood. You have to make sure the wood isn't warped or twisted. I often stand in the aisle of the home improvement store, turning the boards this way and that, inspecting them to make sure they are just right.

The key is knowing what to look for. The Pharisees thought they knew what they were looking for, but they didn't. They totally missed the mark. Psalm 118:22 predicted it: "The stone that the builders rejected has now become the cornerstone." Jesus is the Cornerstone, and the church is built on His life, death, and resurrection.

Paul shared this with the Ephesians: "So now you Gentiles are no longer strangers and foreigners. You are citizens along with all of God's holy people. You are members of God's family. Together, we are his house, built on the foundation of the apostles and the prophets. And the cornerstone is Christ Jesus himself. We are carefully joined together in him, becoming a holy temple for the Lord" (Ephesians 2:19–21).

A firm foundation means security, safety, and longevity. A weak foundation means instability, challenges, and issues. Jesus offers to be that firm foundation on whom we can build our lives. It's up to us to pick Him out of all the options and say, "That's the Cornerstone I want to build on."

Once we start building our lives on God and experiencing His presence, we will be able to say,

> You are my God, and I will praise you!
> You are my God, and I will exalt you!
> Give thanks to the Lord, for he is good!
> His faithful love endures forever (Psalm 118:28, 29).

—Chaplain Kalie

Meeting With Jesus

"And this world is fading away, along with everything that people crave. But anyone who does what pleases God will live forever" (1 John 2:17).

What did you learn about God from this verse?

_____

_____

_____

_____

_____

What stuck out to you in this reading?

_____

_____

_____

_____

_____

What question would you like to ask God about this verse?

_____

_____

_____

_____

_____

An Invitation to Something Better
Luke 19:1–10

M ost of us probably grew up singing about the wee little guy named Zacchaeus and how Jesus went to his house, but I doubt many of us understood the significance behind the invitation.

Zacchaeus was a chief tax collector and a thief. He was rich because he overcharged everyone who passed through Jericho to pay taxes on their merchandise or whatever else the government required. Somehow, he heard about Jesus and learned that Jesus was going to pass through Jericho. Something intrigued him about Jesus, so he followed the crowd to where Jesus was going to pass by, and because he was so short, he climbed a sycamore tree so that he could see above the crowd. As Jesus walked by, He looked up at Zacchaeus and told him to come down because He was coming over for dinner.

Zacchaeus is proof of God's crazy, unconditional love. Zacchaeus was a cheater. He definitely didn't stand out in the crowd in a positive way. In fact, the crowd complained when they heard Jesus say He was going to Zacchaeus's house. What they failed to recognize is that they were just as much sinners as Zacchaeus.

Jesus' kindness to Zacchaeus changed his life forever. How do we know? Well, that very day Zacchaeus said to Jesus, "Look, Lord, I give half of my goods to the poor; and if I have taken anything from anyone by false accusation, I restore fourfold" (Luke 19:8, NKJV). That's a lot of money!

Zacchaeus didn't take God's love for granted. He knew he was a sinner and had done wrong by stealing. In response to His love and forgiveness, Zacchaeus made changes in his life.

Do you take God's love and forgiveness for granted? I think many of us do. We know that God will always be there for us when we mess up, but it doesn't give us the right to do whatever we want just because we know we'll be forgiven. We need to be like Zacchaeus and recognize what a gift God's forgiveness truly is and let that change us.

—Stormie Mitchell, sophomore

Is Seeing Believing?

Matthew 20:29–34; Mark 10:46–52; Luke 18:35–43

F or a few seconds, close your eyes and feel around you. Use your hands to "see" your world. That is the life of a blind person. I know this is stating the obvious, but when you close your eyes, the objects around you are still there even though you can't see them. Blind people have to believe in what they can't see. They never get to see their surroundings. They have to feel their way around and trust that what they are feeling is a table, chair, or bed.

When Jesus walked this earth, He opened the eyes of a number of blind people. Just as the blind could not see the road or the trees or the city walls, they couldn't see Jesus. They had to believe that He was there.

As Jesus traveled, He drew a lot of attention. Whenever He entered the cities, many people called out to Jesus and huge crowds formed to hear what He had to say and witness His miracles. The blind people in the crowd could only hear what was going on around them. They could not see firsthand the miracles Jesus performed. They had to believe in His presence and power to heal. They knew that the opportunity to see the world around them might never come again, so they called out to Jesus to heal them.

One such man was blind Bartimaeus. He was sitting by the roadside begging when he heard that Jesus was nearby. He shouted, "Jesus, Son of David, have mercy on me!" (Mark 10:47, NIV). The people around him told him to be quiet, but he didn't listen to them and shouted even louder. Jesus heard his cry and called Bartimaeus to Him. Jesus then asked him what he wanted, and Bartimaeus replied that he wanted to see. "Go," Jesus said, "your faith has healed you" (verse 52, NIV). He could see immediately, and he followed Jesus down the road.

What if the blind man hadn't believed Jesus was walking along the road? What if he hadn't believed Jesus could help him? Faith is what healed the blind man. No matter what people said around him, he only fought harder to have an encounter with Jesus. So is seeing believing?

—Geoffrey Nkosi, sophomore

The Little Things
2 John 1:5

Last summer I worked at Camp Heritage. I had always heard about how life changing working at camp could be, but I went the whole summer wondering whether I was making a difference in anyone's life. Then something happened the last Friday night of the summer that reminded me that it's all about the small things.

We were getting ready for the Friday evening program, and the campfire director couldn't find the narrator for the play. I offered to go look for him. I looked all over the place, and I finally spotted him in the shadows. As I drew closer, I saw him wipe his eyes. I didn't know what was wrong, but something was definitely up. I went up, gave him a hug, and asked whether he was okay. I told him the campfire director was looking for him because the play was about to start. He said he would be right there, but I sensed that he really needed to talk instead of performing. I asked him whether he wanted to talk, and he said yes. I told him I'd take care of everything. I ran back to the campfire director and filled her in, and she said she'd get someone to cover his part, and then I headed back to hang out with this guy and listen.

I really didn't think anything about the exchange, but two days later I was talking to Miss Gina, the camp mom, and I learned about the difference I had been making all summer in the little ways. She has a porch with rocking chairs, and any staff member who is struggling or having a bad day can come and sit and talk to her. I stopped by to say hi, and she said, "You haven't been on my porch this summer, but your name has been here. You are a bright face. You are kind, and people notice that. If it weren't for you, the staff member you helped the other night told me he would've given up and quit. If it weren't for you, he would've left camp and thrown in the towel."

I'm not the type of person who needs a pat on the back and a bunch of compliments, but it was still nice to hear that I made a difference. I didn't feel like I was doing anything worthwhile, but Jesus calls us to love others. When we love as He loved, we experience joy, fulfillment, and a sense of purpose.

I am a witness!

—Alex Klisches, sophomore

249

Double or Nothing
Luke 19:11–27

How much money do you have? Maybe you have a bank account or maybe you only have a little cash in your wallet. Wherever you have your money stashed, what if you found out about a way to double it? Would you do it? Would you be willing to work to double your money? If it was not easy, would it be worth it?

Jesus was nearing Jerusalem, and His disciples and a lot of the crowd thought this was the moment He would declare Himself king. They thought that He was finally going to set up His kingdom. Jesus knew their thoughts because He told them one final parable before entering Jerusalem.

The parable featured a nobleman (Jesus) who was called away to a foreign country (heaven) where he was crowned king. He promised to return (Jesus' second coming), but he didn't tell his servants when he would return. Before the nobleman left, he gave his servants ten pounds of silver and told them to invest it. Some of the people (Pharisees and unbelievers) who worked for the nobleman didn't like him and didn't want him to be their king.

When the nobleman returned from his trip, he called his servants together and asked them about the money he had given them. The first and second servants doubled their money. The third servant had hidden the money and simply returned what he was given.

Jesus ended the parable with this conclusion: "To those who use well what they are given, even more will be given. But from those who do nothing, even what little they have will be taken away. And as for these enemies of mine who didn't want me to be their king—bring them in and execute them right here in front of me" (Luke 19:26, 27).

Each of us has talents and abilities that Jesus has given us to reach other people for Him. As we wait for His return, let's use our talents like the first two servants to help people get to know God. Then, when Jesus returns to this earth, He will be able to say to us, "You are a good servant. You have been faithful with the little I entrusted to you" (verse 17).

—Uche Nnakwu, freshman

The Heart of Giving

Matthew 26:6–13; Mark 14:3–9; Luke 7:36–50; John 12:1–11

What is the most valuable thing you own? Would you be willing to give it to God? If not, why not? If so, what would drive you to give up something so important?

Six days before the Passover, Jesus was in Bethany at the home of a Pharisee named Simon whom Jesus had healed of leprosy. As He was sitting there for dinner, Mary came in and poured a jar of expensive perfume on Jesus' feet.

The disciples were shocked, and Judas accused her of wasting the very expensive perfume when it could've been sold and the money given to the poor. (Judas didn't actually care about the poor, but he was the group's treasurer and a thief, so the money would've been in his pocket.) The perfume was so valuable that it cost a year's wages.

Jesus defended her actions. " 'Leave her alone,' said Jesus. 'Why are you bothering her? She has done a beautiful thing to me. The poor you will always have with you, and you can help them any time you want. But you will not always have me. She did what she could. She poured perfume on my body beforehand to prepare for my burial. Truly I tell you, wherever the gospel is preached throughout the world, what she has done will also be told, in memory of her' " (Mark 14:6–9, NIV).

Mary gave up a year's wages to buy a small token of her affection for Jesus. Jesus didn't tell her to do this. It was out of her love for Him that she freely gave back. Jesus makes this point in a quick parable He tells to Simon: "Two people owed money to a certain moneylender. One owed him five hundred denarii, and the other fifty. Neither of them had the money to pay him back, so he forgave the debts of both. Now which of them will love him more? . . . Therefore, I tell you, her many sins have been forgiven—as her great love has shown. But whoever has been forgiven little loves little" (Luke 7:41, 42, 47, NIV).

We are all sinners. We all deserve to die, but God sent Jesus to die in our place. He offers us salvation in return for our devotion to Him. The most valuable thing you own is your life. Are you willing to give it to God?

—David Jenkins, junior

Don't Hold Back

Matthew 21:1–9; Mark 11:1–10; Luke 19:29–40; John 12:12–16

As Jesus is approaching the Mount of Olives, He sends two of His disciples into the village and tells them to find a colt that has never been ridden. He tells them that they will find it tied up. Jesus says that if anyone asks what they are doing, they should simply say, "The Lord has need of it" (Luke 19:31, ESV).

The disciples do as they are told, and when they bring the colt to Jesus, they place their cloaks over its back, and Jesus rides on the colt down the Mount of Olives. As He heads down the road, the people spread their cloaks out on the road and wave palm branches. They shout, "Hosanna! Blessed is he who comes in the name of the Lord, even the King of Israel!" (John 12:13, ESV).

As the people are praising Jesus, some of the Pharisees come to Jesus and say, "Teacher, rebuke your disciples" (Luke 19:39, ESV). Jesus responds with, "I tell you, if these were silent, the very stones would cry out" (verse 40, ESV).

The people wanted Jesus to become their earthly king. They still didn't understand His mission—that He was coming to die for their sins. Even though they didn't fully get it, they knew He was worthy of praise, and they shouted for joy as He rode by.

God deserves our praise now just as much as He did then. We need to praise God always, even in the hard times. Sometimes praising can turn awful times into wonderful times as it did for Paul and Silas when they sang in jail (Acts 16). King David often talked about praising God, even when he was going through rough times. Psalm 118:1 says, "Oh give thanks to the Lord, for he is good; for his steadfast love endures forever!" (ESV).

When Jesus returns to this earth the second time, great rejoicing and praises just like those on the Mount of Olives will greet Him. The whole earth will praise Him because the battle between good and evil will finally be finished. Jesus is the true God, and nobody will be able to quiet the praises He deserves.

—Peyton Morrison, junior

Meeting With Jesus

"Faith shows the reality of what we hope for; it is the evidence of things we cannot see" (Hebrews 11:1).

What truth is God sharing in this passage?

What spiritual principle can you take from this verse?

How can you apply this verse to your own life?

Waiting by the Window
Luke 19:41–44

When I was a little girl, the highlight of my brother's and my day was waiting for our dad to get home. We always stood beside our living room window, watching for him to pull into the driveway. We ran back and forth to the window all day, waiting for the moment that he got home so that we could run up to him, hug him, and play with him before dinner. Every day featured the same routine. We anticipated our dad's arrival. We waited for him by the window and then ran to greet him when we saw his car pull in.

This is the same way that our heavenly Father wants us to wait for Him. We are definitely living in the end times. Our world is getting worse by the second, and people's hearts are growing colder and colder. There is only one positive thing that is coming out of all this turmoil—Jesus is coming back very soon! We need to practice living out each day as if Jesus were coming at any moment. This is our temporary home; we do not belong here. Jesus can't force us to be ready. We have to choose.

As Jesus approached Jerusalem on the donkey, He stopped and looked over the city and cried. His heart broke because many people had rejected Him and His message of love, hope, and forgiveness. Many people would be lost because they had pushed away the Savior.

We bash on the Pharisees a lot for being such ignorant and hateful people, but we act like the Pharisees a lot more than we would like to admit. We are ignorant people when we don't spend time with God in prayer and don't study His Word. Just as I waited for my dad to come home each day when I was a little girl, we need to anticipate Jesus' return with excitement. We need to keep God at the forefront of our minds and constantly remind ourselves that our goal is heaven, not this earth. We must all sit patiently and wait at the window for our Lord and Savior, Jesus Christ, to take us home.

—Camila Oleaurre, senior

Auction Block Church

Matthew 21:12–16; Mark 11:15–18; Luke 19:45–48

I t was a beautiful Sabbath morning. The air was fresh and crisp, the sun was up, and the birds were singing. After the opening hymns, the children's story, the offering, and all the other things that happen in a church service, it was finally time for the sermon. The pastor stood up. He was about to walk to the pulpit when a deacon jogged right up to the front. The pastor looked confused, but he sat back down. *Maybe he has to make some sort of announcement,* he thought.

However, instead of making an announcement, the deacon reached into his pocket and pulled out a checkbook. He proceeded to look up at the congregation and say, "This morning I saw a blue and white 2007 Mustang GT for sale in our church parking lot. I wouldn't normally do this in church, but I need a new car to get me and my family to church. So would the owner of this car please come up and discuss a price for this car? I know it's Sabbath and all, but I figured it's pretty much justified since it's for religious purposes."

Before the pastor could regain his composure and stop what was happening, the head elder stood up. He declared that it was his car, and he proceeded to walk up to the pulpit to discuss the price with the deacon. At this moment, everyone seemed confused and unsure of what to do, but most people went with it and started giving advice to the deacon and the elder. Some even started offering bids for the car! A price was about to be reached when the pastor stood up and yelled, "Stop!"

Now, I'm just going to leave the story at that. Assume whatever you want about the ending. This may seem extreme, but is it any different from what was going on in the temple? Jesus shows up in Jerusalem and heads to the temple. Once inside, He finds people buying and selling animals and exchanging money. Don't get me wrong; it's OK to sell things. However, they were doing it in God's temple! The disrespect is unbelievable.

Jesus turns over the tables and drives the sellers out of the temple. Then He begins to teach the people. He says, "My Temple will be called a house of prayer for all nations. But you have changed it into a 'hiding place for thieves' " (Mark 11:17, ERV).

How do you treat God's house? You may not be selling anything, but do you treat it like a holy house of prayer, or is it just another building you sit in like your house or school?

—Miles Ondap, freshman

A Test of Faith

Hebrews 11:1

Georgia-Cumberland Academy (GCA) costs a lot of money to attend, and the summer before my sophomore year, my family didn't have that type of money. My dad warned me that it wasn't looking good and that he didn't know whether I'd be able to attend GCA in the fall.

Every day I woke up and asked my dad how the money was looking. I regret the days I didn't first talk to God about it and then go ask my dad, but I was focused on the money. Every morning I got the same response: "It's not looking good. We have just enough to pay the bills." God was providing for our family's needs, but I didn't know whether He was going to take care of my need to go to school at GCA. I was scared. I didn't want to go to a different school. After just one year, GCA had become like family to me.

Every single day I woke up and asked the same question, and every single day my dad gave me the same response. Summer slowly slipped away. The closer I got to school starting, the more stressed I became. I didn't know what the future held, and that made me nervous.

The countdown kept going. I woke up the Sunday of registration with a smile on my face. I figured God must have pulled through. I went and asked my dad again, "How's the money looking today?" I asked. "Still the same," he said. I went to my room. I felt defeated. Then I had a thought. What if God had different plans for my year? What if He wanted me at a different school? I couldn't tell God to hurry up because then He would just slow down.

School started at GCA without me. Monday came and went. Tuesday came and went. So did Wednesday and Thursday. As the first week of school ticked by, I began to pray a different prayer: "God, I'm giving it all to You. You can have GCA. If You don't want me to go back, I'll go where You want me to go."

On Thursday night, my dad called me into his office. He had a big smile on his face. I, on the other hand, didn't want to get my hopes up. Then he said these words: "Pack your bags, son. You're going to GCA tomorrow." I jumped out of my chair. I thought maybe he was playing a prank on me, but he said he was serious. I couldn't believe it! God had heard my prayers.

The next day as we drove to GCA, my dad told me something I'll never forget. "Have you thought about the word *testimony*? You can't have a testimony without a test."

I am a witness!

—Geoffrey Nkosi, sophomore

Defending God
John 12:20–36

Imagine someone talking behind your back, but a friend of yours hears the conversation. How would you feel if this friend didn't say anything to defend you or maybe even pretended to agree with the mean things being said about you? If you found out that they didn't stand up for you, it would probably hurt quite a bit. You might even wonder why this person would claim to be your friend since when they weren't around you, they didn't act like it.

The same rules we apply to our friendships should also be applied to our relationship with Jesus. If someone has the wrong idea about God, it is our mission to help them understand who He really is. We aren't to sit idly and let criticism be thrown at the One who created us. As Christians, we must lift God up and show the world His true character, which is what Jesus did while He was on this earth. He lived to show us the Father.

John 12:20–36 talks about some Greeks who came to the Passover looking for Jesus, and as always, as these foreigners listened to Jesus speak, He glorified God in what He said. In fact, Jesus said, "Father, bring glory to your name" (verse 28), as He talked about His impending death. God has infinite amounts of power, but He still requires His people to testify about Him just as Jesus did throughout the Gospels.

There was a time in my own life I wish could do over because I didn't defend God when I should have. My cousin and I were talking about the death of her dog and how mad she was at God. Interestingly, prior to this conversation, a massive tornado had swept through Rowlett, Texas, taking my cousin's house with it. Everything was destroyed! It was a miracle from God that my cousin, her husband, and their daughter, along with their pets, had survived. Not long after, their beloved dog passed away. She could not understand why God would allow her precious Harley to survive the tornado only to take her away shortly after. My cousin stood there in tears as she blamed God for this tragedy.

I knew she had the wrong idea about God, but I said nothing in His defense. In that moment I needed to tell her that God doesn't bring about pain and misery; Satan does. I wish I had stood up for God, but I didn't. When situations like this come up, we need to stand behind what we say we believe in. We can't call ourselves Christians if we turn down the opportunity to glorify God.

—Allison Ormes, junior

The Faith Connection

Matthew 21:20–22; Mark 11:20–26

No matter how unadulterated your eyesight might be, without the ultimate Source of light, your sight will be doomed to fail. Your choices will be faulty. Your direction will be misguided. Your decisions will lead you astray.

In contrast, through faith, prayer, and a connection to the Light, you will see the truth. You will find love. You will find security. You will find happiness.

In the week leading up to Jesus' death, He said, "My light will shine for you just a little longer. Walk in the light while you can, so the darkness will not overtake you. Those who walk in the darkness cannot see where they are going. Put your trust in the light while there is still time; then you will become children of the light" (John 12:35, 36).

If we want to walk in the Light, we have to have faith in the Light. We have to believe that what He says is true. There is immeasurable power in faith. Jesus said, "Truly I tell you, if you have faith and do not doubt, not only can you do what was done to the fig tree, but also you can say to this mountain, 'Go, throw yourself into the sea,' and it will be done. If you believe, you will receive whatever you ask for in prayer" (Matthew 21:21, 22, NIV).

Now, I don't believe God is saying that if you ask for a new car with enough faith, you'll get it. But when we ask for His presence in our lives and His guidance, He won't turn us away. When we ask for His help to do impossible tasks or withstand temptation, He won't abandon us. We can believe His promises.

Jesus wants to set us free from whatever is holding us back. He wants to shine a light on the areas of our lives that we try to keep hidden in darkness, but it's only through His light that we can find freedom. Through His love and His light shining in our hearts, He desires to awaken our thirst for Him and only Him. Today He invites us to know Him. To believe Him. To trust Him. To have faith that what He says is true.

What can you pray for today, believing in faith that God hears you and will work things out according to His plan? His light is shining on you today. He wants to hear from you.

—Evangelina Pasos, junior

Don't Miss It

Isaiah 7:10–25

Y ou're at the age where you have to start paying attention to signs. Either you're getting ready to start driving or you already are, which means that you have to pay attention to what the road signs tell you. Most of them, like the red, octagonal stop sign, are pretty self-explanatory, but you still have to pay attention to them to know what is going on. If you get ready to turn on a road that has a sign at the entrance that says, "No Outlet" or "Dead End," you shouldn't be surprised when you have to turn around at the end.

Beyond road signs, there are billboards, sale announcements, and campaign signs that pump information at us while we drive down the road. Signs are great for educating us about a business or sale or person, but they are useless if we don't read them.

The Jews had plenty of signs indicating that Jesus was the Messiah. Beyond His dedication in the temple as a baby, the dove descending from heaven at Jesus' baptism, His many miracles, and His own declarations, the Old Testament pointed to His coming. Isaiah 7:14 says, "Therefore the Lord Himself will gives you a sign: Behold, the virgin shall conceive and bear a Son, and shall call His name Immanuel" (NKJV). This wasn't the only prophecy they were familiar with, and yet they still missed the signs.

We look at the Jews and wonder how they could have been so dense. How could they have missed it? But are we any different? Jesus gave the disciples signs of His second coming, and He told them, and us, to be ready. Matthew 24 and 25 are filled with signs and parables about His coming and what we need to do to be ready. Do we know the signs? That's the first question. The second question is, Are we willing to obey them?

A stop sign is only effective if we obey it. We can see the stop sign and choose to blow through the intersection. Of course, we take the risk of getting a ticket or crashing into someone, but it's our choice to see it and not obey it. The same goes for the signs of Jesus' second coming. We may see them, but do we do something about them? Do we choose to act on what we see and get ready? Or are we simply ignoring the inevitable and running the stop sign?

—Chaplain Kalie

Meeting With Jesus
Hebrews 12:1–3

You are shooting hoops in the gym, but this is not your day. You are usually a good shot, but every time you release the ball, it bounces off the backboard or rim. Nothing is going through the net. With each missed shot, you are getting more and more frustrated.

What's the point? you yell inside your head. *I am a lousy basketball player! This is pointless. I'm clearly not getting any better, even with all of this practice!*

"Having an off day?" a voice asks from behind you.

You turn around wondering whether it is your coach, but it's Jesus. He picks up another ball on the court and takes a shot. Nothing but net. You want to scream because He makes it look so easy. He grabs the ball and takes another shot. This time He misses.

"This feels pointless," you say while He shoots. "I come to the gym every day and practice, but I'm not getting any better, which is really annoying!"

"What's more important? Winning or improving your skills? You can't tell Me you aren't getting any better with all of your practice. I've been watching you. It's slow progress, but it's progress," Jesus says.

"I know that the right answer is improving, but I want to be the best so that our team can dominate on the court," you respond.

"If you were the best, would you practice? And if you didn't practice, would you really be the best? The writer of Hebrews says perseverance is much more important than perfection," Jesus says. "So what do you think about your ball game now in light of perseverance?"

Take some time to talk to Jesus or write down your response to His question.

Read the passage for the day and think about the promise it offers or what it tells you about God.

If you were to talk about these verses with Jesus, what would you say? What would you ask Him?

Doing Right Versus Sounding Right
Matthew 21:28–32

Jesus had a knack for teaching people the truth through stories. It was His little way of having people realize the truth on their own.

Jesus uses this tactic in the parable of the two sons in Matthew 21:

"What do you think? A man had two sons. And he went to the first and said, 'Son, go and work in the vineyard today.' And he answered, 'I will not,' but afterward he changed his mind and went. And he went to the other son and said the same. And he answered, 'I go, sir,' but did not go. Which of the two did the will of his father?" They said, "The first." Jesus said to them, "Truly, I say to you, the tax collectors and the prostitutes go into the kingdom of God before you. For John came to you in the way of righteousness, and you did not believe him, but the tax collectors and the prostitutes believed him. And even when you saw it, you did not afterward change your minds and believe him" (verses 28–32, ESV).

Jesus did not ask which of the sons was good to the father. Instead, He asked which of the sons did what the father wanted. It is clear that the first son did what the father wanted even if it took him a bit to come around.

We are all sinners, but our actions show where our hearts are. The first son did what his father wanted in the end. He obeyed. The second son said he would obey, but he had no intention of following through. Maybe he just wanted to appease his father or get him off his back. Regardless, he lied to his father.

In the end, it all comes down to our motives. Are we repentant and willing to do what God asks, or do we pretend that we want to follow Him and then do our own thing? Jesus wants us to know that doing the right thing is more important than sounding right. To God, faith and obedience are more pleasing than self-righteous behavior. God honors faith rather than false actions. He wants us to know that what we say we will do and what we claim to believe mean nothing without action to follow it up.

—Raina Park, freshman

Story Time

Matthew 21:33–41; Mark 12:1–9; Luke 20:9–16

A parable is a story. Jesus told parables to help people understand what He was trying to teach. He used many farming illustrations because that is what people could relate to in that culture. Let's look at the parable of the tenants from a modern perspective.

There was a businessman who started a successful tech company in Silicon Valley. He purchased a large building, complete with a state-of-the-art security system to protect his product. Once things were up and running, he advertised the company and hired a board of people to run it. He then moved to another part of the country.

Per the contract agreement, the owner was to collect a portion of the profit from the company once a year. One year, he sent a few of his personal employees to collect payment. However, the board members grabbed the employees and beat one, killed another, and tortured the third. Instead of calling the police or the FBI, the owner sent more of his employees. Even though there was a larger group, the board members treated the second group of employees the same way. For some reason, the owner still didn't call the cops. This time he sent his own son as a last resort. He reasoned that they would respect his own flesh and blood. However, the board members figured that if they killed the son, they could take over the company, so they murdered him.

At the end of the story, Jesus asked the crowd what the owner would do in response. They responded that the owner would make sure the board members received what they deserved—death. He would replace them with people who really cared about his company and were willing to pay him what he was owed.

It's easy to figure out that God is the owner and the prophets are the employees. The Jewish leaders are the board members. God sent prophets to work among the people, but the people dismissed what they said and killed them. Then God sent His own Son, but that still didn't work. The Jewish leaders and many people didn't respect God's Son either, and they eventually killed Him. The result? Those who reject God and kill His Son will be lost because of their actions and their refusal to believe. They will not be a part of God's kingdom. God is looking for people who will listen to Him and obey Him. Which category do you fall into?

—Nnamdi Onyeije, senior

Good Plans

Jeremiah 29:11

When I graduated from college, I had my future planned out. I was going to land a great job in public relations, meet and marry the man of my dreams, and start a family, all before I turned thirty. Three years later, I was discontented with my work in the corporate world, I was single again for the second time in two years, and I was approaching my late twenties with little chance on the horizon of starting a family by thirty.

My initial plan seemed like a good one when I mapped it out. Surely God would like it too! It had all the elements of a happy, fulfilled life that could be used to serve and glorify Him. Where had I gone wrong?

I went back over my plan in detail, trying to find some flaw, some clue as to where my life went off track. After several months of frustration and a number of failed first dates, I threw up my hands in defeat, figuratively speaking.

"I don't have the answers, Lord," I prayed. "I don't know what I'm supposed to do with my life or who I'm supposed to spend it with. You're going to have to bring the right person and the right purpose to my life. I surrender my plans and my will to You. Amen."

An overwhelming sense of peace filled my heart. God didn't give me answers right away, but He reassured me in many small ways of His care and provision in my life. He also taught me daily lessons about trusting Him with the unknown and seeking His will before my own.

A few months after praying that prayer of surrender, I met and fell in love with the most wonderful man I've ever known. Being with him was like coming home. Several months after that meeting, I was also able to leave my corporate job and pursue a graduate degree in school counseling.

I'm now married to that wonderful man, and I work at GCA, which allows me to use both my communication and counseling skills in a unique, fulfilling, and God-honoring way.

Is there a secret formula to living a surrendered life? Unfortunately, no. Life is still messy sometimes, but I can rest in the knowledge that God's plans are better than my own. His good plans give me hope for my future, because that is what He promises in His Word, and God always keeps His promises.

I am a witness!

—Jodi Steele, marketing assistant

Broken or Crushed

Matthew 21:42–44; Mark 12:10, 11; Luke 20:17, 18

I magine that ever since you were a kid you've known what profession you wanted to pursue. Since the time you entered elementary school, you've worked hard, knowing that one day you would be at the top of your field. Everywhere you've gone, you've always risen to the top, and now your hard work has paid off. A prestigious university has offered you a full scholarship, and now you are studying there, working harder than you've ever worked before. Finally, after many years of study, you graduate, once again at the top of your class. Finding a job will be easy; everybody wants you. Sure enough, not long after graduation you land yourself a job in a high-level position at a prominent company. Years go by and you become a master of what you do—or so you think.

Imagine now that another man with a mere high school education comes along and starts telling you and others in your field that the fundamental ideas of what you've studied your whole life are flawed and some are altogether wrong.

In the eyes of the Pharisees, this is exactly what happened when Jesus arrived on the scene. They viewed themselves as superior to everyone else, including Jesus, in the area of religion. The Pharisees chose not to believe Him due to their pride. They weren't going to let a Man who didn't go through rigorous years of study in their schools tell them about religion even if deep down they knew He was right. Not only did they reject Him, but they also killed Him for doing the work of God. Of course, all of this fulfilled prophecy.

Psalm 118 talks about the stone that the builders rejected, and Jesus references that in Matthew 21: "Have you never read in the Scriptures: 'The stone which the builders rejected Has become the chief cornerstone. This was the Lord's doing, And it is marvelous in our eyes'? Therefore I say to you, the kingdom of God will be taken from you and given to a nation bearing the fruits of it. And whoever falls on the stone will be broken; but on whomever it falls, it will grind him to powder" (verses 42–44, NKJV).

Jesus is the Cornerstone. He is the foundation of our faith. If we believe, we will be broken and become who He wants us to be. Those who don't believe will be crushed. The Rock doesn't change. The difference is how we approach Him.

—Martin Phillips, junior

Invitation to Enter

Matthew 22:1–14

I'm assuming you've attending a wedding at some point, but if you haven't, maybe you've attending a banquet or another formal event. Once you accepted the invitation, did you think about your suit or dress, or did you just throw on a pair of running shorts and a T-shirt? My guess is that you put at least a little thought into what you were going to wear.

In today's parable, Jesus is talking about the kingdom of heaven and how it is like a king who invited people to come to his son's wedding banquet. When the king's palace was ready for his guests, he sent his servants to tell the people who had been invited to come. However, all the people the king had invited declined his invitation, and some even killed the king's servants. The king was enraged and sent his army to kill the murderers and burn their city.

Then the king told his other servants to go out into the streets and gather people, the good and the bad, to come to his wedding banquet because the ones he had invited did not deserve to come. The servants did as they were told, and the banquet hall began to fill up with guests. However, as everyone was entering the palace, the king noticed one man who had entered was not wearing appropriate wedding clothes. The king asked him why he was not wearing the proper attire, but the man didn't say anything, so the king threw him out.

Jesus has invited everyone to spend eternity with Him. He has given us the free gift of salvation. However, He does ask us to wear the proper clothes for a wedding (Matthew 22:11). The proper attire includes our obedience to God's commands and our love for Him and others. Our faith and relationship with God are what matters. The gift of eternal life is free, but when we accept the invitation, God asks us to do something in return. He asks us to put some effort into preparing for heaven.

At the end of the parable, Jesus says, "For many are called, but few are chosen" (verse 14). You've been called. What will you do with that calling?

—Jenna Peel, sophomore

Giving Back What Is His

Matthew 22:15–22; Mark 12:13–17; Luke 20:20–26

God has made each of us special with unique talents that can be used for His purposes. Do we use our gifts to glorify Him, the One who gave us the ability to do what we do? Or do we use our gifts for our own gain? I respect people who use their special gifts to bring glory to God. There are too many to name, both famous and not famous, but one example is Tim Tebow.

Tim, a former NFL player and current MLB player, is very open about his relationship with God and has used his platform to tell people about his faith. He talks about his faith and the importance of using his talents for God in his book *Through My Eyes*. He grew up in the Philippines and often visited schools and villages to tell people about God. He played football in college and was later drafted to play for the Denver Broncos. Tim is also a group leader for the Fellowship of Christian Athletes, which encourages players to stick up for their faith and to live by Christian standards.

Not only has he used his voice to tell others about Christ, but he also now supports more than forty evangelists working in the Philippines. Speaking to a crowd of twenty thousand on Easter Sunday, he said, "Regardless of what happens, I still honor my Lord and Savior Jesus Christ, because at the end of the day, that's what's important, win or lose. . . . We need to get back to one nation under God, and be role models for kids."*

When I see people using their talents and financial resources for good and not for worldly reasons, I am reminded of what Jesus said to the Pharisees when they were trying to trap Him, again, by asking Him a trick question. They asked him whether they should pay taxes to Caesar, and Jesus' response was this: "Give back to Caesar what is Caesar's and to God what is God's" (Mark 12:17, NIV). When we give our talents to God and use our abilities to glorify Him, we are really giving back to Him what He has given us.

—Cherise Piotrowski, freshman

---

* "Tim Tebow Speaker Information," Christian Speakers 360, accessed May 10, 2019, https://www.christianspeakers360.com/speaker/tim-tebow.php.

Meeting With Jesus

"For the LORD is good. His unfailing love continues forever, and his faithfulness continues to each generation" (Psalm 100:5).

What did you learn about God from this verse?

_____

_____

_____

_____

_____

_____

How should we relate to others based on this passage?

_____

_____

_____

_____

_____

What can you share with others from this verse?

_____

_____

_____

_____

_____

Do You Believe?

Matthew 22:23–33; Mark 12:18–27; Luke 20:27–38

Has anyone ever tried to sidetrack you by focusing on the nitty-gritty instead of looking at the big picture? Or maybe you've tried this ploy with your parents, trying to take the focus off you and direct it somewhere else. Either way, it's a common tactic that some people use when they don't want to address the heart of the matter. And, surprise, surprise, we find the Sadducees doing this very thing in Mark 12.

The group came to Jesus and challenged Him, politely asking Him this question:

> "Teacher, Moses wrote to us that if a man's brother dies, and leaves his wife behind, and leaves no children, his brother should take his wife and raise up offspring for his brother. Now there were seven brothers. The first took a wife; and dying, he left no offspring. And the second took her, and he died; nor did he leave any offspring. And the third likewise. So the seven had her and left no offspring. Last of all the woman died also. Therefore, in the resurrection, when they rise, whose wife will she be? For all seven had her as wife" (verses 19–23, NKJV).

The Sadducees were sophisticated, powerful, and educated religious leaders who wanted to prove their point that the resurrection of the dead didn't exist. Jesus didn't focus on the nitty-gritty. He went to the heart of the matter— whether they believed in God or not. These men had studied the Scriptures, yet they were blind to the truth. Jesus touched on the answer they were seeking by reminding them that there will be no marriage in heaven, and then He addressed the issue for their unbelief. He said, "I am the God of Abraham, the God of Isaac, and the God of Jacob . . . not the God of the dead, but the God of the living. You are therefore greatly mistaken" (verses 26, 27, NKJV).

Jesus knew the Scriptures. He knew the men's intentions and instead of letting them twist the truth by twisting the details He went to the heart of the matter. He reminded them who the King of the universe is and where they should put their trust. They were mistaken because they weren't focused on God.

Where is your focus? Do you believe?

—Florence Phillips, sophomore

What's Most Important?

Matthew 22:34–40; Mark 12:28–34; Luke 20:39, 40

Stories that hold our attention are often based on some type of conflict. Whether fact or fiction, we gravitate toward stories that feature an underdog who is up against a challenge. That obstacle might be another person, a group of people, or an organization that stands in the way of all that is right and good. We cheer when the hero makes some headway, and we cringe when the enemy takes a swing and lands a blow. We get angry when the opposition lies, and we celebrate when the hero lets a good one-liner fly.

I know you might not view these verses as a sassy comeback that puts the opposition in its place, but it is the foundation of our faith, and in the context of the conversation, it is a fighting response to what the Pharisees set up as another trap.

The Pharisees got wind of the conversation Jesus had with the Sadducees about the resurrection, so they called a meeting to discuss what question they could ask Him to silence Him and give them the upper hand. This is what they came up with: "Teacher, which is the most important commandment in the law of Moses?" (Matthew 22:36). Maybe they figured that there was no way for Him to pick one without leaving out another that they could throw back at Him as being more important. They thought they had Him, but the joke was on them.

Jesus responded: " 'You must love the Lord your God with all you heart, all your soul, and all your mind.' This is the first and greatest commandment. A second is equally important: 'Love your neighbor as yourself.' The entire law and all the demands of the prophets are based on these two commandments" (verses 37–40). Mic drop.

Jesus summed up the Ten Commandments and every other law under the sun in two categories—loving God and loving others. Summing it up doesn't make it any easier to follow, but it does put the focus in the right place. Instead of emphasizing a bunch of individual laws and regulations, it reminds us to simply keep our eyes on God, love Him, and let that love spill over onto everyone we meet.

How are you loving God and the people around you?

—Chaplain Kalie

The Impossible Made Possible

Psalm 91:11

When I was growing up, my dad traveled quite a bit for his work, which left my mom to take care of my three siblings and me for a week at a time. This was one of those weeks. My mom had piled all four of us kids in the car, and we headed out to run errands.

I was sitting in the back seat with my younger brother when all of a sudden our car stopped. I don't remember whether we ran out of gas or the car had some type of mechanical issue, but I do remember what happened next.

My mom did her best to get the car off the road, but the car didn't coast far enough to make it to the shoulder. We came to a standstill in the turning lane in the middle of busy suburban traffic. Needless to say, my mom was pretty stressed. She had four kids in the car, and she had no idea what was wrong with the vehicle.

As we were trying to figure out what to do, one of us spotted an auto shop up the road. My mom told us all to pray, and then she suggested that we push the car up the small hill to the auto shop. I must admit that I thought it was an impossible task. I was around nine years old at the time, and I didn't think our little muscles would be able to move the car up the hill. My mom told us all to take our places around the car. She pushed from the driver's side door so that she could also steer the car. My brother and I ended up at the back of the vehicle with my other two siblings on the right side of the car.

It seemed impossible, but just as we began to push, I saw two cars stop. A man from each of the cars got out and came over to the back of our vehicle and helped me and my brother push. Slowly but surely, we made it up the small hill to the auto shop. As quickly as the two men came, they left.

Later that evening while we told my dad the story, I mentioned how grateful I was that those two men had helped us push the car to the shop. I received puzzled looks from my mom and siblings. Nobody had seen the two men except for me. It was then that we realized I had seen two angels help us when we needed it most. God had answered our prayers and provided.

I am a witness!

—Kaleb Leeper, Bible/math teacher

Actions Speak Pretty Loud

Matthew 23:1–12; Mark 12:38–40; Luke 20:45–47

Have you ever heard the phrase, "Do what I say, not what I do"? There are a bunch of memes around this saying. One of them shows a kid asking his dad whether he can play a video game. His dad asks the kid whether he's done his homework. Then the kid asks the dad whether he's cleaned out the garage. The last scene of the cartoon shows both the dad and kid sitting on the couch playing video games.

The Pharisees fell into this trap, and Jesus called them out on it. He said, "Do not do what they do, for they do not practice what they preach. They tie up heavy, cumbersome loads and put them on other people's shoulders, but they themselves are not willing to lift a finger to move them. Everything they do is done for people to see" (Matthew 23:3–5, NIV).

The Pharisees corrupted God's laws and oppressed their fellow people. They had God's teachings, but they took them out of context and used them against those who couldn't study for themselves. People will always corrupt God's Word. They did during Bible times, and there are people today who misrepresent what God says in the Bible to mean what they want it to. That's why we have to rely on God and have a personal relationship with Him. In order to know the truth, we have to study His Word for ourselves and take our relationship with Him seriously.

Jesus reminded everyone listening that they couldn't rely on the religious leaders; they had to rely on God. "But you are not to be called 'Rabbi,' for you have one Teacher, and you are all brothers. And do not call anyone on earth 'father,' for you have one Father, and he is in heaven. Nor are you to be called instructors, for you have one Instructor, the Messiah. The greatest among you will be your servant. For those who exalt themselves will be humbled, and those who humble themselves will be exalted" (verses 8–12, NIV).

What do our actions say about us? The Pharisees didn't practice what they preached. As Christians, are we practicing what we preach? Are we modeling what we say we believe in?

—Ryan Reese, sophomore

A Pretty Bad Nickname
Matthew 23:13–24

In today's passage, Jesus brings to light a bunch of negative stuff the Pharisees do. Starting in verse 13, Jesus says, "What sorrow awaits you teachers of religious law and you Pharisees. Hypocrites! For you shut the door of the Kingdom of Heaven in people's faces. You won't go in yourselves, and you don't let others enter either." The verses continue with pretty much the same message, and then we come to this verse: "What sorrow awaits you teachers of religious law and you Pharisees. Hypocrites! For you are careful to tithe even the tiniest income from your herb gardens, but you ignore the more important aspects of the law—justice, mercy, and faith. You should tithe, yes, but do not neglect the more important things. Blind guides! You strain your water so you won't accidentally swallow a gnat, but you swallow a camel!" (verses 23, 24).

The Pharisees were too busy focusing on the tiniest of details of their made-up laws, such as paying tithe on the herbs from their gardens, when the bigger picture was right there in front of them. They were so focused on how things looked or their cultural rules that they were leaving God out of the whole picture. They weren't worshiping Him; they were worshiping their laws. Even worse, they were doing everything in God's name, thus confusing everyone who listened to them. They were leading the people down the wrong path.

We have a lot to learn from the Pharisees about what not to do. Instead of focusing on the world and unimportant things, we need to focus on God. We need to make sure we are worshiping Him and not ourselves or anyone else. Even when we don't mean to, sometimes we can get too caught up in all the mess of the world. Even when we think we're giving everything to God, we might be too distracted by all the little details that will never even matter.

If Jesus were to visit your church, would He say, "What sorrow awaits you, you hypocrite"? Or would He say, "Well done, good and faithful servant"?

—Ava Ramirez, freshman

The Names of God

Isaiah 9:1–7

I've always loved music, and when I was about five years old, my parents took me to hear George Frideric Handel's *Messiah*. It was a really long performance for a little kid, but my mom said I sat there mesmerized the whole time. Years later, when I was a junior in high school, I sat through hour upon hour of rehearsals learning the *Messiah* and finally presenting it in concert around Christmastime.

The words to my favorite song, "For Unto Us a Child Is Born," come straight from Isaiah 9:6:

> For to us a child is born,
>> to us a son is given;
> and the government shall be upon his shoulder,
>> and his name shall be called
> Wonderful Counselor, Mighty God,
>> Everlasting Father, Prince of Peace (ESV).

Think about those names for a minute.

Wonderful Counselor—Jesus is our guide and cheerleader. He is here to give us advice and to help us along the way. He wants to walk beside us and encourage us through life.

Mighty God—He is also God. He is powerful and has all authority at His fingertips. He is King of the universe. Nothing can stop Him.

Everlasting Father—He is our parent. He loves us with the everlasting love of a devoted father. He will never leave us.

Prince of Peace—Jesus comforts us and gives us peace. He offers us solitude in a chaotic world. Spending time with Him helps us find joy in the midst of sadness.

We can describe Jesus in a number of other ways, with a number of different names, but the picture that Isaiah paints in this prophecy of the Messiah is a complete image of Jesus' mission and His love for humanity.

Which of these names means the most to you, and why? Which name do you need to hold on to right now based on what you're going through?

—Chaplain Kalie

Meeting With Jesus

" 'Bring all the tithes into the storehouse so there will be enough food in my Temple. If you do,' says the LORD of Heaven's Armies, 'I will open the windows of heaven for you. I will pour out a blessing so great you won't have enough room to take it in! Try it! Put me to the test!' " (Malachi 3:10).

What spiritual principle can you take from this verse?

_____

_____

_____

_____

_____

What question would you like to ask God about this verse?

_____

_____

_____

_____

_____

How can you apply this verse to your own life?

_____

_____

_____

_____

_____

Saying It Like It Is
Matthew 23:25–36

It would be unreasonable to have someone who isn't proficient in mathematics teach Algebra II. It would be just as preposterous for a religion teacher not to know the Bible. However, that's kind of what we find with the Pharisees. They were teachers of the law, but they didn't get it. They had memorized every detail of the law, but they didn't understand its principles, leaving them wholly unqualified to teach anyone.

Jesus made it very clear that although the Pharisees looked one way on the outside, they were completely different on the inside. "Outwardly you look like righteous people, but inwardly your hearts are filled with hypocrisy and lawlessness" (Matthew 23:28). Jesus scolded them for teaching one thing and practicing another, calling them hypocrites. He rebuked them for teaching others how to live while not practicing the same lifestyle themselves. Jesus said, "For you are so careful to clean the outside of the cup and the dish, but inside you are filthy—full of greed and self-indulgence! You blind Pharisee!" (verses 25, 26).

Not only did Jesus condemn the Pharisees for their outward appearance in contrast to their inward character, but He also called them out for their treatment of the prophets who preached the truth, including Himself. The Pharisees honored the dead prophets and claimed that if they had been alive during the time when whichever prophet was alive, they would have believed his message. However, that was a flat-out lie because Jesus spoke the truth, and they didn't believe Him. Jesus asked them, "How will you escape the judgment of hell?" (verse 33).

Jesus didn't sugarcoat things. He looked at the hearts of the Pharisees and called them out for their behavior. It might sound like He was being mean, but He was being real because He wanted them to understand the truth and be saved too.

If Jesus was real with the Pharisees, He won't mince words with us either. He wants us to accept the truth and to make the changes we need in order to become the best disciples we can be. Will we listen, or will we dismiss His instruction?

—Isaac Patterson, senior

Willing
Matthew 23:37–39

D o you have a mistake that you keep repeating again and again? No matter what you do, you just can't seem to fix the problem. That was what the Israelites did throughout their lives. Every time God sent Jerusalem a prophet, they disregarded or killed him, arguing that the person wasn't from God, generally because they didn't like the prophet's message.

In Matthew 23:37–39, Jesus cried for Jerusalem. He wanted to help and care for the people, but they kept turning their backs on Him. "How often I have longed to gather your children together, as a hen gathers her chicks under her wings, and you were not willing" (verse 37, NIV). He painted a picture of love and willingness to shield them from the chaos of the world, but they refused. They thought they knew best.

Some time ago, my young cousin was sick. I stayed with my family to help take care of her. It was my responsibility to make sure she got her medicine every day. She didn't like the medicine, and I soon discovered that she was throwing it away or hiding it after I gave it to her. I did everything I could to get her to take it, but she refused. Without the medicine, she got sicker and sicker. One day she looked in the mirror and realized how sick she was. That day she decided to take the medicine. As expected, she started to get better within a few days.

Jesus is the antibiotic to our sin problem. How often do we think we know best and push God aside? He won't force us to take the medicine. He won't force us to accept His gift of salvation. He wants us to realize that we need Him and that there is so much more in life than we think. He wants us to accept Him as our Father. In turn, He promises to gather us to Him when He comes again.

Perhaps we aren't literally killing the prophets, but are we disregarding the truth that God sends us? Are we pushing God away or running to Him like chicks run to their mother hen?

—Ashley Roxas, junior

Challenge Accepted
Galatians 6:9

I have always enjoyed physical challenges, so when a friend challenged me to train and run a half marathon with him, I jumped on it. When I started on this adventure, I had never run more than a 5K. Even that was pathetic because it took me about forty-five minutes to run three miles. As you can imagine, when I started training, even a simple three-mile training run was super hard and took me forever. Doing my weekly, long-distance run was horrible! The first "long" run was only four miles, but it felt like forty!

I kept at it, though, and before I knew it, I had consistently trained for more than ten weeks. After all those weeks of running, I noticed a pattern. During the first half of my runs, I get bored out of my mind, and it takes all I can do to keep going. I get a bit tired and my slightly ADD mind wanders. The mile just before I hit the halfway mark is always the hardest. My legs feel heavy, my lungs ache, and my attention span shrinks. Right after I hit the halfway point, however, it is as if a switch flips inside my body. I am no longer bored, and I get a burst of energy! It doesn't matter how long my run is, from five miles to ten miles, it still happens the same way.

Just the other week, as I was in the first half of my run and bored out of my mind as usual, God showed up in the middle of my boredom and got me thinking. Isn't running just like our relationship with God? We can get bored and distracted. The devil knows that we are prone to giving in to our aching spiritual muscles instead of calling on God to help us push through the pain. We have to decide whether we are going to quit or persevere.

I am running my half marathon in three weeks, and I know I can't do it on my own. I need God's help to run my official race and the race of life. I can't make it on my own strength, but He's proven Himself faithful in the big and little things in my life, so I choose to trust Him and push through whatever challenge is before me.

I am a witness!

—Emily Freeman, freshman

Give It All

Mark 12:41–44; Luke 21:1–4

We reveal our true characters not by *how much* we give but by *how* we give, as is demonstrated in the following story. On His way out of the temple for the last time, Jesus sat down in the courtyard and watched people donate to the church treasury. He saw rich people place large sums of money into the offering box. He also saw a poor widow gently drop in two small coins worth almost nothing.

Jesus gathered His disciples and said: "Truly I say to you, this poor widow put in more than all those who are contributing to the offering box. For they all contributed out of their abundance, but she out of her poverty has put in everything she had, all she had to live on" (Mark 12:43, 44, ESV).

The people watching in the temple saw the widow give very little, but Jesus saw the generosity of her gift. He took this opportunity to teach the disciples an important lesson. Most people contributed from what they did not need, but the widow gave what she couldn't afford to give, donating everything as an offering of hope. This revealed her true character and showed her complete trust in the Lord. She was willing to give all she had and to be left with nothing as an act of devotion to God. God places more value on our willingness to give out of faith than on the actual amount we give.

As youth, giving is often the last thing on our minds. We live hectic lives, and our schedules seem to get busier every week. We usually don't have much money either. That shouldn't stop us from giving, just as it didn't stop the widow. A peace comes with giving. Jesus called us to avoid worldly treasures and to focus our efforts on what really matters. Our own characters are dependent upon our willingness to give. Like this widow, when we are willing to give it all, we cause God to smile. The generous widow remains a model for us; like her, we should be poor in spirit, humble, and completely dependent on God.

—Lismary Rosales, senior

What Are You Reading?

Matthew 24:1–35; Mark 13:1–31; Luke 21:5–33

The Dark Ages was an era when the Word of God was not available in languages that common people could read. The clergy claimed they were the only ones who could comprehend the truths of the Bible. Because of the people's lack of access to the Bible, they were easy prey for religious manipulation and extortion. Many faithful Christians, such as William Tyndale, died for going against the church to bring the Word of God to the masses.

Even though the Bible is readily available to be read today, some people still believe they need an interpreter. Thinking that they can't understand the Bible, they instead read books or devotionals written by pastors or other religious people, and they don't crack open the pages of the Bible to read for themselves. There are many worthwhile religious books out there, but we should not trust what other people say about God's Word when we don't know it ourselves.

Before His death, Jesus warned the disciples about being deceived. He told them that many would claim to have messages from heaven or to be Jesus Himself (Mark 13:5, 6). He warned them to be on guard and stay connected to the truth (verse 9). This same warning applies to us today. The only way we can know the truth is to study the Bible ourselves.

If we are not acquainted with the Word of God, we can be easily fooled and led astray. The Bible is not impossible to understand. In fact, God gave it to us to light our path: "The unfolding of your words gives light; it gives understanding to the simple" (Psalm 119:130, NIV). It is just like learning math or English. It takes time and effort, but the knowledge obtained will take us far. Bible truths become clear with time, study, and the aid of the Holy Spirit. While it is good to read devotionals, such as this one, and other religious books, they are no substitute for spending time in the Word of God. God promises that when we seek Him with all our hearts, we will find Him (Jeremiah 29:13).

—Dane Rhodes, junior

Surprise!

Matthew 24:36–44; Mark 13:32, 33

Have you ever watched YouTube videos in which parents surprise their kids by announcing that they are going to a Disney theme park? In one video, the parents tell their daughter that she is finally going to get what she keeps asking for. The little girl is confused, but she finally catches on. She asks them when they are leaving, and the parents say, "In a few hours. Go pack your suitcase." She obviously freaks out and starts crying and screaming for joy at the same time.

Going to heaven will be much better than a trip to Disneyland, but just like these kids, we don't know when it's going to happen. Jesus told His disciples to "keep watch, because you do not know on what day your Lord will come" (Matthew 24:42, NIV). We know that Jesus is coming back soon to take His children to heaven, but we don't know when. The question is, Are we doing all we can to be ready? Do we have a relationship with God, or are we just hoping it all works out?

It's not easy to have a relationship with God in today's society. Immorality and the vices of this world try to distract us, not to mention social media, video games, TV shows, and all other forms of entertainment. If we know that Jesus is coming back like a thief in the night, what are we doing to get ready?

I struggle to read the Bible because of school, family issues, and a whole host of other distractions, but these aren't good excuses. Our future is at stake. Are we taking eternal life seriously? Are we getting ready for the biggest event in history?

The Lord has given us a voice to touch the hearts of others by sharing the good news about God's love and Jesus' second coming. We need to use our voices and take advantage of the privilege that God has given us. We need to spread the word to every nation so that Jesus' second coming can come faster. The Lord will use you if you let Him. Are you all in?

—Yadir Rodriguez, sophomore

Meeting With Jesus

"Instead, be kind to each other, tenderhearted, forgiving one another, just as God through Christ has forgiven you" (Ephesians 4:32).

How should we relate to others based on this passage?

What did you learn about God from this verse?

How can you apply this verse to your own life?

Wrestling Gone Wrong

Matthew 24:45–51; Mark 13:34–37; Luke 21:34–36

I t was my freshman year, and like many freshmen, my classmates and I didn't make the best decisions. We were settling into life in the dorm and decided it was a good time to wrestle. Of course, wrestling wasn't allowed, but we figured we could get away with it. We often picked a room and wrestled at night or on the weekends. We kept it under the radar—for a while.

I don't know whether we were just getting brave or feeling more comfortable in our surroundings, but one day a match played out in the middle of the day in the upstairs lobby of the dorm. A big group of guys assembled, and we went around the circle challenging each other to a match. (I had grown up in a home with sisters, so I wasn't very good at wrestling, but it didn't stop me from trying. I lost 90 percent of the time, but it was still fun.) Everyone was cheering and having a great time when I stepped into the circle to square off against my friend Josh. We started pretty well, but it wasn't long before he had me in a hold.

It was at that moment that the dean showed up unexpectedly and put an end to the whole thing. We didn't know he was coming. If we had, we would have stopped before he came, or we wouldn't have started in the first place. The fact that we didn't know he was coming caught us all off guard. We knew what the rules were, but we chose to do our own thing, and in the end, we paid for it.

We know that Jesus is coming back, but what are we doing to get ready? Jesus told a parable about a faithful, wise servant and an evil, foolish servant. The wise servant did his job even when the master wasn't around, but the foolish servant partied and messed around while his master was gone, figuring that he wouldn't be coming home soon. Are we ignoring the signs and doing our own thing like the evil servant, hoping we won't get caught, or are we staying true and faithful to God as we wait for His return?

Jesus warns us: "Be careful, or your hearts will be weighed down with carousing, drunkenness and the anxieties of life, and that day will close on you suddenly like a trap. For it will come on all those who live on the face of the whole earth. Be always on the watch, and pray that you may be able to escape all that is about to happen, and that you may be able to stand before the Son of Man" (Luke 21:34–36, NIV). Are we listening?

—Steven Roman, senior

The Hard Truth

Matthew 25:1–13

As Jesus was nearing the end of His life, He told a number of parables about His second coming. He wanted to make it very clear to His disciples—and to us—what we can expect before His return so that we can be ready. It's like a teacher who gives you a review and tells you exactly what to study for the test. You can do what the teacher says and prepare for the exam, or you can disregard the help and wing it, which never goes well.

In the parable of the wise and foolish virgins, Jesus describes a traditional Middle Eastern wedding, and although it is very different from our weddings today, try to imagine the scene. There are five silly virgins and five smart virgins who are going out to greet the bridegroom. It's nighttime, so they have lamps with them. The silly virgins brought their lamps filled with oil, but the smart virgins brought their lamps and lots of extra oil. When they all got to where they expected to see the bridegroom, he wasn't there, so they did the logical thing to do at night and went to sleep.

In the middle of the night, someone yelled that the bridegroom had arrived. The women immediately jumped up and grabbed their lamps so that they could see their way through the streets and meet him. However, the silly virgins realized that their lamps ran out of oil while they slept, and they didn't have any more. They begged the smart virgins for some of their extra oil, but the smart virgins only had enough to refill their own lamps. The silly virgins all ran off to buy more, but by the time they made it to the wedding feast, the door was locked, and no one would let them in.

This story is brutally honest about our need to get ready for Jesus' return. If we aren't ready before He comes, we won't be able to suddenly devote our lives to Him when we see the cloud of angels appear. Some people might look at this story and think God is cruel and unforgiving, not giving people a second chance. That isn't it at all. God created galaxies and ants alike. He created each and every one of us. He will be here in the beginning and the end. He loves all of us, even though we don't deserve it. That is the real truth. But it is also true that time will run out. We have a decision to make. We have to be ready.

—Gabriel Reis, freshman

Power Tool Mishaps

Isaiah 46:4

While I was in college, I took a year off to serve as a taskforce dean at Auburn Academy in Washington State. As the newbie, the dean assigned me the early shift, which meant I was on duty from 5:30 A.M. to 1:00 P.M. This also meant that I had a ton of free time in the afternoon. That was fun for a little while, but then I decided I needed something productive to do.

I found out that one of my friend's dad was a builder, and he needed help on a house he was building, so he hired me. I went straight to work. A few weeks went by and one afternoon my friend Brandon and I were building forms for the foundation of the house. The two of us had agreed that whoever finished last had to buy the other person Taco Bell, so we were focused and working like crazy.

I was cutting boards, nailing them together, putting the rebar in, and tying it together. I was determined to get a free meal! With a bean burrito on my mind, I picked up a two-by-four, cut it, and set the saw down, but as I brought the saw back, the blade, which was still running, caught on the two-by-four and kicked it back—right through my shoe. I looked at my foot and didn't see any blood—at least not at first.

Apparently, ASICS are no match for a saw. I knew I needed to assess the damage, so I pushed down on my big toe, and it went down and didn't come back up. I looked at Brandon, who had no idea what was going on, and I said, "Hey, I think I need to go to the emergency room."

He ran over, looked at my foot, and said, "Oh my goodness!" Then, trying to act calm, he said, "Don't worry about it. It'll be OK."

It was easy for him to say because he wasn't the one who was bleeding all over the place and whose toe was hanging on by a little bit of skin. I was scared!

This wasn't the last time I would find myself in the ER because of a power tool accident. The next one was even more traumatic and involved a chainsaw and my leg. Praise God, who spared me in both instances from permanent damage. In the midst of the crisis, I knew God was with me and would see me through, no matter what.

I am a witness!

—Josh Woods, chaplain

Homework From God

Matthew 25:14–30

In the parable of the three servants, a rich man decides to give some of his servants some of his money since he is going away for a while. Each servant gets an amount according to his abilities: the first receives five bags of silver, the second gets two, and the third gets one. After a time, the master comes back and calls the servants together. He asks them to give a report on how they have invested the money. The first two invested and multiplied theirs, but the last one has done nothing but hide the bag. The master praises the first two servants who earned returns on the money entrusted to them and scolds the last one who hasn't done anything with his portion.

As I was thinking about this story, it dawned on me that it is similar to my experience working on my research paper. My English teacher, Mr. Sigler, is known for having what some students consider exceptionally high expectations. His assignments are certainly time-consuming.

In the days leading up to spring break, we were assigned to write out the three main points of our research papers and then three sub-points. This required a little preliminary research and a lot of time. Mr. Sigler constantly reminded us that it would be very beneficial to our writing process if we actually got into the research and didn't just skim over stuff in order to turn the homework in on time. He gave us many examples during class of how to format the outline, as well as ideas for our topics, and then he let us do the rest. As he was giving us this homework, I realized something. Although it seemed like a pain, he was teaching us a valuable lesson. He gave us all the material and instruction we needed to excel, but it was up to us to really utilize it.

Jesus' parable and Mr. Sigler's homework assignments actually go hand in hand. We receive talents and homework instructions, both of which are good and help us grow, but it is up to us to use them as best we can. We can take the spiritual and physical gifts God gives us and use them to help bring others closer to Christ or to better ourselves spiritually. Alternatively, we can bury our gifts, just as we sometimes ignore our homework, and suffer the consequences later on. God gives us so much. Will we recognize the gifts and utilize them for His glory?

—MariRuth Runyon, junior

Good Crop; Bad Crop
Matthew 25:31–46

My grandfather is a very successful farmer back home in Mexico. He grows a lot of produce: beans, peppers, corns, pumpkins, and more. Every year when the red pepper crop is harvested, there are piles of peppers up to ten feet tall that have to be sorted, bagged, and shipped to grocery stores. During the sorting process, the workers look for any bad spots that will cause the pepper to rot, which will not only make that pepper useless but may even spread to the other peppers in the bag. Although it is very tedious work, my grandfather has experienced workers who are dedicated to sorting. He also puts many of his approximately sixty grandchildren to work! The workers sort the peppers into piles. One pile contains the good peppers that can be sold while the other contains the ugly, rotten peppers that need to be composted.

We are similar to those peppers. We are planted on the earth and cared for by God just as my grandfather plants and cares for the peppers. However, the pepper can't determine whether it will be good or bad, but we have the power to choose our path. Through our choices and the way we live our day-to-day lives, we can determine whether we will be in the "good and faithful" pile or the compost pile. How we treat others affects that outcome too.

"Then the King will say to those on his right, 'Come, you who are blessed by my Father, inherit the Kingdom prepared for you from the creation of the world. For I was hungry, and you fed me. I was thirsty, and you gave me a drink. I was a stranger, and you invited me into your home. I was naked, and you gave me clothing. I was sick, and you cared for me. I was in prison, and you visited me. . . . I tell you the truth, when you did it to one of the least of these my brothers and sisters, you were doing it to me!' " (Matthew 25:34–40).

The way we treat others personally affects God. If we see a person in need and decide not to help them, we are passing up the opportunity to help God. We can choose to focus on ourselves and be selfish, or we can choose to focus on others and be selfless. Let's allow God to help others through us. By doing so, we will be saved when God rejects the unfaithful servants at His return.

—Jonathan Samaniego, senior

Turned Upside Down
Isaiah 11

In the summer of 2018, a BBC news article reported that at least two suspected rhino poachers had been eaten by a pride of lions.* Kind of ironic, right? One might wonder whether, or how, the lions knew they were poachers, but an anti-poaching team found a hunting rifle with a silencer, an axe, and wire cutters near the remains of the men. These are the tools rhino poachers use, so the investigators put the pieces together.

Not only do animals attack and eat people at times, but the whole animal kingdom is built on a predator and prey system. The BBC series *Planet Earth* documents this theory with all of its hunting footage, whether it is of wolves, lions, or polar bears. This makes it hard for us to fathom the scene that Isaiah paints of the new earth:

In that day the wolf and the lamb will live together;
    the leopard will lie down with the baby goat.
The calf and the yearling will be safe with the lion,
    and a little child will lead them all.
The cow will graze near the bear.
    The cub and the calf will lie down together.
    The lion will eat hay like a cow.
The baby will play safely near the hole of a cobra.
    Yes, a little child will put its hand in a nest of deadly snakes without harm.
Nothing will hurt or destroy in all my holy mountain,
    for as the waters fill the sea,
    so the earth will be filled with people who know the Lord (Isaiah 11:6–9).

A day is coming when this world will be turned upside down, and everything will change in the blink of an eye. God will restore the earth to its original design—a place of harmony and beauty. Not only will we live in peace with one another, but we will live in peace with the animal kingdom. We will be able to walk up to a bear or tiger and pet it without fear that our arm will be ripped off. Doesn't that sound amazing? I can't wait to go exploring!

We have the promise of something better. That's why Jesus spent so much of His time telling stories about the future and urging people to get ready. He doesn't want any of us to miss out on what's ahead because it will blow our minds!

—Chaplain Kalie

---

* "Lions Eat 'Rhino Poachers' on South African Game Reserve," BBC News, July 5, 2018, https://www.bbc.com/news/world-africa-44728507.

Meeting With Jesus

Psalm 139:1–3

Y ou set up your hammock between two trees that are brilliant shades of red, and you climb in to soak up the blue skies and the crisp, fall weather. It's the perfect day to do nothing but nap.

Although you were tired a few minutes ago, now that you're settled, sleep seems to be evading you, and your mind is mulling over something you read the other day in your Bible. A friend of yours asked why we should pray, since Psalm 139 tells us that God knows everything about us. If He already knows everything, why do we need to talk to Him? She had a valid point, but it just seems like there is more to it.

"Beautiful day, isn't it?"

You lift your head and peer out of your hammock to find Jesus leaning up against a nearby tree. You immediately feel a peacefulness and comfort in His presence.

"Yes, it is beautiful. I was lying here thinking about something a friend of mind said. She said that if You know everything, there really isn't a point to prayer."

"Sure, I know everything about you, but just knowing about someone doesn't create connection and form a relationship. You may know stuff about your favorite actor. You may know a ton of facts about her. In fact, you probably follow her on social media and know where she's traveling, what she's eating, and who she's visiting, but do you really know her? Knowing stuff about someone doesn't translate into a relationship—there isn't connection without conversation."

"That makes sense. I guess I have more to think about," you respond.

"Here's the other thing, I may know everything about you, but you don't know everything about Me. When we talk, you learn more about Me and My love for you. Prayer is the means by which we communicate, which is honestly My favorite thing to do. So what do you want to talk about today?"

Take some time to talk to Jesus or write down your response to His question.

Read the passage for the day and think about the promise it offers or what it tells you about God.

If you were to talk about this reading with Jesus, what would you say? What would you ask Him?

Twinning
John 12:37–50

W e have six sets of twins at our school this year. Some of them look and act alike while others don't. One pair is hard to tell apart because they look identical, and they act similar too. I don't know whether they play pranks on their classmates or teachers, but we've all heard stories of twins switching places in class or on dates and getting away with it because no one can tell the difference between them. If you've seen one person, you've essentially seen the other because they are so similar.

Jesus came to this earth to save us, but part of His mission was to show us what God is like. They are kind of like twins; if you've seen one, you've seen the other. Here's what Jesus had to say about it: "He who believes in Me, believes not in Me but in Him who sent Me. And he who sees Me sees Him who sent Me. I have come as a light into the world, that whoever believes in Me should not abide in darkness" (John 12:44–46, NKJV).

Not only did Jesus show us the character of God, but He also demonstrated what a loving, obedient relationship with God looks like. Jesus said, "For I have not spoken on My own authority; but the Father who sent Me gave Me a command, what I should say and what I should speak. And I know that His command is everlasting life. Therefore, whatever I speak, just as the Father has told Me, so I speak" (verses 49, 50, NKJV).

If you talk to twins who are close, one thing they often say about their relationship is that they basically know what the other person is thinking and feeling because they are so in tune with each other. They are so close and know each other so well that they can finish each other's sentences. That's the type of close relationship Jesus had with God, and that's the type of relationship He wants us to have with Him. It's possible, but we have to spend time with God in order to reach that point. Why are twins so close? They are inseparable from the beginning, constantly with each other. We can have the same bond with God if we talk to Him throughout our days and spend time with Him.

—Mechael Saint-Val, junior

True Faith

Matthew 26:17–19; Mark 14:12–16; Luke 22:7–16

G rowing up, I learned that God was real and that He cared for me, but as I got older, I wanted to figure out for myself whether God was real. I began to study the Bible and search for answers to my questions. The Bible is like a telescope focused on God. I found answers, but I realized that it still took faith for me to believe in God's existence.

Faith is hard to describe, but then I thought of this illustration: When you sit down in a chair, do you have faith that it will not break? When you walk up a flight of stairs, do you have faith that it won't collapse? Some people might argue that we can see the chair and the steps, so we can trust them, but we can't see God. Here's another thought: When the sun has set, can you see it? No. But do you have faith that it will rise tomorrow? Similarly, you can't see the stars when it's daytime, but do you believe they are in the sky and will be visible when it gets dark?

The disciples had Jesus in their presence. He was a literal being with whom they walked and talked every day, but they still had to have faith in what He said and did. It was the Passover festival, and Jesus sent Peter and John into Jerusalem to prepare the Passover meal. They didn't have a permanent home where they could fix the meal, so they asked Jesus where they should go. He told them that they would meet a man carrying a water jar when they entered the city and that they should follow him and ask the owner of the house whether they could use his guest room (Luke 22:10–12).

Peter and John did as they were told, and it happened just as Jesus said. It took faith for Peter and John to go into the city and follow Jesus' instructions, but that little exercise in faith helped them to trust Jesus in bigger things. After Jesus went back to heaven, the disciples had to exercise their faith even more because they no longer had Jesus right there with them. Without faith, hope, and trust, the early church wouldn't have grown. Their belief in Jesus and their willingness to do whatever He commanded to share the good news with others are what brought many people to God.

How can you practice your faith today?

—Danielle Santana, sophomore

Warrior

Philippians 4:13

As I got off the ski lift, I pulled my scarf up over my face so that the only thing exposed was the tip of my nose. It was very cold, and the snow was falling so thickly that it seemed to drown out all other noise. I skied over to where my family was standing on the top of a ridge. From their spot, the ski run dropped down into a wide-open bowl. Sections of it were very steep, and there were big rocks that protruded out in the middle, even with the heavy snow.

Everyone in my family except me is an expert skier, and we began to take the run that was right in front of us. I am not an expert, and even if I were, I am a semi-fearful skier. I chose to ski around to the far side of the bowl where the drop-offs were not as steep. It was still considered terrain for experts, but it was definitely much more manageable for an intermediate skier. A few of my girls followed me. As we headed off, I heard my husband remark to his father, Ron Scott, that perhaps he should go with us, but Ron opted for the steepest section. At sixty-nine years of age, he was still an adventurous, sports-loving athlete—basketball, football, snow skiing, barefoot water skiing. He loved it all, so I wasn't surprised when he chose to follow my husband.

I didn't see him hit the rocks, but about halfway down, I saw him lying in the snow, and I heard faint shouting. I stopped to catch my breath and then headed over there as fast as I could. When I reached him, he was breathing, but he said he couldn't feel his legs. The ski patrol team arrived, and I skied with the rest of the kids down to the condo to break the news to my mother-in-law. I didn't know the extent of his injuries, but I knew it wasn't good.

It has been more than seven years now since his accident, and each day we are thankful that he didn't die. He very easily could have because he slid 450 feet after landing on his neck. His spinal cord remained intact, but he severely damaged it, leaving him a quadriplegic. As you can imagine, an injury like that is life altering for anyone, especially someone so active.

Before his accident, Ron affected people through his work as a principal, pastor, and youth leader. Since his accident, he has influenced many more. He has refused to let his injuries defeat him or define him. He says that God is faithful and loving and that every day he's alive is a great day. As I've watched him struggle with simple tasks while maintaining his positive, upbeat attitude, I have come to see him as a warrior—a warrior for God.

I am a witness!

—Shannon Scott, science/technology/art/journalism teacher

New Traditions

Matthew 26:26–29; Mark 14:22–25; Luke 22:17–20

I magine that you're one of the disciples sitting with Jesus the night of the Passover feast. You're expecting Jesus to tell the traditional story of the Passover feast and what it symbolizes, but instead of doing that, Jesus prays for the bread and gives a piece to each of you, telling you it is His body and you should eat it. Then He gives you a cup and blesses it, telling you it is His blood and you should drink it. Not only did He do that, but before the meal He washed your feet, the job intended for a servant.

My first thought would have been, *Is Jesus OK? He's acting strange tonight.* My second thought would have been, *Gross! When did cannibalism become acceptable?* We don't know exactly what the disciples were thinking that night, but if their other conversations with Jesus were any indication, they were probably confused. Even though His death was not a new topic of discussion, they still didn't quite understand what He meant.

That Passover meal started a new tradition that we call "Communion." The night of the Last Supper, Jesus created a new covenant, a new promise, with His children through the symbols of the bread and the wine. Communion is our way of showing God that we recognize His sacrifice and understand its worth. This ceremony shows that we remember the covenant and are patiently awaiting Jesus' return. Many people get uncomfortable when it's time for Communion at church, but it's a chance for us to remember Jesus' gift of salvation.

In addition to celebrating what Jesus did on the cross, it's a time for us to remember that Jesus is anxiously awaiting the day when we can celebrate all together in heaven. He told His disciples, "I tell you, I will not drink from this fruit of the vine from now on until that day when I drink it new with you in my Father's kingdom" (Matthew 26:29, NIV).

Communion is a time to look back and a time to look forward—back to God's gift and forward to our reward.

—Toni Sargeant, junior

Called Higher
Luke 22:21–30

The summer before my senior year, I decided to map out my year and figure out what all I wanted to accomplish and be a part of, but there was one thing I couldn't figure out. I couldn't decide whether I wanted to go on the spring break mission trip. It would be my third time going on a mission trip, and I wasn't sure that I wanted to dedicate my spring break to serving others. Don't get me wrong, it wasn't that I didn't want to share the gospel or help others, but I was thinking about my personal need to relax.

Time went by, and I prayed about it. I finally decided to cancel the personal spring break plans I had made and sign up for the trip. The months flew by, and before I knew it, I was on a plane bound for Peru. I wasn't there for more than an hour before the people's severe living conditions and need for help became obvious. The regular conveniences I grew up with were considered luxuries to the people in Iquitos. I felt guilty for even considering placing my own selfish wants above the needs of these beautiful people. As I worked in the community each day, all of those selfish thoughts went away. I realized that my sacrifice was so unbelievably insignificant compared to the one that Jesus made for me and that I need to do everything in my power to embody His character and actions.

God is calling us higher, and serving others is the path. It is a greater duty and is more important than anything else. Jesus made that very clear. He said, "In this world the kings and great men lord it over their people, yet they are called 'friends of the people.' But among you it will be different. Those who are the greatest among you should take the lowest rank, and the leader should be like a servant. Who is more important, the one who sits at the table or the one who serves? The one who sits at the table, of course. But not here! For I am among you as one who serves" (Luke 22:25–27).

Sometimes I feel as if we get so trapped in our routines and obsessed with ourselves that we are deaf to the call to service. We ignore the calling for irrelevant reasons, and we miss the point that Jesus served us. In order to follow Jesus' footsteps, we must get out of our comfort zones and put ourselves last, serving others in His name.

—Laken Scott, senior

A Servant's Heart

John 13:1–17

I enjoy making people feel comfortable when they come to visit my home. Whether it is a cool drink in the summer or hot chocolate in the winter along with homemade goodies, I like to take care of my friends and guests. If they offer to help in the kitchen, I usually turn them down because I don't mind the work and I think they deserve to be waited on. I have a harder time being the recipient of kind gestures. I want to jump up and be helpful. I want to take the burden off them and be useful.

I'm sure I would've been like Peter and told Jesus that He didn't need to wash my feet. I would've probably offered to wash His feet instead. It would've felt more natural to me to serve Him instead of Him serving me. But I, like Peter, would still be missing the point, even if it would've been a noble gesture to serve Jesus.

The foot washing was an act of service and an illustration of how Jesus wanted the disciples (and us) to treat others. It also represents the cleansing we need from Jesus every day. Jesus died for our sins. His blood paid the price for our sins once and for all. However, we make mistakes and mess up every day. Fortunately, Jesus tells us that if we confess our sins and ask for forgiveness, He will erase our sins and wash us clean again (1 John 1:9). We can't cleanse ourselves on our own. No matter how good we try to be, we can never be right in God's eyes on our own merits. We have to have Jesus.

Which brings us back to the exchange between Peter and Jesus. When Peter refused to let Jesus wash his feet, Jesus said, "Unless I wash you, you won't belong to me" (John 13:8). That's some serious language, but it's the truth. We can't save ourselves. We have to humble ourselves and accept Jesus' gift. We have to let Him see all of us, even the secrets we want to keep hidden. We have to get real with Him. When we do, He cleans us up and He calls us to serve other people. He doesn't say that we have to be perfect. He doesn't say that we have to have it all together. He simply invites us to come to Him.

If you were Peter, would you let Jesus wash your feet? If not, what's holding you back from giving yourself over to the one Person who loves you unconditionally? What do you need cleansing from today? Talk to Him about it and let Him clean you up.

—Chaplain Kalie

Meeting With Jesus

"Come now, let's settle this,"
  says the LORD.
"Though your sins are like scarlet,
  I will make them as white as snow.
Though they are red like crimson,
  I will make them as white as wool" (Isaiah 1:18).

What did you learn about God from this verse?

_____

_____

_____

_____

_____

What question would you like to ask God about this verse?

_____

_____

_____

_____

_____

What can you share with others from this verse?

_____

_____

_____

_____

_____

The Elect Killer

Matthew 26:20–25; Mark 14:17–21; John 13:18–30

How often do we reason with ourselves that because we are close to God, we are exempt from betraying Him, from experiencing a time when we would do something entirely against His will? We quickly dismiss the idea, claiming, "That would never happen to me" or "I wouldn't do such a thing." Likewise, the disciples who were sharing the Passover with Jesus were shocked when Jesus said that one of them would betray Him (John 13:22–24).

Judas was one of the twelve disciples, an elect follower of Jesus who spent countless hours with Him learning the ways of God. But somehow, he still missed the boat. So what was the issue? Unfortunately, though he lived and walked with Jesus physically, he lacked a spiritual dedication to the cause of Christ. Judas was simply going through the motions, tagging along to achieve his own selfish desires. We like to think that we are different, but we can fall into the same trap as Judas did if we aren't careful: relying on self and our own plans instead of seeking God and His plans.

I often find myself sidetracked by the craziness of life around me as I run to accomplish the things I have dedicated myself to do. God has blessed me with many talents and abilities, and I have dedicated them to His service. However, if I'm not careful, I begin to take life into my own hands, causing stress. I have soccer practice, homework, gymnastics, band, and praise band—the list goes on and on. When I focus on achieving success in my own eyes, I lose sight of the gifts God has given me and the ways He will help me complete all of my responsibilities. He wants me to rely on Him to accomplish all that I have to do. When I keep my priorities straight and focus on Him, I bring glory to His name in all that I do and say.

This is what Judas lacked. He focused on himself and his own desire for greatness instead of focusing on Jesus and His plans for the future. Rather than accepting that Jesus' sole purpose was to save those who were lost, he turned against Jesus and became His betrayer—the elect killer of the Savior of the world.

—Calvin Scott, junior

True Love

John 13:31–35

H ave you ever been treated unfairly? Most of us have. In response to the unfair treatment, did you retaliate in anger or another unkind way? In those moments it's difficult to respond in love and kindness because we are hurt or offended, so we give ourselves the excuse that the offender deserves our mean treatment. However, Jesus commands us to love each other (John 13:34).

Right after Judas left the upper room to betray Christ, Jesus talked to the disciples about love. Love was to be the one thing that set them apart from everyone else. Jesus said, "So now I am giving you a new commandment: Love each other. Just as I have loved you, you should love each other" (verse 34). Sometimes it's hard to love each other, especially when we get hurt, but Jesus wouldn't ask us do something if He didn't make it possible.

Jesus came to this earth to show us what love is, and He did. He treated everyone with kindness and compassion, even when they made fun of, spit upon, falsely accused, and beat Him. He died because of His love for us. He had the strength to carry out the plan of salvation because of His relationship with His heavenly Father. The only way we can truly love others is to have a relationship with our Lord.

To love others as Jesus loved us means that we first need to love God with all our hearts. Then we need to ask Him to give us the compassion, patience, and understanding that only He can give. If you really mean it when you ask for this, He will give you the ability to love others as He loves us.

Jesus summed up the importance of loving others: "Your love for one another will prove to the world that you are my disciples" (verse 35). When we show loving-kindness toward others, people will see that we're different and special. They will want what we have. They will see Jesus' love pouring out of us. That love proves that we are His disciples.

In what ways can you show love to those around you? Think of some specific ways to show God's love to your family, classmates, teachers, or whomever else you encounter today, and then sit back and watch God work.

—Brianna Self, freshman

Answered Prayers
1 John 5:14

G od has done so many amazing things for me that I could write a number of testimonies, but one story that sticks out in my mind happened this past summer. I was canvassing in South Georgia. It was a sunny Tuesday afternoon, and I had been talking to people all day, but I had not made many sales, and I was dying from the heat. If you've ever been in the South during the summer, you know what I mean when I say that it was hot. I had been rejected so much that day that I was discouraged, and my will to keep going was minimal. My friend Calvin and I were working in the same neighborhood, and he was having the same challenges.

We knew we needed some encouragement and a boost of energy, so we stopped and bowed our heads right there on the side of the road and talked to God. I've learned that prayer helps in every situation, so we spent some time sharing our challenges with God and asking Him to give us strength and to help us sell some books.

After we finished praying, we continued to go door-to-door. No one was home at the house I visited immediately after the prayer, so I went to the next house anticipating that God would answer our prayer. I knocked, but there was no response. Just before I was about to knock a second time, a friendly man opened the door. I told him about the books I had with me. The whole time I was talking, he smiled and seemed interested. When I had finished, he invited me into his home, which doesn't happen too often, but when it does, that means something good is about to happen. He offered me a bottle of water, which I gladly accepted. While I drank the water, he and his wife looked through my books. They decided to get two of the children's books I had with me. I explained that there wasn't a set price for the books and that we accepted whatever donation the customer offered. They ended up donating a large amount.

That donation began a string of blessings from God in that neighborhood. As I walked from house to house, I thanked Him with great joy for His providence. After that incredible experience, I was encouraged for the rest of the week. God's love is infinite, and He stands ready to help us when we ask.

I am a witness!

—Dylan Waters, sophomore

Not So Sure

Luke 22:31–34; John 13:36–38

Have you ever said something outrageous because you were trying to act as if you knew what you were talking about in the heat of the moment? Peter had a knack for finding himself in these types of situations.

Jesus has just finished the Passover meal with the disciples. He's revealed Judas as His betrayer, and He's told the disciples to love each other. He's been talking about His death and how He's going to leave them, but the disciples still don't catch on to all that is happening. Peter asks Jesus, "Lord, where are you going?" (John 13:36, NIV).

Jesus says that where He is going Peter can't follow now but that he will later. Peter turns around and makes a bold statement: "Lord, why can't I follow you now? I will lay down my life for you" (verse 37, NIV). And, in Luke's version, "Lord, I am ready to go with you to prison and to death" (Luke 22:33, NIV).

Peter seemed as if he was ready to go all in for Jesus. You'd think Jesus would be proud, but He knew the future. He knew that Peter wasn't ready to stand strong in the face of persecution. Jesus simply says, "I tell you, Peter, before the rooster crows today, you will deny three times that you know me" (verse 34, NIV).

It's easy to look at Peter and think, *How could you?* Yet how many times have we denied God? Many of us are more similar to Peter than we may think or want to admit. When we are alone with God, everything is good. We tell Him we love Him, and we thank Him for the many blessings He has given us. We act as if we are all in for God. However, like Peter, we deny God in front of others.

We might not say that we do not believe in or follow Christ, but we can deny Christ without speaking a word. We deny Him through our actions and decisions. We tell God we would go to great heights to follow Him, yet we seem to forget all about Him when we hang out with our friends or coworkers. By acting like the world, we dismiss the sacrifice that Jesus made for us on the cross so long ago. If we tell Him we love Him, we need to reflect it every day in everything that we do. Instead of denying Christ, let's fully show others what it means to be all in for Jesus and the faith we believe in.

—Cameron Shatus, senior

One and the Same
John 14:1–15

Peple tend to ask questions after they've developed a relationship with Christ. I know I've had conversations with God that kind of go like this: "God, where are You? How come I can't see You? I want You to be present in my life, so show up!" It's as if I've been waiting for a spiritual high, a moment when I just know God is present. If you've ever asked one of these questions, don't feel bad. The apostles, the people who were in daily contact with Christ, still asked questions.

Jesus is in the middle of telling the disciples about heaven and that He will be preparing a place for them, and Thomas asks, "Lord, we do not know where you are going. How can we know the way?" (John 14:5, ESV). It's OK to ask questions and even to doubt, but, like Thomas, we need to keep talking to Jesus and seeking answers. Jesus gives him this simple answer: "I am the way, and the truth, and the life" (verse 6, ESV).

When Jesus says this, He is not talking about the way to a physical location; He is talking about the way to the Father. If you're looking for God in an experience, in something you can see, you're looking in the wrong place for the wrong thing. Instead, you should be studying the Bible and looking to Jesus, relying on the relationship you have already established with Him—that's how you see God and learn about who He is.

Philip asks Jesus to show them God, and Jesus reminds the disciples that He and God are a mirror image of one another: "Whoever has seen me has seen the Father. . . . Believe me that I am in the Father and the Father is in me, or else believe on account of the works themselves" (verses 9, 11, ESV).

There are going to be plenty of spiritual highs and lows in life, so don't get discouraged. Just look to Jesus and keep building a relationship with Him. As you get close to Jesus, you will get close to God.

—Amie Shelley, junior

Would You Rather?

Isaiah 25

W ould you rather go skydiving or bungee jumping? Would you rather eat only cold cereal or waffles for the rest of your life? Would you rather visit Africa or Asia? Some "would you rather" questions are easy to answer while others are harder. Of course, all of it is purely for fun. But what about this question: Would you rather live forever with God in heaven or die the second death and be lost forever? This one seems like a no-brainer.

In one of today's passages, Jesus is getting ready to die for the sins of every person who has ever lived, but before He does, He gives the disciples a glimpse of the bright future in store for them if they choose to stay close to Him: "Let not your hearts be troubled. Believe in God; believe also in me. In my Father's house are many rooms. If it were not so, would I have told you that I go to prepare a place for you? And if I go and prepare a place for you, I will come again and will take you to myself, that where I am you may be also" (John 14:1–3, ESV).

In the midst of the impending misery that would consume their minds for the next few days, Jesus provides this ray of hope. The Bible is full of the juxtaposition of good and bad, joy and sorrow, praise and lament. Isaiah 25 features such a comparison. The challenges that faced Israel were overwhelming, but Isaiah pictures what the future looks like when God restores the nation to its former glory. The scene he describes also depicts the hope of heaven:

O Lord, I will honor and praise your name,
    for you are my God.
You do such wonderful things!
    You planned them long ago,
    and now you have accomplished them. . . .
There he will remove the cloud of gloom,
    the shadow of death that hangs over the earth.
He will swallow up death forever!
    The Sovereign Lord will wipe away all tears. . . .
In that day the people will proclaim,
"This is our God!
    We trusted in him, and he saved us!
This is the Lord, in whom we trusted.
    Let us rejoice in the salvation he brings!" (Isaiah 25:1, 7–9).

The future is bright when we think about all God has in store for us.

—Chaplain Kalie

Meeting With Jesus

"He has removed our sins as far from us as the east is from the west" (Psalm 103:12).

What truth is God sharing in this passage?

What did you learn about God from this verse?

What stuck out to you in this reading?

Faith Amid the Pain

John 14:16–31

S ometimes we feel so consumed by our trials that we wonder whether God is with us. Hardships and temptations can get in the way and cloud our vision of the truth. When that happens, it can be very hard not to blame God for the challenges even though we know that God is not the author of suffering and adversity.

Jesus said, "Peace I leave with you; my peace I give you. I do not give to you as the world gives. Do not let your hearts be troubled and do not be afraid" (John 14:27, NIV). Jesus reminded us that when the rough days come, which they will, we can trust Him and find peace in knowing that He has a plan.

There are times when I feel very disconnected from God, but that's not because He has moved away from me; it's because I've moved away from Him. God is always trying to reach us. He wants to be close to us. He wants to have a relationship with us. Jesus came to earth to live with us, and then He promised to send the Holy Spirit to live in us.

"And I will ask the Father, and he will give you another advocate to help you and be with you forever—the Spirit of truth. The world cannot accept him, because it neither sees him nor knows him. But you know him, for he lives with you and will be in you. I will not leave you as orphans; I will come to you. . . . But the Advocate, the Holy Spirit, whom the Father will send in my name, will teach you all things and will remind you of everything I have said to you" (verses 16–18, 26).

All of this proves how much God wants to be near us. If you are feeling like God is far away, ask Him to give you a new understanding of who He is. Ask Him to fill your heart with the truth of His love. Ask Him to send the Holy Spirit to impress upon your mind the things you need to learn to grow. He will honor your prayer because He loves you and wants what's best for you.

—Lexie Skiwski, sophomore

Broken Promises

Matthew 26:30–35; Mark 14:26–31

When you work at a boarding school, you often have to transport students into town. Town trip is once a week, but if a student needs last-minute supplies for a class project, breaks their phone, or "needs" Starbucks, they beg for a ride to town. Some days my schedule allows me to drop everything and make a quick trip to town, but other days I have meetings and appointments that I can't rearrange. When that happens, I usually try to schedule the town trip for another day.

One week a student asked me whether I could take her to town so that she could pay her cell phone bill. I told her I would be happy to, and we picked a day and time to make the trip. I added the event to my calendar so that I wouldn't forget. I had the best intentions of upholding my end of the deal, but when the appointed day rolled around, I got busy doing other stuff and completely forgot about my promise. I hadn't set an alarm for the event in my calendar, so it never alerted me. When I didn't show up to the dorm as promised, she texted to ask whether we were still going. I felt awful because at that point I was tied up with something and couldn't get away. We had to reschedule for later in the week.

I know this is insignificant compared to Peter promising to never leave Jesus—"Even if all fall away, I will not" (Mark 14:29, NIV)—but the principle is still the same. We make promises, we agree to do things, and many times we break those promises. Some of our failures are unintentional, like me forgetting about my appointment; other times we intentionally go back on our word whether out of fear or anger or a misunderstanding.

Even after Jesus tells Peter that he will deny Him, Peter says, " 'Even if I have to die with you, I will never disown you.' And all the others said the same" (verse 31, NIV). They all made a promise, and they all broke it. If the story ended there, it would be a crummy ending, but, fortunately, we know what happened. Peter messed up. They all did. Not one of them stayed true to their word. Nevertheless, Jesus offered them grace and forgiveness. He restored them, and they went on to spread the gospel to the whole world.

You've probably made promises to God that you haven't been able to keep, but He's used to that. Fortunately, He offers us the same grace He offered Peter, and then He encourages us to try again. What seems like failure can be turned into an opportunity to grow.

—Chaplain Kalie

A Pinch of Salt and a Pound of Faith
Matthew 10:29–31

My grandmother was one of my favorite storytellers when I was growing up. At a young age, she learned what it meant to trust God with the big and small things in her life, and her faith stories always inspired me.

Grandma married my granddaddy in 1945 when she was nineteen, and they moved from Brooklyn, New York, to his family's farm in eastern North Carolina. As they started their life together, money was scarce. There were times when they weren't sure that their weekly groceries would hold out until the next paycheck.

One day, Grandma was making oatmeal for breakfast. As always, she reached for the salt in the cabinet only to find that the box was almost empty. There was just enough for that morning's breakfast. However, after emptying the box, she put it back in the cabinet out of habit.

The next morning, while making their oatmeal, she reached up for the salt box, remembering that it was empty. However, it didn't feel empty. Shaking it, she realized there was salt inside. She poured out just enough salt for the oatmeal and saw that the box was definitely empty. Grandma wondered whether she had imagined the box being empty the day before. Curious, she set it back in the cabinet, deciding to wait and see what would happen tomorrow. Every morning for the rest of the week there was just enough salt for the oatmeal. Grandma emptied the box each morning and then put it back in the cabinet for the next day.

When Granddaddy came home with his paycheck at the end of the week, Grandma checked the salt box. Empty. God had met their needs all week as they made their small budget stretch to accommodate their expenses. Now they could replenish the salt on their next trip to the store.

Whenever I wonder whether something in my life is too small to bring to the Lord, I think of my grandparents and the salt box. God cares about every part of our lives. We're told in Matthew 10:29–31 that our heavenly Father cares for the tiny sparrows and He knows when even one of them falls to the ground. The lives of His children are worth more to Him than a sparrow.

What is your salt box today? God already knows everything about you, and He is just waiting for you to bring your concerns to Him. Who knows what miracles He may have in store?

I am a witness!

—Jodi Steele, marketing assistant

Me Without You
John 15:1–8

Have you ever relied on someone so much that when they weren't around you almost felt lost? Maybe it's your parents, friends, siblings, pastor, or teachers. No matter how much they might be there for you or how lost you'd feel without them, the truth is that they are human and they will eventually let you down or disappoint you. Thankfully, we have a solution to this problem—we have God.

This may seem like a cliché, and maybe it is, but is that such a bad thing? God is our source of connection in this crazy world. "I am the vine, you are the branches. He who abides in Me, and I in him, bears much fruit; for without Me you can do nothing" (John 15:5, NKJV). We need to be connected to God, not others, to get strength and guidance in this world. God is the only reliable source because He knows everything and has all the time in the world to help us.

The Bible is full of stories of people who lived this close connection with God, but the one I think of is Moses. Moses may have started out a bit unsure and indecisive, but once he decided to follow God's plan, he fully relied on God. When Pharaoh refused to let the Israelites leave Egypt, Moses didn't give up. He turned to God for the next move and then he did as he was instructed. Once the people were freed, Moses trusted God for everything: food, water, shelter, and protection. Any time he had an issue, he went to God for the answer.

It's easy to think that Moses relied on God because back in Bible times, things were different. However, Moses was an ordinary person just like you and me. He had speech difficulties and was shy. When God called him to help, he was terrified, just as we sometimes feel today when God asks us to follow Him or to stand up for the truth. All we have to do is have faith that God will provide whatever we need. All we have to do is stay connected to God like branches stay connected to a tree. The only way to live fully for God is to devote yourself completely to Him and to stay connected to Him. What are you connected to?

—Annslie Staton, sophomore

Promoted

John 15:9–17

When I was in the seventh grade, a new music teacher, Ms. England, started working at our school. I had been taking piano lessons for years from a church member, but my parents switched me to taking lessons from Ms. England. By the middle of my seventh-grade year, she asked me to accompany the choir. I felt quite special and jumped at the opportunity. I continued to learn and grow so much under her instruction. Then, during my eighth-grade year, she asked me to help her teach a piano class to preschoolers. Once again, I jumped at the opportunity.

By my ninth-grade year, I had a few beginning students of my own. Ms. England cheered me on, giving me the confidence to teach others a skill I started learning when I was six years old. She saw something in me that she nurtured and helped me develop as her student. I went on to teach piano lessons all through high school, and I decided to get a music minor in college to further develop my skills so I could become a better piano teacher. None of this would have happened if it hadn't been for Ms. England pushing me.

Something about being chosen, being picked, being selected, gives you a little boost of confidence. Right before Jesus' death, He gives the disciples a pep talk. They are about to go through the darkest days of their lives, and He wants them to remember how much He loves them. Not only does He want them to feel His love, but He calls them to stand firm and hold fast to what they know to be true. Here are His words:

"As the Father loved Me, I also have loved you; abide in My love. If you keep My commandments, you will abide in My love, just as I have kept My Father's commandments and abide in His love. . . . You are My friends if you do whatever I command you. No longer do I call you servants, for a servant does not know what his master is doing; but I have called you friends, for all things that I heard from My Father I have made known to you. You did not choose Me, but I chose you and appointed you that you should go and bear fruit, and that your fruit should remain, that whatever you ask the Father in My name He may give you" (John 15:9–16, NKJV).

I love the line in which Jesus says that they didn't choose Him; He chose them. He says the same thing about us. Jesus chose to come to this earth and die for your sins and mine. He has chosen us to show others what He is like. He has a job for us to do, and He promises to equip us.

—Chaplain Kalie

The Unpleasant Side
John 15:18–16:4

"I f the world hates you, remember that it hated me first.... Since they persecuted me, naturally they will persecute you" (John 15:18, 20). Sounds fabulous, doesn't it? You don't have to look very far to know that Jesus spoke the truth when He said these words. History is full of stories of Christians persecuted for their faith, from the early church through the Dark Ages and up to now. We don't necessarily think about it today because we live in a country where Christianity is currently acceptable, but there are countries where the gospel is not welcome and those who proclaim the name of Jesus are imprisoned, beaten, or killed. This is the side of the gospel we don't want to talk about. It's not pretty.

This side of being a Christian scares me. I don't want to think about it. I don't want to imagine the possibility of being hated, or worse, for my faith. However, Jesus said we are in good company when this happens because that's what He dealt with the whole time He was on earth. Fortunately, Jesus didn't say, "You will be hated. Good luck." He gave the disciples, and us, the promise of His presence.

"But I will send you the Advocate—the Spirit of truth. He will come to you from the Father and will testify all about me. And you must also testify about me because you have been with me from the beginning of my ministry. I have told you these things so that you won't abandon your faith" (John 15:26–16:1).

This doesn't alleviate all of my fears, but it does help shift my focus away from the unknown—persecution—to the known—Jesus. I've experienced His love and protection at different times in my life, so I know I can trust Him. That trust, that relationship I've developed with Him, will help me if a day comes when I face persecution like the disciples did.

Jesus told the disciples these things so that they wouldn't be surprised when it happened. That in itself gives me courage, knowing that Jesus doesn't want us to be in the dark about anything. He wants to prepare us for whatever we will face in this life.

—Katelyn Kelch, freshman

Meeting With Jesus

"Look! I stand at the door and knock. If you hear my voice and open the door, I will come in, and we will share a meal together as friends" (Revelation 3:20).

What did you learn about God from this verse?

_____

_____

_____

_____

_____

_____

How should we relate to others based on this passage?

_____

_____

_____

_____

_____

What spiritual principle can you take from this verse?

_____

_____

_____

_____

_____

_____

Training Program
John 16:5–15

Have you ever watched a military or police dog working with its human partner? It's impressive. They move as a fluid unit. The dog trusts its partner, and the partner trusts the dog. There is extreme loyalty between the two. There are plenty of stories of dogs risking their lives to save their partners.

Think about our relationship with God as a loving relationship between a law-enforcement dog and its partner. We are the dog, and God is the partner. Dogs go through rigorous training to learn the necessary skills to attack criminals; sniff out bombs, drugs, or illegal weapons; and protect their partners in dangerous situations. Without their partner teaching them, they would just be regular dogs who wag their tail and run around the yard chasing a ball. Military dogs have a purpose and a mission to accomplish.

Similarly, when we become Christians, we sign up for a training program with God. He has a mission for us and a purpose for our lives. He doesn't send us out without training us and giving us the necessary resources. We just have to have willing hearts to learn. We have to be engaged in the process. How do we learn?

Jesus told His disciples that it was actually good that He was leaving because He could send them the Holy Spirit to help reach more people than Jesus could by Himself on the earth. "When the Spirit of truth comes, he will guide you into all the truth, for he will not speak on his own authority, but whatever he hears he will speak, and he will declare to you the things that are to come. He will glorify me, for he will take what is mine and declare it to you" (John 16:13, 14, ESV). The Holy Spirit is our Teacher. He is our Guide.

The question is, Are we willing to learn? Are we willing to take the time to train? Spending time with God is crucial to developing a trusting relationship just as it is with police and military dogs. Because we are humans with free will, we have a choice to make. We can commit to the training or sit on the sidelines. What's it going to be?

—Daniel Skyler Hoke, sophomore

Scattering the Darkness
John 16:16–33

I am a worrier. I tend to think about all of the horrible things that could happen and then obsess about them. In general, these things are not significant, just minor bumps in the road, but I blow them up in my mind. There are so many different things to be afraid of that it's hard to pick just one. Here's an example of a fear that I've exaggerated in my mind.

As a kid, I was taught about the end of time. Messages about the end always portrayed it as something to be afraid of. For the longest time, the only reason I wanted to have a relationship with God was that if I could go to heaven, there was hope at the end. I wanted a way out of the pain. I was terrified of how much persecution we, as Christians, would have to endure. I made plans that would minimize the amount of pain I might have to feel.

Gradually, as I have grown, the end of time is not as scary as it once seemed. I still see the potential pain, but I also see the bigger picture. In Christ we have peace. If you have invited Jesus into your heart, then you know that you are not alone. If we ask Jesus to be with us, He will be there through the hardships. We know that the ultimate winner of the battle of good and evil is Jesus. If we believe Jesus has already won, then we should not be afraid of whatever lies before us, even if it is persecution.

Jesus knew His disciples were in for a bumpy ride, so He tried to prepare them the best He could. He told them repeatedly that He was with them, that the Holy Spirit would come to them, and that their sorrow would turn into joy. At the time, they didn't get it. They didn't fully understand what He was saying until after His death, but they had this promise: "I have told you all this so that you may have peace in me. Here on earth you will have many trials and sorrows. But take heart, because I have overcome the world" (John 16:33).

Think about this: if we know Jesus has overcome sin, is living inside of us, and gives us peace, we have nothing to fear. It's like a child who discovers that she doesn't need to be afraid of the dark because light always overcomes the darkness. Jesus is our lamp.

—Katie Shelley, junior

God's Hands and Feet

Mark 16:15

L ast summer I spent a week at Cohutta Springs Camp as a counselor-in-training. I went during adventure week with the seven- to nine-year-old kids, and before I left, my mom warned me that dealing with ten young girls might be tough. I assured her it would be fine because I love watching kids and spending time with them.

When I arrived at camp, I found my cabin, and I immediately connected with the counselor. She was great. Then I met the little girls I would be hanging out with all week. They were great, too, but there was one girl in particular who seemed to latch on to me.

As the days slipped by, I began to understand my mom's warning. It was emotionally and physically draining to have all these young girls looking up to me. I loved every minute, but I felt the weight of the responsibility to be a positive influence on their lives.

One night this one little girl asked to talk to me. She opened up and told me a little about her family. She lived with her aunt and sister because her parents were abusive. She talked about how hard it had been growing up in her home, and she was only seven! It was a lot to process. I wasn't sure what to do, so I went and talked to my counselor. The little girl said she was more comfortable talking with me than the counselor, so my counselor told me to just keep listening and to pray with her. I went back outside and did that. After my prayer, this little girl looked up at me and said, "No one has ever prayed with me. I've learned so much this week about Jesus. I didn't know there was a Man who could love me so much. I didn't know there was anyone who cared."

My heart broke thinking about how young this girl was and how much she had already gone through in her short life. Sure, the kids were difficult at times, and the hours were long, but knowing that I had played a small part in showing Jesus to this girl made it all worthwhile.

I am a witness!

—Annslie Staton, sophomore

A Picture of Selflessness
John 17:1–5

According to *Merriam-Webster*, the definition of selfless is "having no concern for self."* Jesus is the embodiment of this word. His name should be in the dictionary as a real-life example of this word.

Right before His death, Jesus prayed that His death would bring glory to God. He never sought glory for Himself; He always sought glory for His Father. Here's Jesus' prayer: "Father, the hour has come. Glorify your Son, that your Son may glorify you. For you granted him authority over all people that he might give eternal life to all those you have given him. Now this is eternal life: that they know you, the only true God, and Jesus Christ, whom you have sent. I have brought you glory on earth by finishing the work you gave me to do. And now, Father, glorify me in your presence with the glory I had with you before the world began" (John 17:1–5, NIV).

I think that this should be everyone's prayer every day. Our whole goal should be to glorify God, not ourselves or anyone else on this earth. Glorifying God can be as simple as talking to one different person every day and showing them love. This simple act could help 365 people in one year, and that's only if one person did it. If we all took the time to reach out to someone every day, we could impact hundreds of thousands of people. Who knows how many people would be in heaven if we each took the time to show God's love to those around us?

This type of movement starts with you and me. You, the person reading this devotional, can change the world. Start the movement! Do something right now that positively affects someone else. Maybe that is telling them that you love them or standing up for someone who can't defend themselves. Philippians 4:8 says, "Finally, brothers and sisters, whatever is true, whatever is noble, whatever is right, whatever is pure, whatever is lovely, whatever is admirable— if anything is excellent or praiseworthy—think about such things" (NIV). Do something positive. Always smile. Always show love. Always be kind. Always look out for other people. Always be selfless. Together we can change the world. Together we can glorify God by the way we act.

—Waylon Spicer, freshman

---

* *Merriam-Webster*, s.v. "selfless (*adj.*)," accessed May 12, 2019, https://www.merriam -webster.com /dictionary/selfless.

We Belong
John 17:6–19

It was 2014, and the biggest thing in my young adult life was about to begin—high school. I lived in the beautiful state of Florida, but my parents decided that I would attend boarding school in Georgia. The reason was that they wanted me to expand my horizons and have a chance to try a wide variety of extracurricular activities and academics. Even though I'd had the privilege of living overseas and in multiple states, it's safe to say that I was still a bit anxious about attending GCA.

At first the lifestyle change was rough, but as time went on the faculty and students went above and beyond to make me feel like I belonged. Fast forward four years, and I have made friends and memories that will last a lifetime. GCA has become my family. The people here have seen me fail, mess up, and repeat mistakes, but they have also seen me grow scholastically, physically, and spiritually. God has worked hard in my life these past four years thanks to the prayers of many people, and I have come out a better man in Christ because of it.

There is no way we can go through life without prayer. As Jesus neared His death, He prayed a prayer that is recorded in John 17. He prayed for Himself and for His disciples, asking God to give them strength in the midst of the trials to come. Not only does this prayer reveal Jesus' love for us, but it reminds us whom we belong to: "I am not praying for the world but for those whom you have given me, for they are yours. All mine are yours, and yours are mine, and I am glorified in them" (John 17:9, 10, ESV).

Jesus addresses the gift of belonging, the gift of the Father's name, and the gift of the Word in His prayer. In other words, we belong to the Father, but God has also given us to Christ, and we have a place with them wherever we go. We also have God's name, and with that comes everything He stands for, including the life, death, and resurrection of Jesus Christ. Because of that, we have the assurance of eternal life. Lastly, we have the Word into which we must delve into to grow closer to Christ.

—Adriann Stahl, senior

Hide-and-Go-Seek

Isaiah 29:13–24

Sometimes we think we can get away with things when it's dark outside because no one can see us. Because I attended a boarding school, I have friends and family who went to boarding schools, and I work at a boarding school, I know all too well that plans get made and carried out at night. Perpetrators believe that darkness protects them from being caught. I know of one guy who tied a bunch of sheets together to make a rope to sneak out of his third-floor dorm room. His girlfriend was a village student, and his mission was to go over to her house. He managed to make it out of the dorm. Then he rode a bike five miles to her house, jumping into a ditch every time he saw headlights to avoid being spotted by anyone.

Some people get away with stuff. Some don't. The guy who went on a midnight bicycle ride managed to fly under the radar, but I've known many more students who have been busted for breaking the rules. Even if they weren't caught red-handed in the middle of the night, word gets out and makes its way back to the deans or administrator, and the truth eventually comes out.

Isaiah warned the people of Israel about trying to hide from God. He said,

What sorrow awaits those who try to hide their plans from the LORD,
    who do their evil deeds in the dark!
"The LORD can't see us," they say.
    "He doesn't know what's going on!"
How foolish can you be?
    He is the Potter, and he is certainly greater than you, the clay! (Isaiah
      29:15, 16).

The Pharisees fell right into this trap arresting Jesus at night. They thought they were above the law, above God Himself. Look where it got them—into a heap of trouble! We're not much different. We think we can get away with stuff. We think we know better. We rationalize and think it's no big deal. We may even think God doesn't see. But, like Isaiah said, "How foolish can you be?"

God knows everything, and He's set before us commandments to guide us and help us to live the best life possible. He calls us to live in the light, His Light. "But you are not like that, for you are a chosen people. You are royal priests, a holy nation, God's very own possession. As a result, you can show others the goodness of God, for he called you out of the darkness and into his wonderful light" (1 Peter 2:9).

—Chaplain Kalie

Meeting With Jesus
Isaiah 40:29

You enter the cafeteria and make your way to the serving line. You grab a tray and wait in line impatiently because you're super hungry. They are serving your favorite meal—lasagna with garlic bread and salad. You finally make it to the front of the line and serve yourself a huge slice of lasagna. You grab three pieces of bread and head to the salad bar. You fill a bowl with lettuce, add your favorite salad toppings, and then drown it in Italian dressing. You pick up your tray and survey the cafeteria for a place to sit.

"Mind if I sit with you today?" asks a voice behind your right shoulder.

You turn and see Jesus with His own tray piled high with food, and you turn back to scanning the seating options. "Sure," you say, but your mind is racing. *Do I sit with those friends over there? Or do I head to that table in the corner? No, he doesn't get into religious stuff. I'm not sure how he would react if Jesus came and sat with us. How about that table? She's always speaking up in Bible class and Sabbath School. That would probably be a safe combination of friends to sit with.*

"Is something the matter?" Jesus asks. "You seem to be hesitating. I don't have to sit with you if you don't want Me to."

"No, no. It's fine. I want You to sit with me. I'm just looking for the right table."

"Is there a wrong table?" Jesus asks. You catch His drift. "What makes you feel comfortable around Me with certain friends and uncomfortable around Me with other friends?"

It's an honest question that deserves an honest answer. "Let's go eat outside where we can talk more," you suggest.

Take some time to talk to Jesus or write down your response to His question.

Read the verse for the day and think about the promise it offers or what it tells you about God.

If you were to talk about this verse with Jesus, what would you say? What would you ask Him?

A Prayer of Love

John 17:20–26

Are you a follower of Jesus? Do you walk in His steps and boldly share the Gospel? Maybe you merely cheer from the sidelines. Are you just a spectator, mildly interested but not sure whether you want to commit? Perhaps you'd rather watch than get involved.

Some time ago, I started to look at my life, and I decided that I wanted God to be a bigger part of it. I realized that I was more of a spectator than a follower. I think many us can admit to that. About the time that I came to this conclusion, a few of my friends came back from a prayer conference, and they were super excited and wanted to start a Bible study. This seemed to fit perfectly with my plan to strengthen my relationship with God. My roommate and two other classmates decided to start a sophomore girls' Bible study in the mornings. We invited everyone on our hall, but the next morning, only the four of us who had planned it were there. We were disappointed, but four were better than none.

I also committed to reading a few Bible verses every night before going to sleep. I stuck with both for a little while, but I'm sad to say that we all let life's demands slowly push out our early morning Bible studies. We drifted back to our normal routines.

Jesus knew we would face challenges in this world. He knew we would face distractions, persecution, and whatever else Satan can dream up to pull us away from God. That's why Jesus prayed. Have you ever stopped to think that Jesus, our Savior and the King of the universe, prays for us? If He took the time to mention us in the final moments before His death, I'm sure He still prays for us.

This is what He said, "I am praying not only for these disciples but also for all who will ever believe in me through their message. I pray that they will all be one, just as you and I are one—as you are in me, Father, and I am in you. And may they be in us so that the world will believe you sent me" (John 17:20, 21).

God wants us more than we want Him, which means He is easy to find. It's not as if He is hiding or something. He wants to spend time with us. He's ready and waiting for us come to Him. In the meantime, while He's waiting, He's praying for us.

—Alyssa Stojkic, sophomore

Resisting Temptation

Matthew 26:36–46; Mark 14:32–42; Luke 22:40–45

T he night of Jesus' arrest must have been awful. I can't imagine the amount of stress He was under knowing what lay before Him. Jesus clearly relied on His heavenly Father, but He also asked His disciples to support Him by praying for Him. The group of disciples had come to the olive grove in the Garden of Gethsemane. Jesus left eight of the disciples in a small group nearby and took His three closest friends—Peter, James, and John—with Him further into the grove of trees. Jesus told them to pray, and then He moved a little distance from them and poured out His heart to God.

When Jesus came back to the three, He found them asleep. He said, "Couldn't you men keep watch with me for one hour?" (Matthew 26:40, NIV). I'm guessing they felt terrible leaving their Friend and Master hanging while they gave in to their own tiredness and fell asleep. Jesus warned them that even with the best intentions, without prayer, they would fall prey to temptation, which in this case turned out to be sleep. Jesus urged them to stay awake and pray while He went to talk more with God. Sure enough, they went to sleep again.

A relationship isn't something we can tend just when it's convenient. It has to be nurtured constantly, like a manicured garden, or it will be ruined. The disciples let Jesus down when they failed to pray for Him the night of His betrayal. They had the ability to support Him and lift Him up in prayer, but they let their own needs crowd out His needs.

Deuteronomy 29:18 warns us to not "let down your guard lest even now, today, someone . . . gets sidetracked from GOD, our God" (*The Message*). We need to do what Jesus told the disciples to do: "Watch and pray so that you will not fall into temptation. The spirit is willing, but the flesh is weak" (Matthew 26:41, NIV). We need to be mindful of what's going on around us, and we need to keep God at the center of our lives. Through prayer and a connection to godly people, we can gain the strength we need to withstand temptation. We're in this together. Don't let your guard down. Stand firm. Pray continually. Support one another.

—Disney Smith, junior

Needle in a Haystack
Ephesians 1:18

We had an agreement with our kids that we would throw them birthday parties with their friends when they turned ten, thirteen, and sixteen. We celebrated every year with family, but we decided to make birthday parties a big event on "bigger" birthdays. My daughter Katelyn's birthday is in July, and the summer she was set to turn ten, we were moving from Maryland to Georgia. I didn't want her to miss celebrating with her friends, so we decided to have the party in May before we moved in June. I planned a big scavenger hunt at our town park with clues and activities for the kids to complete at each station.

The day of the party, I headed out to the park two hours before the event to hide all of the clues and set up the picnic table with the food and drinks. I was running all over the park hiding clues in the gazebo, under the slide, by the barn, and a gazillion other places. I kept checking my phone to make sure I had enough time to go decorate the picnic table and get the food ready. I had about forty-five minutes left by the time I hid the last clue.

I started jogging to the van to get the food out. Naturally, I reached in my pocket to grab the keys to unlock it, and that's when I discovered they weren't there. I felt in my other pocket, but they were nowhere to be found. I panicked! I had crisscrossed all over the park. They could be anywhere! I retraced my steps to the gazebo where I had last been. I searched in the gazebo and around the outside. Nothing. I was at a complete loss as to where the keys were. Before going to the gazebo, I had walked through a huge open field. I couldn't even remember the route I had taken, so walking back through it seemed hopeless.

I couldn't even call my husband to bring me a spare set of keys because this was our only set! I felt my blood pressure rising, but then I told myself to calm down and pray about it. There was no use stressing. I needed to turn this over to God and let go. I stood in the gazebo and asked God to help me find my keys, as well as for peace and patience.

I opened my eyes and decided to head back toward the van and comb the field between the gazebo and the parking lot. I continued praying while slowly walking, my eyes scanning the grass. I had taken maybe thirty steps when I spotted my keys. I was so thankful that God answered my prayer and took care of my needs.

I am a witness!

—Chaplain Kalie

The Face of Mercy

Matthew 26:47–56; Mark 14:43–52; Luke 22:47–53; John 18:2–12

Think of a time when you were betrayed by a good friend. How did you feel when you heard they betrayed your friendship, perhaps by saying things about you that weren't true? How did you respond? Did you get angry or remain calm? Did you confront your friend or let it go? Did you hold a grudge or offer forgiveness?

Jesus took the high road the night He was betrayed, giving us an example to follow when we face challenging situations. Jesus is praying, and a mob shows up in the Garden of Gethsemane. He goes to meet them and asks who they are looking for. They respond, and then Judas steps forward and kisses Jesus. Instead of getting angry with Judas for betraying Him, Jesus remains calm even though He knows this is the beginning of the end. In Matthew's iteration of the story, Jesus even goes as far as to call Judas "friend" (Matthew 26:50).

Jesus allowed Judas to be one of the twelve disciples even though He knew Judas's heart was not with Him. His assignment, just like all the other disciples', was to assist Jesus in His ministry. He was constantly in God's presence, witnessing miracle after miracle. Yet he chose to turn in his master for a bit of money. If I were Jesus, this would have made me furious.

As if the scene weren't crazy enough, Peter jumped in to defend Jesus with the sword and cut off the ear of the high priest's servant. Jesus reprimanded Peter, and then He showed mercy to the servant by healing his ear. Jesus had no reason to heal the man. He was in the mob of people coming to arrest Him. Jesus could have justified this incident. But perhaps Jesus' act of kindness completely changed the servant's view of Him. We'll find out in heaven.

We can learn a lot from Jesus' demeanor during His arrest, trial, and crucifixion. First, we should always keep our tempers under control. Anger can get out of control quickly, as evidenced by the large number of violent acts in our world today. If we show kindness to those who aren't kind, it will touch them more than if we lose our tempers. Also, mercy is powerful. It can change a person's life. Jesus showed each one of us mercy by dying on the cross. He didn't deserve death because He didn't do anything wrong. We did. Yet His love manifests as mercy. He asks us to do the same with others.

—Jonathan Stover, senior

In Denial of Denying

Matthew 26:59–75; Mark 14:53–72; Luke 22:54–62; John 18:12–27

During the summer of 2016, I embarked on a six-week dance camp with the Joffrey Ballet School, spending three weeks in New York City and another three weeks in San Francisco. I had spent thirteen years of my life learning ballet in a Christian studio where my faith wasn't questioned, but this summer was different. It tested my faith in ways I never imagined.

The people I met weren't as kind, nor were they supportive of my faith. Some people asked me about God and what I believed. Some asked me about my church and why I kept the Sabbath. Some asked me why I was going to a Christian boarding high school in "the middle of nowhere" Georgia. I found it hard to answer their questions; no one could relate to or understand my life since it was so different from theirs.

These questions pushed me to think about my life in a different way. Two months before I officially started high school, I realized that I was trying to figure out who I was and how I was going to act.

After Jesus' arrest, He was taken before the high priest to be questioned. Peter followed along and waited in the courtyard to see what would happen. While he was standing around, three different people approached Peter and told him that they had seen him with Jesus. Each time, Peter flat-out denied their accusations. After the third instance, the rooster crowed, and Peter remembered Jesus' words. This cut him to the core, and he left the courtyard and wept.

I have never really denied God in front of my friends or teachers, but I have avoided talking about God. By not talking about Him, I have concealed my faith and missed the opportunity to share God with others. He says to go out and tell the whole world about Him so that people will know of the love and joy that come from God. Although I didn't deny God, I didn't advertise the fact that I was a Christian.

In my eyes, denying and hiding are about the same. Either way, we aren't acknowledging our connection to God. Have you ever denied God or hidden your faith? What can you do differently next time to own your relationship with God so that others can see?

—Jensen Sutton, sophomore

On Trial

Matthew 27:1–14; Mark 15:1–5; Luke 22:66–71; 23:1–4; John 18:28–38

Have you ever watched one of those TV court shows like Judge Judy? They can be crazy. The judge asks them to stick to the facts, but most people resort to accusing the other person, the angry words start to fly, and the judge bangs the gavel to silence everyone.

If you've never been to court or watched a case on TV, there is generally a plaintiff and a defendant. The plaintiff is the person who is bringing a complaint to court against the other person, who is the defendant. The defendant is defending his or her name against the complaint, upholding the idea that you are innocent until proven guilty.

Jesus went through multiple trials the night of His arrest. If He were in today's legal system, the Pharisees would have been the plaintiff, and Jesus would have been the defendant. The Pharisees hated Jesus and wanted to see Him killed, but they had a weak complaint. When Pilate asked them what accusation they were bringing against Jesus, they said, "If He were not an evildoer, we would not have delivered Him up to you" (John 18:30, NKJV). Talk about avoiding the question! They had nothing, so they responded very vaguely.

Jesus was innocent! Yet, they treated Him like a criminal. He was treated unfairly, but He endured the trials and death on the cross because of His love for us. He had a mission to complete, and He didn't give up when it got tough. He carried it out until the very end.

We will never experience all that Jesus went through, but we, too, will have tests and trials. Just think of all the Bible characters and Christians today who have endured tests of faith. Each situation helped them grow in their relationship with God and prepared them for what was next in their lives. Although it pales in comparison to Jesus' trial, I have faced my own individual trials, such as moving to Georgia from Texas and leaving all my friends behind and starting at a new school. However, it was all in God's plan, and I've grown because of the experience. It's helped me to trust God more, which I believe is why we have trials. The rough days teach us to rely on God and stay focused on Him, trusting that He will help us through whatever we are facing.

—Parker Taglavore, freshman

Meeting With Jesus

"This is real love—not that we loved God, but that he loved us and sent his Son as a sacrifice to take away our sins" (1 John 4:10).

How can you apply this verse to your own life?

_____

_____

_____

_____

_____

What can you share with others from this verse?

_____

_____

_____

_____

_____

Why is this message included in the Bible?

_____

_____

_____

_____

_____

Undeserved

Luke 23:5–12

I grew up with three older siblings: Joe, Jonathan, and Ashley. As the youngest, I was always picked on. I could share plenty of stories of mistreatment, but the following happened when I was around four years old. My brother Jonathan had taken our mom's cell phone without her permission. After doing on it what he wanted, he decided to hide it in my closet so that I would get in trouble. He tried to bribe me with a piece of gum not to tell our mom what he did. Of course, at that young age I had a one-track mind—everything sugar—so I agreed to his plan. However, when my parents found the phone in my closet, I didn't uphold my end of the bargain with Jonathan, and I told them it was his fault. Sadly, they didn't believe me, and I got the consequences he deserved.

Even at that age, I felt betrayed because I was accused of doing something that I didn't do. I know I had a fit about it. Even though no one listened, I made it clear that I hadn't done anything wrong.

It's hard to fathom that Jesus, who was innocent of all wrong, didn't complain once during His trial, not even when they whipped Him, spit on Him, made fun of Him, and shouted at Him. Jesus held tight to the Father and kept His mind focused on the end goal—our salvation.

Jesus is our role model. We need to look to His example when troubles come our way and approach each situation without complaint and with full dependence on God. Nothing that we will ever face in this life will be as tough as what He experienced during His ministry and especially in His last twenty-four hours. If He can do it, so can we because He promises to give us His strength. What trials are you currently facing? How can you trust God and avoid falling into the trap of complaining about your circumstances?

—Alyssa Thomas, sophomore

Choose Wisely

Matthew 27:15–23; Mark 15:6–14; Luke 23:13–23; John 18:39, 40

I t seems absurd to think that a group of people would choose to save a murderer over a gentle preacher who healed people, but that's exactly what happened. Pilate thought he could get out of the sticky situation with the Pharisees by offering what seemed to be an easy choice—either set free a murderer or an innocent man. However, Pilate underestimated how much the Pharisees hated Jesus and how much influence they had over the crowd.

The chief priests and elders persuaded the crowd to choose Barabbas over Jesus. The crowd was easily swayed. Some of them may even have been in the crowd at His triumphal entry into Jerusalem, praising and welcoming Jesus and hoping He was about to set up His kingdom. Then, just a short time later, they were cursing His name.

We think it's crazy that the crowd could've picked Barabbas, but are we any different? The crowd listened to the Pharisees' accusations and let themselves be swayed by the loudest voices. We, too, are often persuaded to make bad decisions when we listen to the voices of popular culture and media. The crowd knew that Barabbas had done horrible things, but they still chose him over Jesus. We know the outcome of sin and the effect it has on us, yet we are still fascinated by it and sometimes choose sin over staying connected to God.

If we were to look at Barabbas as representing evil and at Jesus as representing good, we often choose evil just like the crowd chose Barabbas, allowing ourselves to be influenced by those around us in a negative way. We may have been worshiping God in church just a few days before, but in the heat of the moment, when everyone around us is choosing evil, we feel the pressure of the crowd and conform to what we know is wrong.

Peer pressure is a very real thing, and it's hard to resist. Do you want to go along with the crowd and choose evil, or will you stand up for what is right, true, and pure, and pick Jesus?

—Vanessa Thurman, junior

In the Wind
Psalm 51

Last summer I attended DiscipleTrek, a three-week Bible camp at Cohutta Springs Youth Camp. We spent our days studying the Bible and learned about what we believe as Christians in addition to participating in regular camp activities, such as swimming, canoeing, horseback riding, and crafts.

After breakfast the first Sabbath of camp, we took our Bibles and spread out across camp to have some quiet time with God. I walked down to the creek that flows into the lake and sat on a large rock by the water's edge. I dangled my feet in the water and started to pray. I had been feeling distant from God that school year, so I poured out my heart to Him and asked Him to come back into my life. I asked Him for forgiveness for all the stuff I'd done that had pulled me away from Him.

As I was sitting there praying, I remembered a passage in Psalms I had just read that week in which David asked God to cleanse him and restore him to right standing with God. I picked up my Bible and began to flip through it, but I couldn't find the verses I was looking for. I was a little frustrated, so I set my Bible down on the rock next to me. It was open to Psalm 57.

I began to pray again. I was sharing more of my heart with God when a light breeze began to blow. I heard the pages of my Bible rustling, and then the breeze stopped. I opened my eyes and looked down at my Bible. It was open to Psalm 51, the very chapter I had been looking for!

I sat in amazement of God's goodness. I was amazed that He would reveal Himself to me in such a tangible way. I read the words that David penned thousands of years ago and prayed them anew for myself, knowing full well that God heard my cry and was faithful to forgive me.

> Create in me a clean heart, O God.
>   Renew a loyal spirit within me.
> Do not banish me from your presence,
>   and don't take your Holy Spirit from me.
> Restore to me the joy of your salvation,
>   and make me willing to obey you (verses 10–12).

I am a witness!

—Florence Phillips, sophomore

The Test

Matthew 27:24–32; Mark 15:16–22; Luke 23:24–31; John 19:1–17

This is too hard! Why can't life be easy?"

"Why are people so mean? I'm so tired of all the drama!"

"I'm so stressed out! I just don't know how I can keep up with everything!"

"Why does bad stuff always seem to happen to me? I'm tired of it!"

I'm sure you could add your own complaints to this list. We often vent about how life treats us harshly. We grumble about how unfair things are. We whine about our circumstances. But do we need to? How should we handle injustice, challenging situations, and trying circumstances?

I was thinking about all of this in light of reading the account of Jesus' sentencing and subsequent mocking. If it weren't bad enough that He was sentenced to death, the soldiers led Jesus into the courtyard and tormented Him. They dressed Him in a purple royal robe, stuck a crown of sharp thorns on His head, saluted Him, taunted Him, hit Him, spit on Him, and pretended to worship Him (Mark 15:16–19). "When they were finally tired of mocking him, they took off the purple robe and put his own clothes on him again. Then they led him away to be crucified" (verse 20).

The physical pain must have been excruciating, not to mention the emotional pain of being mocked and tortured by the people He created and loved. Yet through it all Jesus remained silent. Not because He was weak or wimpy but because He knew He had a job to do, and it wouldn't make it any easier to fight back or lash out or pout and cry about it. He was very capable of showing strong emotion. Remember Him clearing out the temple? Talk about being in charge and making His presence and authority known! He could have done so again.

Jesus could have stopped the soldiers from mocking Him, but He didn't. He could have complained about the mistreatment and His innocence, but He didn't. Jesus understood His mission, and He embraced it even though it meant going through the worst physical and mental pain possible. So that brings me back to us. We know rough stuff is going to happen. We know bad days are going to come. How will we respond? Will we complain, or will we remember that Jesus suffered far worse and that if He could get through it, so can we? May we trust in God and the fact that He will eventually make all things right!

—Chaplain Kalie

The Tempest in Our Lives

Matthew 27:33–44; Mark 15:23–32; Luke 23:32–43; John 19:18–24

E very day we follow a routine. For most of us, it's one class after another, maybe broken up by work or studying or extracurricular activities. Throughout the course of the day, there are things that affect our moods; how we are treated is one example. Some days you may be walking through the hallway at school and be ignored by your friends, left alone at the lunch table, excluded from a certain group of people, or ridiculed for your beliefs.

All of these types of negative moments are thanks to the devil and the fact that he wants to do everything in his power to disrupt our lives and bring us pain. Should we be surprised? Jesus told us that as His followers we would suffer with Him. Even if you don't follow Jesus, the devil still likes to bring chaos to your life.

At Golgotha, as Jesus was nailed to the cross, the mockery and torture continued. Onlookers spit on, yelled at, and mocked Him for being the "King of the Jews." The soldiers even gambled for His clothes (John 19:23, 24). The crowd "hurled insults at him, shaking their heads and saying, 'You who are going to destroy the temple and built it in three days, save yourself! Come down from the cross, if you are the Son of God!' " (Matthew 27:39, 40, NIV). Some of these people may have witnessed His miracles or heard Him preach, but now they taunted the King of the universe.

When I look at what Christ went through, my problems seem very insignificant. However, Jesus went through all of this because He loves us. He lived in this messed-up world so that He could relate to the struggles we face each and every day, and He died on the cross to take our punishment for sin so we can enjoy His eternal life.

The exchange between Jesus and the thieves on the crosses next to Him proves this point. He knew the pain they were suffering. He was on a cross just like theirs. When one thief recognized his own sin and Jesus' righteousness, he asked Jesus to remember him when Jesus came back to set up His kingdom (Luke 23:42). Jesus' response was the best gift ever—the promise of salvation.

Jesus understands what we're going through. He's lived the life of a human. He defeated the power of sin, and He offers us eternal life if we will just ask.

—Luana Torres, junior

Pointing in the Right Direction

Isaiah 35

I have a love-hate relationship with my GPS. I love the fact that I can type in any address and it will tell me exactly how to get there. I hate the fact that sometimes I still can't decipher when it wants me to turn. My husband would say this is user error, and I'm sure he is right. Nevertheless, I struggle sometimes with knowing when to turn, especially if I'm driving with the sound turned down low or off, at which point I'm trying to follow the outline on the map.

One time I got turned around in Atlanta. My poor GPS kept having to reroute me because I missed one turn. By the time it rerouted me, the next turn was around the corner, and I missed it, too, because I wasn't ready. The streets came up too quickly. I finally pulled over and let it calibrate and then looked at the route to get my bearings so that I wouldn't miss any more turns.

The Jews had the prophecies of the Old Testament as a GPS pointing to the Messiah, but somehow when Jesus walked their streets, they missed the signs. They got confused and all turned around, so they gave up. Isaiah 35 points to the miracles that Jesus performed during His ministry:

And when he comes, he will open the eyes of the blind
and unplug the ears of the deaf.
The lame will leap like a deer,
and those who cannot speak will sing for joy! (verses 5, 6).

Right before this promise of healing, Isaiah wrote these words:

With this news, strengthen those who have tired hands,
and encourage those who have weak knees.
Say to those with fearful hearts,
"Be strong, and do not fear,
for your God is coming to destroy your enemies.
He is coming to save you" (verses 3, 4).

We are all tired and weak and afraid, but we don't have to fear because Jesus came and destroyed Satan once and for all when He died on the cross. He crushed the head of the serpent and defeated the grave. The signs are all there. He is the Messiah and the coming King. He saved us from our sins, and He is coming back again to take us to heaven. Are you looking for Him? Are you watching the signs?

—Chaplain Kalie

Meeting With Jesus

"But you are not like that, for you are a chosen people. You are royal priests, a holy nation, God's very own possession. As a result, you can show others the goodness of God, for he called you out of the darkness into his wonderful light" (1 Peter 2:9).

What did you learn about God from this verse?

_____

_____

_____

_____

_____

How should we relate to others based on this passage?

_____

_____

_____

_____

_____

How can you apply this verse to your own life?

_____

_____

_____

_____

_____

Moving On

John 19:25–27

Have you ever felt like the issues you are dealing with are just too difficult to bear and that no one understands, not even God? Well, think about this: Jesus was hanging on the cross dying. He was dealing with excruciating pain, and yet He was concerned that His mother would be left alone.

Jesus adored His mother. He loved her unconditionally. He didn't want her to grieve without support. He didn't want her to suffer. Right before His last breath, Jesus took care of His mother. "When Jesus therefore saw His mother, and the disciple whom He loved standing by, He said to His mother, 'Woman, behold your son!' Then He said to the disciple, 'Behold your mother!' " (John 19:26, 27, NKJV).

Jesus took care of His mother in a very practical way. This showed how much He cared for her and how much He values relationships. Jesus knew that with Mary in John's care, they would have each other to rely on in the midst of the sadness that they would experience after His death. That's what relationships are all about, whether those of blood family or adopted family. Jesus wants us to support and encourage one another, especially through the challenging times of life.

I decided to come to GCA because my older brother was here and loved it. Getting out of the house and living with a bunch of my friends sounded exciting too. However, once I arrived, I was a mess. There wasn't a day in the first six weeks of school that I didn't want to be back in the comfort of my own home. I constantly begged my parents to take me out of school and let me move home. They encouraged me to hang in there. I'm glad they did because if I had left, I wouldn't have made all the friends and memories that I have now.

My parents supported me through the adjustment period of my freshman year. They encouraged me and helped me stick with it even though it was hard. That's the beauty of a loving relationship.

—Emma Tol, sophomore

The Death of the Savior

Matthew 27:45–56; Mark 15:33–41; Luke 23:44–49; John 19:28–37

Just from the title of this devotional, you may be thinking that you have heard this story a million times and that there is nothing new you can learn from it. If you believe this, it will become true for you. However, if you choose to look a little deeper into the story, you will find new perspectives on the extent of Jesus' love for us. It doesn't matter how many times you read the Bible; you can always learn something new even from familiar stories.

I challenge you to look up today's verses and read them before finishing this devotional. What stands out to you about Jesus' final moments on the cross? Is it what He said? Is it the curtain in the temple being torn from top to bottom? Is it the resurrection of the righteous? Is it the centurion who said, "Surely this was a righteous man" (Luke 23:47, NIV)?

As I read these passages, I was reminded of what a true gentleman Jesus is. He doesn't force us to follow Him—He invites us. Jesus does not push Himself on us; He allows us to choose whether to accept Him or not. Some may ask why the Lord doesn't continue to actively pursue us if we don't pursue Him. If you think about it, that is true love because in a good relationship, if someone does not want you, you respectfully give them the space they desire. This shows Jesus' character. He will gently try to bring you to Him through your conscience and through the people around you, but ultimately, He doesn't push. You are free to choose to reject His sacrifice.

Jesus knew that many would reject His offer of salvation, but He chose to give them the opportunity through His death. He wants everyone to have an equal chance at salvation, which is why it is given freely to anyone who asks. God wants all of His children to go to heaven with Him. All we have to do is say yes.

—Jack Smith, junior

The Fast-Food Prayer
Matthew 10:29–31

I had always heard young people at my church talk about how God had answered their prayers and was working things out in their lives, but I didn't feel that real connection with God. I prayed every day, and I definitely knew God was real, but I felt like He wasn't really my Friend. I was fourteen years old, and I felt like I was just going through the motions with God because I knew it was the right thing to do. Every revival, every call to action, every tear-jerking campfire play at summer camp all seemed the same to me. It wasn't that I didn't want a relationship with God, but I felt like He saved most of His attention for the avid Bible readers. (Not the ones who start to read the Bible in a year program and end up reading Genesis six times because they can't remember where they stopped last.)

Then something happened. Last summer, I went on a mission trip to Guatemala with my church. If you're thinking that I'm going to talk about how the people, the poverty and the atmosphere changed my life, think again. It was a great trip, but something a lot more interesting than that happened.

If you've ever been on a mission trip out of the country, you know that they usually don't serve you American food. I love Latin American cuisine as much as the next person, but our mission trip was almost a month long. At the beginning of week three, I was craving a burger. Anyone who knows me knows that I have two main loves: sleep and good food. The food on the trip was good, but it was very different.

Every morning our mission team had worship and took prayer requests before starting the day. After a slightly disappointing breakfast, I felt like snacking. When our youth pastor asked for prayer requests, I said very seriously, "I would like French fries for lunch." Since my request was sincere, I was appalled when the table burst into laughter. I'm glad we prayed for my fries anyway. At midday, my brother banged on the door of our tiny hotel room, hollering for me to come to lunch. Our entire church group gathered in front of a table of papas fritas!

My connection with God took a step in a new direction, thanks to the answer of a trivial prayer request.

I am a witness!

—Becky James, freshman

The Worst and the Best

Matthew 27:57–66; Mark 15:42–47; Luke 23:50–56; John 19:38–42

If you have ever lost a family member to death, you know it is one of the hardest things to go through. The sadness swallows you up and tries to suffocate you. Jesus' disciples, His mother, and His other close friends were devastated when He took His last breath and died. There was no hope of Him using His power to get down off the cross. It was over, and He was gone.

Jesus had told them many times that He would be killed and then rise up after three days (John 2:19–22; Matthew 16:21; Mark 8:31). They either thought His words were figurative or they just refused to hear it. So, with great sadness, they buried His body. Joseph of Arimathea asked Pilate for Jesus' body. Those who loved Him wanted to see that He got a proper burial. Pilate agreed to the request, so they took the body down and laid Jesus in Joseph's tomb, which was cut out of a large rock. Then they rolled a huge stone across the entrance of the tomb.

Luke makes it a point to say that on the Sabbath the disciples and women "rested according to the commandment" (Luke 23:56, ESV). What were the Pharisees doing? They went to ask Pilate to station soldiers there to secure the tomb because they remembered that Jesus had said He would rise in three days. "Therefore order the tomb to be made secure until the third day, lest his disciples go and steal him away and tell the people, 'He has risen from the dead,' and the last fraud will be worse than the first" (Matthew 27:64, ESV). The Pharisees remembered what the disciples forgot! Maybe some of them even believed it was true, but they played it off by claiming that the disciples would steal His body and lie about His resurrection. Either way, they were so worried about Jesus, even after His death, that they took time on the holy Sabbath to go talk to Pilate.

Fortunately, the story doesn't end there. It has a life-changing ending! The burial of Jesus is one of the saddest events in the Bible, but it is also one of the most hopeful.

—Cole Turner, sophomore

Rise Up

Matthew 28:2–15; Mark 16:1–11; Luke 24:1–11; John 20:1–18

After Jesus' death, the disciples feared for their lives. The priests and religious leaders had finally gotten their way and killed the Master. Then the Pharisees asked that the tomb be sealed and guarded by Roman soldiers. The disciples were so overcome by grief that they forgot the words Jesus said about His resurrection. While the men were lying low, fearing for their lives, the women were taking action.

Sunday morning rolled around, and Mary Magdalene and some of the other women went to the tomb to anoint Jesus' body. When they arrived, they were shocked to find the stone rolled back and His body missing. An angel there told the women, "Do not be alarmed. You seek Jesus of Nazareth, who was crucified. He is risen! He is not here. See the place where they laid Him. But go, tell His disciples—and Peter—that He is going before you into Galilee; there you will see Him, as He said to you" (Mark 16:6, 7, NKJV).

Jesus showed compassion toward Peter, who denied Him even after he had said he would never leave Jesus. Mary ran and told Peter and John the news, and they took off for the tomb. When they arrived, they went inside. They saw that the burial cloth was neatly folded. John saw this and believed, for Christ was a diligent man, and if someone else had stolen His body, they would not have taken the time to fold the cloth.

Mary also returned to the tomb. She was crying when she heard a man's voice asking her why she was sad. She did not recognize that it was Jesus' voice. The Bible doesn't tell us why she did not recognize Him at first. Maybe it was God's will, or perhaps she was overcome by grief. Then Jesus said her name—Mary—and she immediately knew who it was. She had the distinct honor of sharing the good news with all the other disciples that she had seen Him alive. This was shocking because in that culture, a woman was not considered a viable witness in court. However, Jesus chose to reveal Himself to a woman first, a woman whom Mark points out had been demon possessed (Mark 16:9). God works through those who are most willing to be used, even people whom society deems insufficient or insignificant.

What a beautiful ending to what seemed like the worst event in history!

—Serena Van Fossen, senior

Always With You

Luke 24:13–35

It's Thursday, and nothing has been going right this week. In fact, nothing went right last week or the week before that either. You currently have three piles of homework on your desk that you need to finish, not to mention that you're about to be late to work for the third time this week. You spilled juice on yourself—again. You wonder, *Why does this keep happening to me? Why do I feel so alone?* The weight of the world is on your shoulders, and it feels like no one understands, not even God. For some reason He feels distant, as if He has left you to deal with all the madness on your own.

I don't know whether the two friends walking to Emmaus felt like life was against them, but they sure were upset about Jesus' death, and they might have felt as if God had abandoned them. Then Jesus approached them and asked what they were talking about. The Bible says that "they were kept from recognizing him" (Luke 24:16, NIV). The two friends couldn't believe that this fellow traveler wasn't up on the latest news, so they filled Him in. Then Jesus had a Bible study with them. He showed them from Moses' and other prophets' writings how they had misinterpreted the role of the Messiah (verses 25–27). As they approached their destination, they invited Jesus to stay with them. It was not until Jesus broke bread with them that they recognized who He really was. Then Jesus vanished.

As we go through the stress of our day-to-day lives, it is sometimes hard to trust that God is in control. Instead of praising Him for giving us another day of life and for loving us, we go around moping about the discouraging things just like the disciples on the road to Emmaus. Even when we are at our lowest point, God is with us! God is always there offering us peace in the midst of our trials.

We can't see God or our guardian angels, but they are there. We just have to believe. "For God has not given us a spirit of fear, but of power and of love and of a sound mind" (2 Timothy 1:7, NKJV). As long as God is by our side—and He is, no matter what—we should live our lives with joy, peace, and the assurance that we do not have to go through it alone.

—Jahsoulay W. Walton, junior

Meeting With Jesus

"By his divine power, God has given us everything we need for living a godly life. We have received all of this by coming to know him, the one who called us to himself by means of his marvelous glory and excellence" (2 Peter 1:3).

What stuck out to you in this reading?

What question would you like to ask God about this verse?

What did you learn about God from this verse?

You Have Been Called
Luke 24:36–44

Days after Jesus was crucified, He appeared to the disciples. Instead of rejoicing, they shrank back in fear thinking they were seeing a ghost. "Why are you troubled? And why do doubts arise in your hearts? Behold My hands and My feet, that it is I Myself. Handle Me and see, for a spirit does not have flesh and bones as you see I have" (Luke 24:38, 39, NKJV).

Jesus didn't scold them for not believing. Instead, He invited them to come and see that it was really Him. He then ate with them. Before leaving, He reminded them that Scripture is accurate and foretold all of this: "Everything must be fulfilled that is written about me in the Law of Moses, the Prophets and the Psalms" (verse 44, NIV).

This got me thinking about the importance of sharing the Bible with others. We all struggle with knowing what to say and how to do it. We may even discount our ability because we are just teenagers. This reminded me about a movie clip we watched in Freshman Experience class. It was about a class that was given an assignment to figure out a way to impact the world. The main character devised a plan by which he could affect multiple people. If he showed kindness to just three people, and each of those three people showed kindness to three more people and so on, soon a whole bunch of people would be reached.

Why can't we use the same technique to tell people about Christ? Sure, we all have excuses: "I don't know what to say." "I don't have enough time." "I don't know my Bible that well." But just as Jesus was patient with the disciples, He is patient with us. Just as He gave them strength to tell others about Him, He will give us what we need to be successful in sharing Him with others. In Ephesians 3:14–21, Paul talks about the job that we have to share God's amazing love with others, but he reminds us that we don't have to do it with our own power. God is the one working through us. "Now to Him who is able to do exceedingly abundantly above all that we ask or think, according to the power that works in us, to Him be glory in the church by Christ Jesus to all generations, forever and ever. Amen" (verses 20, 21, NKJV).

—Maurille Smith, sophomore

All of Us All In
John 20:20–29

The disciples were ecstatic when they found out that Jesus, whom they had watched die on the cross, was alive. All their sorrow and grief disappeared the minute they saw Him, standing with arms open wide. However, one of the disciples was missing from this joyous scene. Thomas was out when Jesus stopped by the first time, and when he heard the news from his friends, he didn't believe them. He doubted their story and told them that he wouldn't believe until he could touch the wounds in Jesus' hands and side.

Eight days later, Thomas got his wish. The doors are locked, but suddenly Jesus was standing in the room. Jesus invited Thomas to touch Him and believe that He really was risen from the dead. In that moment, all doubt was erased from Thomas's mind. Then Jesus said, "You believe because you have seen me. Blessed are those who believe without seeing me" (John 20:29).

I see Thomas as rather rational for not wanting to believe without seeing. That's a very normal human response. However, as followers of Christ, we are not called to be normal. We are called to dive headfirst into whatever mission God has for us. God asks us to have faith in what we cannot see because it sets us apart from the ordinary—it gives us purpose and hope. Life is not meant to be easy or comfortable. We are called to be bold and strong. Although we may feel blind, we must be willing to believe and serve despite how difficult it may seem.

Imagine what would happen if all of us, all of Christ's followers, stopped doubting. Imagine we all decided to go all in, to stop holding back because we are afraid. Everything would change. If we placed our lives fully into the hands of our Creator instead of doubting His plan or providence, we could change the world. Our fragile faith hinders the work we are meant to do. We must strive to have a faith that never dies, and we must urge one another to do the same. If we build each other's faith, we will destroy doubt and become catalysts for change. We all experience uncertainty and unbelief sometimes, but we must stand firm and fight against doubt. We must believe Jesus' promise that we will be blessed by believing in Him and working for Him without seeing. Are you in?

—Tori Waegele, senior

God's Faithfulness
1 Corinthians 1:9

I t was a normal day of canvassing, but as I was working in some high-rise office buildings, I started to feel unwell. I had developed a fever and a headache, so I asked my supervisor whether I could rest in the van for a while. I rode around in the vehicle, and by 5:00 P.M., I was starting to feel a little bit better. I still wasn't feeling great, and there was part of me that wanted to just hang out and not do anything, but I felt like there was someone out there who needed to hear about Jesus, so I decided to head back out and work for a bit.

That morning I had been reading in 1 Corinthians where Paul wrote "God will do this, for he is faithful to do what he says, and he has invited you into partnership with his Son, Jesus Christ our Lord" (1 Corinthians 1:9). As I got out of the van, I prayed, "God, You promised that You are faithful, and I need you to come through in a big way to help me reach people and my goal for the week. God, please bless me enough to cover a full day of canvassing."

I headed to the first house, and God indeed blessed! The man bought a book from me. That got me praising God because it was a direct answer to prayer. I went to a few other houses, and I realized that I didn't feel bad anymore. God had taken away my headache! I continued knocking on doors, and I met a nice woman, but she said she didn't want to buy a book. Instead of making a sale, I got to pray for her and her two little kids.

As I was walking up the steps to the next house, I prayed, "God, please show Yourself faithful." An elderly gentleman came out, and I told him that I was selling books to raise money to attend a Christian school. The man was genuinely interested in what I was doing, and he donated enough money to buy eight books. That alone made up for all of the hours I had been sick. God continued to bless over the next two hours, and I finished the day with an above-average number of book sales. This showed me God's faithfulness.

I am a witness!

—Jared Freeman, junior

More Fish; More Love
John 21:1–14

The story in today's passage has always amazed me because it demonstrates Jesus' power and willingness to forgive even when we let Him down. His love for us is unending even though He can see our hearts and knows our sinful tendencies.

As you remember, the disciples flaked out on Jesus when He was arrested. Peter, James, and John, along with the others, left Jesus alone to pray and agonize before the mob showed up. They totally let Jesus down. Then, after His arrest, Peter denied knowing Jesus three times. As humans, we hold on to hard feelings. We distance ourselves from, talk bad about, or try to get even with the people who hurt us.

Because of this mentality, we often think that Jesus will treat us the same way we treat others. We fear that when we mess up, Jesus won't forgive us unless we do something to make up for our crimes, such as going to church more or otherwise making amends. This is wrong thinking. Jesus will always forgive us when we ask. We are all humans who sin each day, and no one sin is worse than another because sin is sin. Jesus came to the beach that day to reinforce His love for His disciples, even with all of their human flaws and mistakes.

The disciples had been fishing all night, but they hadn't caught anything. Jesus called out from the shore, but they didn't recognize Him. He asked whether they had caught any fish. They said no. Jesus then told them to throw their net on the other side of the boat. They listened to the stranger on the beach—who knows why—and were rewarded with a catch of 153 large fish. There were so many fish that they couldn't haul the net back into the boat.

Soon Peter realized that the man on the beach was Jesus. Excited about seeing his best Friend again, Peter jumped in the water and swam to shore. When Peter and the other disciples got to shore, they found that Jesus had cooked them breakfast.

Jesus not only provided for their monetary needs by bringing in a huge catch, but He provided for their physical needs by making them breakfast. I can just imagine the smile on His face as He sat talking with His friends, retelling stories from the three years they hung out together. Jesus didn't hold it over their heads that they had deserted Him in His darkest hour. Nope. He forgave them, loved them, and blessed them.

—Nicholas Walton, sophomore

Do You Love Me?

John 21:15–24

Jesus first met Peter by the Sea of Galilee, and now He is spending His last days on earth with the disciples at the place where it all began. They've finished breakfast and probably had a few laughs over the surprised looks on their faces when Jesus performed yet another miracle involving fish. Then the conversation turns serious in John 21:15–17:

"Do you love me?" Jesus asks Peter.

Peter responds with a simple, "You know I love you."

Then Jesus instructs Peter, "Feed My lambs."

Jesus asks the same question two more times, and each time Peter tells Jesus that he loves Him, and then Jesus tells him to take care of His sheep.

Many people say they love Jesus but aren't willing to show Jesus the love He deserves by serving others. Some people think that Jesus just wants us to pay tithe, pray, and go to church. All of those are good things, but Jesus also asks us to tell others about Him and meet their needs. Whether we give money or our time to help others, Jesus wants us to serve in any way we can.

Peter said he loved Jesus, and he backed up those words when he did what Jesus asked him to do—taking care of others. Peter was prepared to live out what Jesus had been teaching His disciples for three years.

" 'For I was hungry, and you fed me. I was thirsty, and you gave me a drink. I was a stranger, and you invited me into your home. I was naked, and you gave me clothing. I was sick, and you cared for me. I was in prison, and you visited me.' Then these righteous ones will reply, 'Lord, when did we ever see you hungry and feed you? Or thirsty and give you something to drink? Or a stranger and show you hospitality? Or naked and give you clothing? When did we ever see you sick or in prison and visit you?' And the King will say, 'I tell you the truth, when you did it to one of the least of these my brothers and sisters, you were doing it to me!' " (Matthew 25:35–40).

We need to do a better job of taking care of God's children. He's called us to step into this important role, and He will help us along the way.

—Joshua Walker, senior

Shepherds, Parents, and God
Isaiah 40:1–11

I wonder what job in today's society would be comparable to being a shepherd during Bible times. It wasn't a glamorous position, but it was an important job. Someone had to do it because sheep were to Israel as cows are to the United States. They provided people with food and clothing, not to mention the important role they played in the spiritual lives of the Jews.

Jesus called Himself the Good Shepherd in John 10, but that wasn't the first reference to Him being a shepherd. Isaiah uses this analogy in Isaiah 40:

> Yes, the Sovereign LORD is coming in power.
>> He will rule with a powerful arm.
>> See, he brings his reward with him as he comes.
> He will feed his flock like a shepherd.
>> He will carry the lambs in his arms,
> holding them close to his heart.
>> He will gently lead the mother sheep with their young (verses 10, 11).

It might be tempting to look on and think that a shepherd doesn't have much personality or purpose because he spends his day in the field wandering after a bunch of animals, but Isaiah uses rich language to describe Jesus as our Shepherd. First, he reminds us that Jesus will rule with power. He isn't a pushover or a pansy. Jesus is God, and He rules with authority. In His role as our Shepherd, Jesus takes care of our physical needs (He feeds His flock), and He takes care of our emotional needs (He carries us in His arms, comforts us, and gently leads us).

Not everyone has the privilege of growing up in a loving home with good parents, but if you've ever watched devoted and loving parents take care of their children, you will see all of these characteristics at play. They protect their little ones. They provide for their physical needs, such as clean diapers, clothes, and food. They soothe them when they cry. They carry them when are tired and can't walk any further. They rock them to sleep at night when they have scary dreams, offering security and comfort.

God wants to be that loving parent that you may or may not have on earth. He is our Good Shepherd. Will you let Him step in and fill that role?

—Chaplain Kalie

Meeting With Jesus

"And we know that God causes everything to work together for the good of those who love God and are called according to his purpose for them" (Romans 8:28).

What truth is God sharing in this passage?

What can you share with others from this verse?

What spiritual principle can you take from this verse?

Childlike Excitement

Matthew 28:16–20; Mark 16:15–19; Luke 24:45–53; Acts 1:6–14

Anyone who deals with kids knows how eager they are to blurt out little bits of information—some important, some not so much—to anyone who will listen. As long as the child thinks of it as an accomplishment, the whole world needs to know. Thus, in most households, incessant talking is the norm for toddlers and little kids.

I remember when I was younger that everything in the day was exciting to me. A grasshopper making its way down the sidewalk was more than enough entertainment, and terror, to keep me busy for quite a while. Toys used to amaze me with their odd shapes and bright colors. Mind you, I moved on from one trinket to the next because I got bored of them quickly. I got bored because the world had so many opportunities in store for me that I wanted to explore the next thing. The world seemed like such a big place when I was little that even my backyard seemed to be a wilderness of crazy adventures and awe-inspiring feats. All these things were important aspects of my childhood, but one thing was the most exciting for me—impressing my parents. Any little achievement I made was never a secret. If I touched a miniscule frog for even a second, I might as well have been awarded an Oscar.

What happens between childhood and adulthood that we lose the wonder of exploration? Fear. Peer pressure. Worry. The list could go on and on, but those are a few of the many things that threaten to crowd out our sense of discovery and joy.

When Jesus shared these parting words with His disciples, He was calling them to go on a grand adventure: "All authority in heaven and on earth has been given to me. Therefore go and make disciples of all nations, baptizing them in the name of the Father and of the Son and of the Holy Spirit, and teaching them to obey everything I have commanded you. And surely I am with you always, to the very end of the age" (Matthew 28:18–20, NIV).

What would happen if we approached Jesus' commission with a sense of adventure? What would happen if we embraced each new day with enthusiasm to see what God had in store for us and how we could serve others? What would happen if we shared all of our accomplishments and failures with God? I think it's safe to say that a lot would happen!

—Eve Tol, sophomore

The Unexpected
Acts 2:1–13

O n the day of Pentecost all the believers were meeting together in one place. Suddenly, there was a sound from heaven like the roaring of a mighty windstorm, and it filled the house where they were sitting. Then, what looked like flames or tongues of fire appeared and settled on each of them. And everyone present was filled with the Holy Spirit" (Acts 2:1–4).

Who would have thought that the Holy Spirit would be represented by something as crazy as little tongues of fire? Jesus told the disciples when He left that they needed to wait for the Holy Spirit, but He didn't tell them how the Holy Spirit would come or when He would show up.

The Bible doesn't tell us how the disciples reacted when they heard the wind. Some of them may have been scared. Some may have been startled. It's funny to imagine one of the big, burly fishermen jumping in surprise. I know I probably would have jumped or been frightened by the unexpected rush of wind in a closed house.

When the Holy Spirit filled them, Jesus' followers received the ability to speak in different languages. This enabled them to spread the gospel to people groups all over the world. The disciples weren't the only ones who heard the rush of wind. The Bible says that other people heard the loud noise and came running. The believers emerged from the house and the gathering crowd was "bewildered to hear their own languages being spoken by the believers" (verse 6). The disciples took this opportunity to share God with the crowd, but some discredited the miracle and said they were drunk.

I've been on a few mission trips to countries that don't speak English. It's tough to talk about God with people who don't speak your own language. In those times, I wish the Holy Spirit would allow me to speak their language so I can tell them about God. God hasn't blessed me that way yet, although I've heard stories of this very thing happening in modern times. People have either been able to speak in the other person's language, or they spoke in English, but the other person could hear in their own language. Just because this hasn't happened to you doesn't mean that you aren't filled with the Holy Spirit. Each day we should pray and ask God to fill us with the Holy Spirit so that He can guide our decisions and help us reach people who are in need.

—Dylan Waters, sophomore

Wrong Turn
Psalm 91:11, 12

I grew up in Port Charlotte, Florida, and my grandparents on my dad's side lived in Miami, Florida, so a few times a year we made the three-hour drive to visit them for the weekend.

The trek across the state was boring. We traveled along Alligator Alley, also known as "Everglades Parkway" or I-75, through Florida Panther National Wildlife Refuge, Big Cypress National Preserve, and a portion of the Everglades. I'm sure these places are really cool with plenty of wildlife to see if you get off the beaten path, but from the highway, there wasn't anything to look at—just swamps and scrubby trees as far as the eye could see.

We had spent the weekend with my grandparents and were leaving Miami to head back home when my dad missed the road we were supposed to take. We were still trying to get out of Miami, and it took us about thirty minutes to get back on the correct road and headed home. My brother and I were a bit annoyed at the delay, but we obviously couldn't do anything about it.

It was overcast the whole way back, and then the storms rolled in and the rain began to fall. This type of weather is typical for Florida, so we didn't think anything about it, but when we turned into our neighborhood, we met an unexpected sight. We saw flashing lights, fire trucks, and emergency vehicles at the end of our street. There were tree limbs down and roof tiles strewn across the road. Then we noticed that our neighbor across the street was missing his garage door, which was now sitting on the roof of another neighbor's house.

We pulled into our driveway and went to investigate. We talked to our neighbors and learned that thirty minutes before, a tornado had touched down on our street and hit their house. It was then that our little detour seemed more like a blessing than an inconvenience. That evening we thanked God for His protection because if we hadn't missed our turn, we could've been driving down our road at the same time the tornado hit.

I am a witness!

—Chaplain Kalie

Whose Interpretation?

Acts 2:14–36

There are only two sides. There is no middle ground. You are either on His team or against Him. When Jesus was on this earth, people either accepted Him as the Messiah and looked at His miracles in wonder and praise, or they rejected His message and thought the things He said and did were crazy. The same was true after His death, and it still remains true today.

When the Holy Spirit filled the disciples at Pentecost, some people praised God for the miracle and others accused Jesus' followers of being drunk. What was the difference? Everyone was amazed and confused, but some people saw it as an act of God and others saw it as the work of the devil. Peter made it clear that

> "In the last days, God . . .
> 'will pour out [His] Spirit on all people.
> Your sons and daughters will prophesy,
> your young men will see visions,
> your old men will dream dreams' " (Acts 2:17, NIV).

Some of the people in the crowd failed to recognize the prophecy and made up their own interpretation of what they saw. Avoiding mistakes like this comes down to whom we are focused on. Are we focused on God and His Word, or are we focused on ourselves and our own thoughts?

From the time we wake up until we go to bed, we are surrounded by life and all of its chaos and distractions. The first thing we do in the morning is usually check our phones to see whether we have messages or notifications on social media. We like to see everything that is happening around us through the lenses of our phones so much so that we fail to see what is actually happening around us. The world is ending, and the signs all tell us that Christ's second coming is quickly approaching. There are many distractions taking our focus away from what's important and turning it to things that really don't matter.

Like those who thought the disciples were drunk, we may not realize the signs because we aren't paying attention. It is important for us to study our Bibles so we can know what to expect and how to handle things that happen. Today I challenge you to not be distracted by the things of this world. Instead, watch, wait, and prepare yourself for the second coming of Christ our Savior.

—Kaitie Williams, junior

Becoming More Like God
Acts 2:37–47

Many people in America take necessary things for granted, such as clean water, a place to sleep, transportation, education—the list goes on. They don't realize how fortunate they are until they no longer have those things available. In America, we also take freedom of religion for granted. We forget that many people in other countries around the world have to sacrifice greatly because of their relationships with God.

I didn't realize how much all of this meant to me until I went to India for three weeks on a mission trip. We were building a church and holding evangelistic meetings. I was shocked at how hard it is for the people to get common things that are readily available in America, such as clean water and a safe place to sleep at night. It is even harder for them to maintain a church group, because many members struggle to travel to church every Sabbath. In many cases, they have to be willing to sacrifice money, which they already have very little of, in order to attend church. Many people work seven days a week just to make ends meet, so attending church means they miss work and sometimes incur travel expenses, which may mean they don't eat. This factor alone makes it so that many families never get to know Jesus. As we met people and invited them to our meetings, we heard these excuses and others for why they couldn't come. It was a challenging situation.

In spite of many people turning us down, many did come to the meetings thanks to God's influence. At the end of the three weeks, more than 130 people were baptized! This trip was a revelation for me.

Peter and the disciples began their evangelistic work on Pentecost, and on the first day, they baptized three thousand people! Peter said, "Repent, and let every one of you be baptized in the name of Jesus Christ for the remission of sins; and you shall receive the gift of the Holy Spirit" (Acts 2:38, NKJV). We have the privilege of finishing what Peter and the disciples started. Let's go share God with others and call them to a life of faith. Will you put God to the test and see how He can change your life as He did mine?

—Stephen Williams, sophomore

Paralysis
Acts 3:1–26

One night when my son was a baby, I heard him crying, so I jumped out of bed to head to his room. However, there was one problem. My legs didn't work. The minute my feet hit the floor, I collapsed in a heap. It was the weirdest thing ever. I tried to stand, but I couldn't. I ended up crawling to his room. By the time I got to his crib, I pulled myself to a standing position, and my legs started working again. The only thing I can figure is that both of my legs had fallen asleep, so when I jumped out of bed, they couldn't support my weight, and I fell to the floor. It was definitely the most bizarre thing I'd experienced.

My paralysis lasted all of five minutes. I can't imagine being born lame and not being able to walk or move around freely without the help of other people, but that's the life the lame man was living when Peter and John walked past him. This man was sitting by the temple gate begging. This was his daily routine. He didn't even look up. He just held out his cup and asked for money as the people streamed past him. Yet his life was about to change. Peter and John looked at him, and then Peter told the man to look up. "So the man gave them his attention, expecting to get something from them" (Acts 3:5, NIV).

He was only looking for money. He had no idea that these two men could give him so much more. Peter then uttered these words: "Silver or gold I do not have, but what I do have I give you. In the name of Jesus Christ of Nazareth, walk" (verse 6). Peter then took his hand and helped him up. Immediately, his legs worked, and he could walk! The Bible says that he walked, jumped, and praised God (verse 8).

We all experience different types of paralysis in our lives, whether it be physical, mental, spiritual, or emotional. There are things that trip us up and keep us from experiencing true freedom. Sometimes we think paralysis is our lot in life and we can't do anything about it, so we don't even try. Sometimes we like what we are doing, so we don't want to change. However, if we do that, we will never fully live the life God has planned for us. We must look up and let God heal us.

What are you holding on to today? Are you willing to turn it over to God and let Him make you whole?

—Chaplain Kalie

Meeting With Jesus
Matthew 6:19, 20

Y ou flip the price tag over, and your heart sinks a bit. You've just found the perfect outfit for the Christmas banquet, but it's way out of your price range. Why does everything have to be so expensive?

You move on to another rack of clothes and being searching for something you can afford, but nothing catches your eye. All you can think about is the other outfit—the perfect one! You begin tossing around ideas of how you can buy it. Maybe I can ask Mom whether she'll give me some money and skip buying me presents. Or maybe I could convince the neighbors to go shopping and let me babysit their twins.

"Do you have it all figured out?"

"I'm working on it," you say. "I know what You're thinking, Jesus."

"OK, what am I thinking?"

"Well, you're going to tell me that I shouldn't buy that outfit because I don't have the money, that I need to be careful about my priorities, and that I shouldn't focus on stuff that's going to be here today and gone tomorrow," you say in a huffy tone of voice.

"Actually, what I was going to ask you is this simple question, What's the motive of your heart? What is driving your desire for this outfit? Is it to fit in with your friend group? Is it because you want others to admire your body or your beauty? Is it because you just really like the look of the outfit? There's always a motive behind our decisions. What the Father desires is pure motives and a heart set on Him," Jesus says. He pauses before continuing. "Take a bit to figure out what is driving you to make this purchase, and then see whether that aligns with My ways."

Take some time to talk to Jesus or write down your response to His question.

Read the passage for the day and think about the promise it offers or what it tells you about God.

If you were to talk about these verses with Jesus, what would you say? What would you ask Him?

I Am the Cripple

Acts 4:1–22

The Jewish religious leaders hated Jesus so much that they killed Him. It was only natural that they would hate His disciples too. They thought that when Jesus died, all of His teachings would die with Him. They didn't take into account the power of God working through His followers. Now they had an even bigger mess than when Jesus was alive. The message of His noble life, unjust death, and miraculous resurrection was spreading like wildfire.

Peter and John and the other disciples spent their days preaching and healing people. In Acts 4, we find Peter and John arrested and thrown into jail. The next day, the religious rulers brought them before the council and questioned them about the recent healing of the lame man, recorded in Acts 3. They asked them by what power they performed this miracle. The Holy Spirit filled Peter, and he told them it was through the power of Jesus Christ working through them.

This is not the only story in the Bible of a cripple being healed. Jesus healed many during His life, and there are other recorded stories of the disciples bringing healing to those who couldn't walk. All are miracles, but in today's story, I'm struck by the fact that this man had never walked in his entire life. When babies are learning to walk, they get up and fall—again and again. They stumble and teeter, and it takes them a while to learn. Even though this man was grown, he was still a baby in the sense that he had never learned to walk. When Peter healed him, he walked right away as though he'd been walking all his life. Maybe he stumbled a bit like a newborn giraffe, but he must've found his footing quickly because the story shows him jumping around and praising God minutes later.

From a spiritual standpoint, I am that crippled man; you probably are too. We may not be physically crippled, but we are crippled spiritually by sin. Sin is an inevitable thing we deal with as humans on this planet. We can try never to sin, but on our own that isn't possible. We will always trip and fall short. However, when Jesus is in the picture, everything changes. He lived a perfect life, and He gave His life so that we could be saved. On our own, we can do nothing, but through Christ, we can live perfect lives. Peter tried to share this good news with the religious rulers, but they didn't want to hear it. "This Jesus is the stone that was rejected by you, the builders, which has become the cornerstone. And there is salvation in no one else, for there is no other name under heaven given among men by which we must be saved" (Acts 4:11, 12, ESV).

—Joella Weaver, sophomore

Give Me Boldness
Acts 4:23–31

It was ten o'clock at night in the middle of December. I was packed and ready to fly home for Christmas break. Flying doesn't scare me, but I was feeling unsettled. A few nights before, I had prayed a prayer that went like this: "God, give me boldness to reach the ones You want me to reach. Lead me and give me courage." I was not ready for what He had planned.

Ironically, my friends would consider me quite bold. I confront them without hesitation. Public speaking doesn't faze me. My opinions are no secret even when they're politically incorrect. Yet if there is something that freaks me out more than heights, cockroaches, and a world without Wi-Fi, it is talking to strangers. The thought of walking up to a total stranger and talking to them creeps me out. So honestly I had no idea what I was thinking when I prayed that prayer, but as I prepared to head to the airport, I knew I would have to face my fears because I would spend the next twenty-four hours surrounded by strangers.

The next morning after I passed through security, I looked around to see whether anyone stuck out as someone I was supposed to help. Nope. I didn't see a crying woman holding a Bible or a lost child with a "Jesus Loves Me" T-shirt. The masses were not coming to ask for prayer. I was freaking out because I realized I would have to go to them. I panicked. *God! This is not what I asked for! I can't walk up to these people and talk to them. They might think I'm crazy!*

As I was getting ready to board the train for my concourse, the lyrics to "Walking in the Light of God" popped into my head.* "It's a great thing to serve the Lord . . ." I stopped. I could take the train and be at my gate in a few minutes, or I could walk. I felt God prompting me to walk, so I did. I ended up meeting so many people on that concourse whom I still pray for today. Alex, the cleaning man who asked for strength for his family, and Janae, a woman battling cancer. Those people gave me courage to talk to others. I ended up praying for a woman I met later at the bus station who was grieving the death of a family member, for Denise who asked for peace and an understanding of Jesus, and for Mrs. Pitcher whose grandson was in prison.

So many blessings unfolded that day, but ultimately, I was reminded that when we pray for boldness, God will equip us to get the job done. He did it for the disciples and the early church, and He longs to do it for us today. What are you praying for?

—Ashlee Wilson, junior

---

* Lou Rawls, "Walking in the Light of the Lord," *The Pilgrim Travelers*, 1962.

An Unexpected Blessing

Lamentations 3:22, 23

L ast summer I spent my days going from business to business and house to house telling people about Jesus by sharing books with them. It was hard work, but it was very rewarding. Every day I prayed that God would lead me to the people He wanted me to reach.

One day as I was in a neighborhood, I knocked on a door and a man answered. I shared with him what I was doing, but he quickly dismissed me and said he wasn't interested in purchasing anything and that I should just move along.

It's hard, but rejection is just part of the job, so I left his house and headed to the next one, and the next one, and the next one. As I was walking along the street to another house, a car pulled up beside me, and a woman rolled down her window and yelled, "What are you selling?" I stopped to respond, and she continued. "My husband was the one who answered the door when you stopped at our house. I was in the kitchen cooking. I know he turned you away, but I felt something stir within me, and I need to know what you wanted."

I explained that I was selling books to raise money to attend a Christian school. She told me that she was a Christian and that she would like to help me by making a donation. She gave me $10, and I told her she was an answer to prayer. We prayed together, and she left.

A few minutes later, I saw the same car come down the street. This time the husband was driving. I got a little worried, but he pulled up and said, "Chris, my wife told me what you are doing, and I'd like to help. I'm sorry that I didn't listen when you came to our door. Can I write you a check?"

I showed him the books and asked whether he was interested in any of the titles as a gift for his donation, but he said he didn't want any books. He just wanted to give me some money. When he handed me the check, I was blown away. It was for $100!

I am a witness!

—Chris Barrera, sophomore

Lombardi the Legend

Acts 4:32–37

V ince Lombardi, former football player, NFL coach, and general manager of the Green Bay Packers, once said, "Individual commitment to a group effort—that is what makes a team work, a company work, a society work, a civilization work."

We talk about teamwork a lot in sports because the ones who get it, like Lombardi, know that a single player cannot win in a team sport like football or baseball or soccer. It takes the effort of everyone on the field working together to pull off the victory.

Fred "Fuzzy" Thurston was a left guard on the Green Bay Packers. Fred had been rejected by three other football teams but had been picked up by the Packers. Lombardi was coaching the team at that time, and he saw potential in Fred. He taught Fred never to quit. He also taught him to work together with his teammates to be the best they could be. The team played hard, and they found themselves going to the first Super Bowl in the history of the NFL.

As a guard, Fred's job was to protect the quarterback, but he couldn't do it alone. He had to lock in with his teammates to hold off the defense. Fred and his teammates went on to win the very first Super Bowl, which secured their status as legends in the world of football. They will forever be remembered as champions. The Packers won as a team; each player played a part in their historic win.

God is our Coach, and He has called us to work together as a team to share the gospel with the world. The early church was so committed to teamwork that the Bible tells us they shared everything, even their personal belongings. "There was not a needy person among them, for as many as were owners of lands or houses sold them and brought the proceeds of what was sold and laid it at the apostles' feet, and it was distributed to each as any had need" (Acts 4:34, 35, ESV). That may seem like a crazy idea to us, but the bottom line is that they were all in with Jesus and the work He asked them to do. Whatever it took, they were ready to do, including financially supporting the other members of their team.

What about you? Are you pulling your weight as part of the team? Do you have teammates you trust and whom you know will support you as you work for God? Don't do it alone. God doesn't ask us to. Find a team to surround you.

—Preston Waters, freshman

Natural Tendencies

Acts 5:1–11

There is a fable that goes something like this:

There was once a scorpion that wanted to cross a river. Since he was a scorpion, he couldn't swim, so he was stuck. Luckily for him, there was a frog nearby. The frog and the scorpion started to talk, and the scorpion asked the frog to take him across the river on his back. The frog said no because he figured the scorpion would sting him. As you can guess, the scorpion disagreed, telling the frog that would be stupid because then they would both drown. After further debate, the frog finally agreed to the arrangement. All went smoothly at first, but when they were about halfway across the river, the scorpion stung the frog. As they were sinking, the frog asked the scorpion why he lied. The scorpion answered, "I could not help myself. It is in my nature."

In Acts 5, we find a sad story about a couple who let their sinful nature get the best of them. Ananias and Sapphira decided to sell some land they owned and give a certain amount of money to the church. Then greed got in the way, and Ananias decided to keep some of the money and give the rest to the church. When he came before Peter and gave him the money, Peter said, "Ananias, why has Satan filled your heart to lie to the Holy Spirit and to keep back for yourself part of the proceeds of the land? . . . Why is it that you have contrived this deed in your heart? You have not lied to man but to God" (Acts 5:3, 4, ESV). Then Ananias died.

Later that day Sapphira came by, and Peter asked her how much they had made on the land sale. She lied about the total, and she, too, died on the spot.

Ananias and Sapphira lied to God. Their greed, which is part of our human nature, got in the way and ended up killing them. We can never overcome our sinful human natures by ourselves. In the fable, the scorpion promises that he will control himself until he gets to the other side, but in his own power, it's not possible. In our own power we cannot beat sin, but God is willing to help us. Jesus overcame our sinful human tendencies, and He stands ready to help us be like Him. We just have to ask.

—Kori Wilkens, junior

Beauty in the Midst of Ugliness
Isaiah 52:13–53:12

We're entering that time of year with Christmas programs galore. The classic school or church program features a dramatic play about Jesus' birth complete with a doll in the manger and little girls dressed up as beautiful angels. Don't get me wrong; I enjoy Christmas plays and remembering Jesus' birth as much as the next person, but I got to thinking that there seem to be many more Christmas plays than Easter plays. Yes, we celebrate Jesus' resurrection, but I think we shy away from putting together dramatic presentations because, unlike the glorious vision of angels announcing the arrival of the King to a group of sleepy shepherds, there wasn't anything pretty about Jesus' crucifixion.

It was a gruesome event. Isaiah prophesied about Jesus' death, and it's not a pretty picture:

But many were amazed when they saw him.
    His face was so disfigured he seemed hardly human,
    and from his appearance, one would scarcely know he was a man. . . .

But he was pierced for our rebellion,
    crushed for our sins.
He was beaten so we could be whole.
    He was whipped so we could be healed (Isaiah 52:14; 53:5).

Nothing about that is beautiful. It's raw and dreadful. And yet without the pain and suffering that Jesus went through, we wouldn't have the amazing hope of salvation.

And because of his experience,
    my righteous servant will make it possible
for many to be counted righteous,
    for he will bear all their sins.
I [God] will give him the honors of a victorious soldier,
    because he exposed himself to death (verses 11, 12).

Without Jesus' death, we don't have life. During this season when we celebrate Jesus' birth and think about all things sparkly and beautiful, let us also contemplate Jesus' death and all that He endured on our behalf. From beginning to end, the account of Jesus' life is the most important story you'll ever hear.

—Chaplain Kalie

Meeting With Jesus

"He saved us, not because of the righteous things we had done, but because of his mercy. He washed away our sins, giving us a new birth and new life through the Holy Spirit. He generously poured out the Spirit upon us through Jesus Christ our Savior. Because of his grace he made us right in his sight and gave us confidence that we will inherit eternal life" (Titus 3:5–7).

What spiritual principle can you take from this passage?

What can you share with others from these verses?

Why is this passage included in the Bible?

The Source of Our Power

Acts 5:12–16

A s a kid, I had a very vivid imagination. I clad myself in any identity but my own, whether it was as a famous movie star or a rugged mountain climber. Eventually, my imagination always settled on the notion that I was some superhero with a set of powers available to no one but me. I imagined that people from around the world would benefit from my presence if only I was feeling benevolent that day. Luckily for them, I was the nicest superhero there ever was. As I've grown older, I've come to terms with the fact that I never did, and probably never will, possess such abilities that will draw the world to my feet.

Unlike me, who dreamed up superhero powers, the apostles had superhero powers because God saw fit to work many signs and wonders through them. They had the privilege of acting out the works of Christ by performing miracles, healing those around them, and preaching confidently the Word of God. "And believers were increasingly added to the Lord, multitudes of both men and women, so that they brought the sick out into the streets and laid them on beds and couches, that at least the shadow of Peter passing by might fall on some of them. Also a multitude gathered from the surrounding cities to Jerusalem, bringing sick people and those who were tormented by unclean spirits, and they were all healed" (Acts 5:14–16, NKJV).

We know that the apostles didn't possess special powers on their own, although they could have easily become proud and taken the credit. Instead, the apostles regularly gave glory to God, making it clear that nothing good came from them.

Although our own lives may seem to be relatively normal compared to the apostles', we can still take a cue from them. Every chance we get, we can be kind to those around us, taking the time to talk with them and help them to the best of our abilities. When we show love to others, we are giving them a glimpse of our God, the One who gives us power to impact the world for good.

—Caleb Tol, senior

Envious of God?

Acts 5:17–42

T he Jewish leaders were plagued by jealousy. They were jealous that people looked to an outsider for religious guidance, and they hated that Jesus called out their sin and hypocrisy. The leaders got so jealous that they killed Jesus. They thought that would solve all their problems, but then Jesus rose from the dead and the disciples took up the campaign of proclaiming His resurrection and death for our sins.

This only further infuriated the Jewish leaders. They were probably envious of the powers that the disciples displayed, not to mention the crowds who turned out to listen to the disciples' every word. In anger, they arrested the disciples and threw them into prison at every opportunity. In today's passage, an angel opened the prison door and told them to go preach in the temple the next day, so they did as they were told.

When the Jewish leaders heard this, they were furious. All they wanted was revenge. They arrested them again, but because they were afraid of the people, they didn't kill them. Instead, they threatened them and told them to stop preaching. "But Peter and the other apostles answered and said, 'We ought to obey God rather than men. The God of our fathers raised up Jesus whom you murdered by hanging on a tree. Him God has exalted to His right hand to be Prince and Savior, to give repentance to Israel and forgiveness of sins. And we are His witnesses to these things, and so also is the Holy Spirit whom God has given to those who obey Him' " (Acts 5:29–32, NKJV).

Out of the whole group of Pharisees, only one man spoke up and actually said something logical: "Gamaliel, a teacher of the law held in respect by all the people," said, "Keep away from these men and let them alone; for if this plan or this work is of men, it will come to nothing; but if it is of God, you cannot overthrow it—lest you even be found to fight against God" (verses 34, 38, 39, NKJV). Finally, a voice of reason! This one Pharisee didn't let jealousy cloud his mind, and he spoke with wisdom, reminding them that if these men were truly on God's side, no one could stop them.

—Ethan Williams, sophomore

The Light That Penetrates Darkness
Psalm 116:3

It was dark, and I was scared. I was crying. I really wanted to scream and wail, but everyone else in the house was asleep, and I didn't want to wake them up. *I don't like the dark with those shadows that move,* I thought. *They get closer every night, and now there is another one by the door. That makes three of them.*

It had been four years since I started reading books that pulled me into a very dark world. *They seem ready to grab me at any second,* I thought. My mind raced with ideas of how to get them to leave my room. *I have a street lamp outside my window. If I open the curtains, the light will slip into my room, and the shadows will have to go away!* I ran from my bed to the window and threw the curtain open. *There—wait! The new one. Why isn't it gone? How can it stand in the light?*

The shadow didn't go away when the light shone on it, and that frightened me more than anything else could have. Suddenly I felt out of control. All I could think to say was "Lord, save me!" It was the first time I had prayed in years. I had ignored God so I could live in my sin, and as a result, I did not have His protection from Satan. I had allowed the shadows to come into my life, but God was ready and waiting for me to call on His name. That night He sent the shadows away when I called out to Him. He reminded me that I believed in Him. I was His child.

The words of Psalm 116 took on a new meaning after going through this experience. They say,

> I love the LORD, for he heard my voice;
> he heard my cry for mercy.
> Because he turned his ear to me,
> I will call on him as long as I live.
> The cords of death entangled me,
> the anguish of the grave came over me;
> I was overcome by distress and sorrow.
> Then I called on the name of the LORD:
> "LORD, save me!" (verses 1–4, NIV).

I felt as if no one could understand my fear or pain. I felt as if no one could hear me crying out for help, but as soon as I opened the door of my heart just a crack for God, even though it was out of fear, He stepped in and rescued me from the evil I had brought into my own life. He didn't ask me to change my ways before He sent the demons away; He saved me first. He heard my cry and answered, and because He did that, I gave up my sin to be with Him.

I am a witness!

—Noelle Lucas, junior

Chosen

Acts 6:1–7

T he wheels of the plane sped down the runway, signaling the start of my journey to Peru. This was my first mission trip, my chance to bring aid to those in need. I was so excited to share my love for God with others who needed His influence in their lives! I was a little nervous about going to a foreign country. I worried about my safety. However, I figured that it was all in God's hands. We were on our way!

One thing I learned while on the trip was that we never know what kind of impact our actions will have on others, no matter how small they may seem to us. On one of our days in Iquitos, we were responsible for distributing food bags to people in the neighborhood. We split into groups and headed out. At each home, we took time to talk with the families and get to know them, thanks to our translators. The families at the first three homes we visited were nice, but we were in for a surprise when we arrived at the fourth house.

When we knocked on the door and it opened, we were welcomed inside with open arms, smiles, and singing. As we visited, we found out that the family members were newly converted Christians. They had only been going to church for about two months prior to our visit. Our visit was a divine appointment. They praised God for our gift of food. As we asked the family questions, they began opening up about how they had been praying to God for a sign of His providence. It turns out that we were that sign sent from God. We were their angels. God had used us to do His work.

Looking back, all the days of travel, hard work, and time spent raising money were worth it because of the valuable experiences I received.

This spiritual experience ties into God's call for us to serve others by spreading His Word. God can work through us to reach people for Him when we step out of our comfort zone and are willing to help others. The early church is a perfect example of how a remarkable movement can happen when people dedicate themselves to God: "So the word of God spread. The number of disciples in Jerusalem increased rapidly, and a large number of priests became obedient to the faith" (Acts 6:7, NIV). God has chosen you and me to share the news of His love with those around us. Are you willing to be a witness?

—Anabella Stevens, senior

The Face of an Angel
Acts 6:8–15

Did your parents ever say to you, "You're such an angel?" I've heard a few parents refer to their kids as angels, but most have other things to say about them.

What does that phrase even mean? We don't know what angels look like or how they act. We just assume that because they are heavenly beings, they are perfect (which is probably an accurate assumption), but we don't really know much about angels. We do know that they are messengers from God and do His bidding on this earth, often protecting or helping God's followers.

In Acts 6, we find the story of Stephen, one of the early church leaders, who was "full of faith and the Holy Spirit" (verse 5, NKJV). Like most of the other apostles, he preached and performed "great wonders and signs" (verse 8, NKJV). This got him into trouble with the religious leaders, and they pulled him in before the council and debated with him about the things he was teaching. Because he was filled with the Holy Spirit, they couldn't win the discussion. Their arguments fell flat in the face of the truth. Instead of recognizing the flaws in their own thinking and being open to what Stephen was saying, they got defensive and accused him of blasphemy. In the midst of this discussion, as the council members looked at Stephen, the Bible says that they "saw his face as the face of an angel" (verse 15, NKJV).

How cool is it to be so close to God that even when you are being attacked, He shines through you so clearly that your face looks like that of an angel! Sometimes when I read these stories, I feel like it is impossible to reach the same level of connection these people had with God, but then I stop and remember that they were just like me. They didn't possess any superpowers or more spiritual DNA than I have. They were humans just as I am. However, they were sold out for God. They were all in. They were so in love with Jesus that they couldn't help but tell others about Him.

You may think it isn't possible, but it is. We can be like angels on this earth. We can be messengers of good news to a world that is hungry for hope. Are you in?

—Chaplain Kalie

Story Time
Acts 7:1–53

Young kids love stories. Whether they are about forest creatures on a mission to collect enough food for the winter or a family exploring the beach in Hawaii, stories capture the minds of kids (adults, too, actually). When they have a favorite story, they ask for it to be read again and again until they have it memorized.

The Jewish people loved stories too. Because not everyone knew how to read or write, oral history was a very important part of ancient cultures. They told stories and recounted the history of their nation and how God had led them from slavery in Egypt to freedom in the land they now called home. They knew their history, but many of them didn't know the God behind the stories.

Standing before the council and looking like an angel, Stephen launched into the history of Israel. He talked about Abraham and Joseph and Moses. He detailed the Exodus and the time that the Israelites spent in the wilderness because of their disobedience. He then talked about Joshua and David and Solomon.

Those listening would have been familiar with the stories he recounted but not the conclusion that he drew at the end of his sermon: "You stiff-necked and uncircumcised in heart and ears! You always resist the Holy Spirit; as your fathers did, so do you. Which of the prophets did your fathers not persecute? And they killed those who foretold the coming of the Just One, of whom you now have become the betrayers and murderers, who have received the law by the direction of angels and have not kept it" (Acts 7:51–53, NKJV).

This wasn't a welcome message, but it was one they needed to hear if they were ever going to snap out of their false thinking and take an honest look at their relationship with God and His Word. The truth can hurt, especially when we don't want to hear it. However, accepting the truth and becoming who God intended for you to be is certainly better than living a lie and becoming the worst version of yourself.

Ask God what one truth He wants to share with you, even if it hurts. Are you ready to listen? Are you ready to make a change?

—Makaya Williams, senior

Meeting With Jesus

"And I will give them singleness of heart and put a new spirit within them. I will take away their stony, stubborn heart and give them a tender, responsive heart" (Ezekiel 11:19).

What question would you like to ask God about this verse?

_____

_____

_____

_____

_____

_____

How can you apply this verse to your own life?

_____

_____

_____

_____

_____

_____

What can you share with others from this verse?

_____

_____

_____

_____

_____

_____

It's Still Happening

Acts 7:54–8:3

Stephen wasn't the first person to die for his faith in Christ, and he certainly wasn't the last. In January 2017 the Center for Studies on New Religions released a report stating that ninety thousand Christians were killed for their faith in 2016. "The Christian population in Iraq alone has plummeted from 1.5 million in 2003 to current estimates of 275,000 and could be gone for good within just a few years, according to activists."*

While most of us will never have to die for our faith, this does beg the question, Are you willing to stand up for God even if your life is on the line? I have worried whether I would have enough strength to stay strong. Is it really all up to us? On our own, we can do nothing, but through God we can do anything. Stephen stood strong because God gave him strength. "He, being full of the Holy Spirit, gazed into heaven and saw the glory of God, and Jesus standing at the right hand of God, and said, 'Look! I see the heavens opened and the Son of Man standing at the right hand of God!' . . . And they stoned Stephen as he was calling on God and saying, 'Lord Jesus, receive my spirit.' Then he knelt down and cried out with a loud voice, 'Lord, do not charge them with this sin.' And when he had said this, he fell asleep" (Acts 7:55–60, NKJV).

It's sad to think about someone dying for their faith, but there's something beautiful about this story. In the midst of immense pain and suffering, God allowed Stephen to see heaven. What an amazing blessing in the midst of persecution! As Stephen took his last breath, Saul, who later became Paul, stood by approving of the whole thing. One man gave his life for God, and one man sold his soul to the devil. The good news is that as long as we are alive, we can be redeemed, and God wasn't done with Saul.

The stoning of Stephen unleashed a time of persecution for the early church, but it didn't stamp out the movement as the religious leaders hoped. Instead, it fueled the flames.

—Conner Wood, sophomore

---

* Perry Chiaramonte, "Christians the Most Persecuted Group in World for Second Year: Study," *Fox News*, January 6, 2017, http://www.foxnews.com/world/2017/01/06 /christians-most-persecuted-group-in-world-for-second-year-study.html.

Can You Buy God?

Acts 8:4–25

Most of us live in a privileged world where if we want something, we buy it. Many people even buy things without having the money, using credit cards to get what they want or taking out loans to purchase big-ticket items. Do you want an iPhone? Buy it. Do you want a bag of Doritos? Buy it. Do you want a pair of jeans from Gap? Buy it. Do you want a car? Buy it. Do you want God's power in your life? Sorry; that's one thing you can't buy. However, there was a man who thought he could.

Because of all the persecution in Jerusalem, Philip headed out to the city of Samaria. As he preached, large multitudes accepted Jesus as their Savior, including a man named Simon. This guy had been a sorcerer in the city. The townspeople had attributed his power to God when in reality he was working for the devil. Nonetheless, Simon believed Philip's message and was baptized. After his conversion, Simon hung out with Philip and followed him around.

Word got back to Jerusalem that Philip was doing good things in Samaria, so Peter and John traveled to Samaria and, upon arriving, laid hands on the people who had been baptized and prayed that they would receive the Holy Spirit. And they did. Simon was watching this, and for some reason, he offered Peter money, saying, "Give me this power also, that anyone on whom I lay hands may receive the Holy Spirit" (Acts 8:19, NKJV).

Peter is quick to point out that it doesn't work that way. "Your money perish with you, because you thought that the gift of God could be purchased with money! You have neither part nor portion in this matter, for your heart is not right in the sight of God. Repent therefore of this your wickedness, and pray God if perhaps the thought of your heart may be forgiven you" (verses 20–22, NKJV).

You probably haven't ever thought of trying to buy God's power, but I do think we often wish there was some way to get in on God's favor. We want a shortcut to the good life. Christians prosper and live an easy life, right? That's not what God promises. He promises us His presence and His gift of eternal life. Both of those things require us to have a relationship with Him, which takes time and can't be bought.

—Zach Negron, sophomore

The Missing Cat
Psalm 50:10, 11

We had just moved into our new home that morning, and my wife and I were on a mission to unpack as much as possible and get settled because my parents were coming for a visit later that week. We had been working all day, and it was now about nine o'clock at night. We had been steadily making a dent in the number of boxes sitting in the garage. As my wife finished unpacking each box, I went to retrieve another one from the garage and bring it inside. We had a good system, and were making good progress.

It was getting late, and we were slowing down. We told the kids to get ready for bed, but as they did, we realized our cat, Simon, was missing. We frantically searched the house but came up empty. He wasn't under any of the beds or in any of the closets. We checked the open boxes to see whether he had crawled in one and fallen asleep, but he was nowhere to be found. We grabbed flashlights and headed outside. We searched all around the house and in the woods. Still nothing. We stopped and prayed together, and I headed back outside to keep looking in the woods. I started at the back of our property and made my way toward the house. There was no sign of him. I kept praying, and then an idea struck me. Check under the hood of the van.

It seemed like a crazy idea, but I couldn't shake the thought. I remembered a story I had heard before about a cat climbing up under the hood to stay warm. It was cool outside since it was the first part of March. I figured I didn't have anything to lose. I headed to the house and turned on the outside lights. Then I popped the hood of the van and shone my flashlight all around. Sure enough, Simon had wedged himself up under the hood. I managed to extract him and take him inside to get cleaned up.

There were tears of joy from the kids and thankful prayers to God for helping us find our kitten. This may seem like a small thing, but I've found that God cares about everything we are going through. We're the ones who label things as small or big.

I am a witness!

—Randy Kelch, IT director

Called to Lead Others

Acts 8:26–39

There are many amazing stories in the Bible of great heroes, and I often find myself feeling very small in relation to characters like Moses, David, John the Baptist, Stephen, and Paul. These characters led great nations and endured trials, conflicts, shipwrecks, prison, and death at the hands of those who hated them.

Phillip, however, seems a bit more relatable. God told him to head south along the road leading from Jerusalem to Gaza. Philip did was he was told, and as he walked, he came upon an Ethiopian eunuch who served under Candace, the queen of Ethiopia. This man was reading the prophecies of Isaiah while sitting in his chariot. God prompted Philip again, telling him to catch up to the chariot and ask the eunuch whether he understood what he was reading.

Upon catching up with the chariot, Philip asked the man what he was reading, and the eunuch responded that he could use some help digesting the prophecies. God gave Philip wisdom to help the eunuch understand the Bible. Not only did Philip help him read the Bible, but he also told him all about Jesus. As they traveled down the road, they passed a body of water, and the eunuch asked to be baptized. Thanks to Philip's testimony, it didn't take long for the Ethiopian to seek a relationship with God and want to be baptized.

Sometimes preaching the Word of God and talking to others about Him can seem tricky. I am not big on public speaking, and most of the time I find myself being quite antisocial. However, I'm learning that you don't necessarily have to go up front to tell others about Christ. God gives us opportunities, such as mission trips and regular personal conversations with others, to talk about what He's done for us. We may even find chances popping up in our work environment or in public places such as the grocery store. This is exactly the kind of job we are called to do—lead others on the right path to Christ, no matter the setting.

Some of my personal mission involves talking on the phone with friends and helping them through their problems. This is kind of like what Philip did: serving where God places you with your own special talents. You can be a Philip in your own town or sphere of influence. You just have to be open to His voice and leading and watch for opportunities to help others come to a deeper understanding of who God is and how much He loves us.

—Isabelle Woods, junior

Not the Same
Acts 9:1–9

W hat has been your favorite Christmas present from the time you can remember until now? Was it a LEGO set, a life-size doll, video games, or a bike? Now that you're older, is it clothes, books, sports gear, or electronic stuff?

Around this time of year, we talk about the fact that Jesus is the best Gift the world has ever received, but do we really believe it? Do we really believe that Jesus' birth is the best thing that could've happened to us? Is Immanuel, God with us, really that special? Some people say yes, and some people say no. It all depends on whether you've had an encounter with God.

Saul hated the people "who belonged to the Way" (Acts 9:2, NIV). It didn't matter whether they were men or women; Saul arrested them and threw them in prison if they professed to follow Jesus. It says that he was constantly "breathing out murderous threats against the Lord's disciples" (verse 1, NIV). He wanted to stamp out the movement, but God had other plans.

While Saul was traveling to Damascus to go and arrest believers in that city, a light flashed down from heaven and stopped him dead in his tracks. The Bible says, "He fell to the ground and heard a voice say to him, 'Saul, Saul, why do you persecute me?' " (verse 4, NIV).

I'm sure Saul must have been confused and terrified. Saul asked, "Who are you, Lord?" and the voice from heaven replied, "I am Jesus, whom you are persecuting" (verse 5, NIV). Bam! Saul met Jesus on the road to Damascus. Now, what was he going to do about this encounter? When he opened his eyes, he was blind. His traveling companions led him into the city and got him settled.

Jesus had told Saul to go into the city and wait for further instruction from God (verse 6), and that's exactly what Saul did. For three days he didn't eat or drink anything. I'm guessing he prayed and searched his heart to figure out why he had been so bent on persecuting the believers when they were connected to Jesus.

Jesus is the greatest Gift to the world, but do we recognize it? If you don't, He might just hit you over the head as He did Saul.

—Kara Wei, senior

Behind Bars
Isaiah 61:1, 2

L enora had taught home economics when my mom was in high school. For those of you who don't know, back in the day, home economics was a class that taught you how to sew, cook, clean, garden, and take care of other household responsibilities. Lenora was an amazing tailor and cook, and she taught for a number of years before moving on to work as a dietician for the prison system in Frederick, Maryland.

My junior year of high school, our family moved to Hagerstown, Maryland, which was twenty minutes west of Frederick. Naturally, my mom wanted me to meet Lenora. She had been more than a teacher; she had been like a second mother to my mom. We met Lenora at her home, and she showed us all around her beautifully manicured garden and home, which was filled with a wide assortment of antiques. After visiting for a while, she said she wanted to show my mom where she worked, so off we headed to the prison.

Lenora drove up to the gate, showed them her badge, and told the guard that we were with her. We followed her car through the gate, which was topped with barbed wire. I wasn't sure whether I should be intrigued or nervous. We pulled around to a large building, and I surveyed my surroundings. There were fences with barbed wire around the perimeter with a variety of buildings inside. There were also other fences in the interior creating corridors to walk through from one building to the next. Lenora took us inside and showed us around what appeared to be a normal-looking cafeteria. I knew it was far from normal—the men who lived there couldn't leave. They weren't free to go where and when they wanted. They were stuck.

In reality, we are all prisoners to sin. We are born with sinful natures into a sinful world. However, there is good news! Unlike the men at the prison we visited, we can choose to be free by simply accepted Jesus' gift of salvation. Jesus "sent me to bind up the brokenhearted, to proclaim freedom for the captives and release from darkness for the prisoners" (Isaiah 61:1, NIV).

Jesus quoted these words from Isaiah when He was in the synagogue in Nazareth (Luke 4:14–30). He is our Savior, and He wants to set us free from the bondage of sin. He's just waiting for us to ask for His help.

—Chaplain Kalie

Meeting With Jesus

"This means that anyone who belongs to Christ has become a new person. The old life is gone; a new life has begun!" (2 Corinthians 5:17).

What did you learn about God from this verse?

_____

_____

_____

_____

_____

_____

How should we relate to others based on this passage?

_____

_____

_____

_____

_____

_____

What spiritual principle can you take from these sentences?

_____

_____

_____

_____

_____

_____

Living the Best Life
Acts 9:10–19

Imagine it's the last month of the school year, and everything is going great. You have straight As, you are doing amazingly in all of your extracurricular activities, and it looks like everything is going to end on a high note. Then all of a sudden, your life goes for a spin. You have multiple tests in one week and extra practices for the end-of-the-year programs. You do your best, but things begin to snowball, and you feel like you are getting buried under the homework and tests and pressures of everything else you're involved in. Just when you thought life was going great, bam, it kicks you in the face.

Life is like a roller coaster, full of ups and downs. The challenge is that we're riding the roller coaster blindfolded, so we aren't quite sure when the ups and downs will occur. We have to hold on for the ride and trust that the car will stay on the track. This is where faith comes in. We have a loving God who is managing the ride. When we have faith, we choose to believe that, no matter how dark life may seem, God is always watching over us.

Saul found himself in a dark place, literally, after seeing the bright light of God on the road to Damascus. He became blind on the spot, and he sat in darkness waiting to see what God had planned for him. After three days, God sent Ananias to heal Saul of his blindness. Ananias was skeptical because he had heard about Saul and his hatred of those who followed Jesus. He questioned God, but God told him that He had chosen Saul to carry the gospel to the Gentiles (Acts 9:15). Even though Saul had done many terrible things, God had a plan for him.

There are two pieces to this story: God's forgiveness of Saul and Saul's trust in God. God didn't hold over Saul's head that he had murdered and imprisoned God's children. No, He called Saul to repent and then get busy working for Him. There was no time to waste. Saul had a job to do. This took a great amount of trust on Saul's part. He had to believe in God's forgiveness and be willing to surrender to God's plan.

The same goes for us today. What do you need to trust God with today?

—Devin Schlisner, sophomore

Assumptions

Acts 9:20–31

The summer before I went into ninth grade, I tried out for the East Hall High School varsity volleyball team. I was going to be in Puerto Rico during tryouts, so I made an agreement with the coach that I could try out after I got back. I was very surprised that the coach was willing to do that.

The day came for my tryout, and I was excited. However, when I walked into the gym, the nerves set in because the whole team was there, and everyone seemed to be staring me down. I'm short, and most volleyball players are tall, so I felt the other girls immediately judging me and sizing me up. No one said hi to me or introduced themselves. It was uncomfortable.

To make a long story short, I made the team, but it took me a while to fit in because they had judged me for coming in late, and they resented me for getting special treatment. We all became good friends by the end of the season, but the first little bit was rough.

Saul found himself in a similar situation. He had persecuted believers his whole life, but when he met God, he changed. God told Saul to preach and share the good news of salvation with everyone he met, but the disciples weren't so sure about this plan. They were afraid of him, and with good cause. They didn't believe in his transformation. They judged him for his past actions, not his current behavior. Fortunately, the disciples did accept Saul into their community, and they all worked together to spread the gospel.

It's easier to judge people than to get to know them, but when we jump to judging, we miss the opportunity to get to know someone who may turn into a close friend. We need to learn not to judge too quickly and to take the time to get to know people instead. It's better to be like God, who doesn't judge anyone for their past mistakes but looks at their potential instead.

—Ariana Hernandez, sophomore

So Much More

John 21:24, 25

We have spent a year exploring the Gospels in an effort to get to know Jesus better. Yet there is so much more we will never know. At the end of John, the disciple penned these words: "This is the disciple who is bearing witness about these things, and who has written these things, and we know that his testimony is true. Now there are also many other things that Jesus did. Were every one of them to be written, I supposed that the world itself could not contain the books that would be written" (John 21:24, 25, ESV).

Do you wonder what the other stories might be? What other miracles did He perform? What other sermons did He give? Were there more confrontations with the Pharisees? What family stories could've been recorded? What funny mishaps weren't mentioned? What other encounters happened that changed people's lives?

Jesus lived on the earth for thirty-three years, and He was engaged in ministry for only three years. There is so much more we don't know about Jesus and His life. However, what we do know is enough.

He is God, and He is human. He is loving, kind, caring, considerate, and loyal, while still being authoritative, majestic, powerful, determined, and intense. He is full of questions and full of answers. He is meek and mild and bold and unflinching. Most importantly, Jesus has the power to save us through His death and resurrection. That is more than enough.

We will spend eternity getting to know Jesus better, and I'm sure we'll be able to hear the untold stories that weren't written down in Matthew, Mark, Luke, and John. Until we go to heaven, we should constantly seek to get to know Him better by spending time reading the Bible and talking to Him through prayer.

Jesus loves you so much! He wants to be your Friend! Be intrigued by the many facets that make up His character. Get to know Him as your personal Savior. And take the good news and share it with someone else.

—Chaplain Kalie

Your Turn
Matthew 5:16

"L et your light so shine before men, that they may see your good works and glorify your Father in heaven" (Matthew 5:16, NKJV). That sums up our job. It's our mission to be a light in this dark world. Will you accept the mission?

Paul challenged the church at Philippi to accept the mission: "Do everything without complaining and arguing, so that no one can criticize you. Live clean, innocent lives as children of God, shining like bright lights in a world full of crooked and perverse people. Hold firmly to the word of life; then, on the day of Christ's return, I will be proud that I did not run the race in vain and that my work was not useless" (Philippians 2:14–16).

That sounds like a tall order, especially in today's society in which we all like to rant about the things that annoy us or make us mad. However, it's possible with Jesus because He is the one working in and through us to transform us into new people. Paul also said, "And so, dear brothers and sisters, I plead with you to give your bodies to God because of all he has done for you. Let them be a living and holy sacrifice—the kind he will find acceptable. This is truly the way to worship him. Don't copy the behavior and customs of this world, but let God transform you into a new person by changing the way you think. Then you will learn to know God's will for you, which is good and pleasing and perfect" (Romans 12:1, 2).

Paul understood the change that can take place when you give yourself over to God. He went from hating people so much that he was willing to kill them to being joyful about sitting in a prison cell in chains because he was preaching about Jesus. He was a living testimony of God's power to change someone's heart and give them purpose. Paul was a witness to God's working in his life, just like the disciples, the prophets, and millions of people since the Creation of the world.

God is alive and working around you. Do you see it? If you don't, ask Him to reveal Himself to you. If you do, go share it! You are a witness! There will never be another you with your perspective of who God is and how He is working in your life. Don't miss the opportunity to share that with someone! You never know what type of impact you will make. It's a matter of life or death.

You are a witness!

—Chaplain Kalie

Bible Verses That Mean a Lot to Me

Things I Want to Pray About

Things I Want to Pray About

How God Answered My Prayers

How God Answered My Prayers

Different Ways I Can Be a Witness

Different Ways I Can Be a Witness